·exlibris·

Discourse and the Construction of Society

DISCOURSE
and the
CONSTRUCTION
of SOCIETY

Comparative Studies of
Myth, Ritual, and Classification

Bruce Lincoln

New York   Oxford
OXFORD UNIVERSITY PRESS
1989

Oxford University Press

Oxford   New York   Toronto
Delhi   Bombay   Calcutta   Madras   Karachi
Petaling Jaya   Singapore   Hong Kong   Tokyo
Nairobi   Dar es Salaam   Cape Town
Melbourne   Auckland

and associated companies in
Berlin   Ibadan

Published by Oxford University Press, Inc.,
200 Madison Avenue, New York, New York 10016

Oxford is a registered trademark of Oxford University Press

Library of Congress Cataloging-in-Publication Data
Lincoln, Bruce.
Discourse and the construction of society : comparative studies
of myth, ritual, and classification / Bruce Lincoln.
p. cm.
Chapters originally written in Italian and English 1980–1984.
Bibliography: p. Includes index.
ISBN 0-19-505757-0
1. Myth. 2. Ritual. 3. Classification. I. Title.
BL304.L56   1989
306'.6—dc 19   89–2874   CIP

2 4 6 8 9 7 5 3 1
Printed in the United States of America
on acid-free paper

Ai miei amici senesi,
Pier Giorgio e Teresa Solinas,
Pietro e Ida Clemente

Contents

Discourse and the Construction of Society

Introduction

The studies that follow pursue the question of how certain specific modes of discourse—myth, ritual, and classification—can be, and have been, employed as effective instruments not only for the replication of established social forms (this much is well known), but more broadly for the construction, deconstruction, and reconstruction of society itself. Before we can turn to this topic, however, there is another that must be treated: No consideration of discourse is complete that does not also take account of force. Together, discourse and force are the chief means whereby social borders, hierarchies, institutional formations, and habituated patterns of behavior are both maintained and modified.

Force and Discourse

Force (i.e., the exercise or threat of physical violence) is an instrument open to a variety of uses by individuals and groups within any society. It is regularly employed by those who hold official power to compel obedience and suppress deviance. Thus they preserve generalized social stability and, what is more, a specific configuration in which they—and certain others with whom they have close and complex relations—occupy positions of privilege and enjoy disproportionately large shares of those classic scarce and desired resources Weber identified as wealth, power, and prestige as well as such other desiderata as education, information, health, leisure, and sumptuary goods of various sorts. Further, force may also be used by ruling elites to effect significant social change, for instance, when they direct the violence at their disposal beyond the borders of their own society in campaigns of expansive conquest through which ever-larger social aggregates with more varied and complex patterns of organization can be constructed.

Moreover, elites hold no monopoly on the exercise of force, and however much they attempt to define all that lies outside their control as illegitimate, nondominant groups of all sorts always retain some measure of force—if only that of their own bodies. This they can employ in a variety of ways disruptive to the established order, including scattered assaults on persons and property as well as more organized struggles in which they seek (1) to remove themselves from an encompassing and exploitative social aggregate (secession), (2) to dislodge and replace those in positions of power and privilege (rebellion), or (3) to reshape established social forms and habituated patterns of behavior in sweeping and fundamental ways (revolution).

In all instances, however, force—be it coercive or disruptive—remains something of a stopgap measure: effective in the short run, unworkable over the long haul. The case of imperial expansion (already mentioned) is an instructive one: Although new territories may be added by conquest, successful integration of the populations within those territories depends on—better yet, *amounts to*—the transformation of these peoples' consciousness so that they come to consider themselves members of an imperial society rather than the vanquished subjects of a foreign nation. Such a radical recasting of collective identity, which amounts to the deconstruction of a previously significant sociopolitical border and the corollary construction of a new, encompassing sociopolitical aggregate, can hardly be accomplished through force alone. Nor is the exercise of force an adequate long-term response to the episodes of revolt and rebellion that occur in empires within which conquered peoples remain imperfectly integrated and retain their preconquest loyalties to a large degree, because force can quell these outbreaks only at the cost of further alienating subject populations.

Similarly, it must be recognized that although force can surely be used to protect the interests of a ruling elite against the agitation of subordinate strata, this is quite different from saying it can ensure social stability. The coercive violence employed by elites itself effects change, in that it removes certain persons and groups from their previous places within society—for example, by death, banishment, incarceration, and the like—thereby modifying the size, shape, and nature of the total social aggregate. Genocide is the extreme case. Further, the employment of coercive force by a ruling elite modifies the affect of all members within society, sometimes dramatically so: Some groups and individuals may be emboldened, some intimidated, some depressed, some enraged. Such shifts are always significant, both in and of themselves and for the way they inform actions that produce still further change.

Discourse supplements force in several important ways, among the most important of which is ideological persuasion. In the hands of elites and of those professionals who serve them (either in mediated fashion or directly), discourse of all forms—not only verbal, but also the symbolic discourses of spectacle, gesture, costume, edifice, icon, musical performance, and the like—may be strategically employed to mystify the inevitable inequities of any social order and to win the consent of those over whom power is exercised, thereby obviating the need for the direct coercive use of force and transforming simple power into "legitimate" authority. Yet discourse can also serve members of subordinate classes (as Antonio Gramsci above all recognized) in their attempts to demystify, delegitimate, and deconstruct the established norms, institutions, and discourses that play a role in constructing their subordination.

Myth, Ritual, and Ideology

It has been common, ever since Marx and Engels coined the term, to contrast *ideology* with some other mode of thought and discourse, called variously knowledge, science, consciousness, or the like, but always characterized as both accurate and illuminating in its representations and thus an appropriate instrument of criticism, analysis, and demystification. Among other studies that implicitly adopt this position—and one of considerable importance to the present inquiry—is Roland Barthes's brilliant and influential essay "Myth Today," in which he characterized myth in an unusual but insightful fashion as a second-order semiotic system, that is, a form of metalanguage in which preexisting signs are appropriated and stripped of their original context, history, and signification only to be infused with new and mystificatory conceptual content of particular use to the bourgeoisie. Myth, Barthes argued, "has the task of giving an historical intention a natural justification, and making contingency appear eternal. . . . This process is exactly that of bourgeois ideology. If our society is objectively the privileged field of mythical significations, it is because formally myth is the most appropriate instrument for the ideological inversion which defines this society."[1] To myth—the most ideological form of speech—he contrasted a form he took to be its dialectic opposite: the direct and transformative speech of labor and of revolution.[2] Barthes maintained:

> There is therefore one language which is not mythical, it is the language of man as a producer: wherever man speaks in order to transform reality and no longer to preserve it as an image, wherever he links his language to the making of things, meta-language is referred to a language-object, and myth is impossible. This is why revolutionary language proper cannot be mythical. Revolution is defined as a cathartic act meant to reveal the political load of the world: it *makes* the world; and its language, all of it, is functionally absorbed in this making. It is because it generates speech which is *fully*, that is to say initially and finally, political, and not, like myth, speech which is initially political and finally natural, that Revolution excludes myth.[3]

More recently, a line of analysis similar to that which Barthes proposed for the category of myth has been advanced with equal verve and brilliance by Maurice Bloch regarding the category of ritual, which he defines broadly to include "greetings, and fixed politeness formula, formal behaviour and above all rituals, whether social, religious or state."[4] Such phenomena, he argues, are characterized first by severely attenuated parameters of discourse and second by thought categories that, being socially determined, render criticism of society quite impossible insofar as they are "already moulded to fit what is to be criticised."[5] Such criticism—and the contingent potential for social change—becomes possible only through thought and discourse that originate within a nonritual sphere, where they are shaped by something other than society and thus afford an objective, nonmystified perspective that allows one to talk *about* society and not just *within* society. This sphere Bloch locates in the experience of productive labor, where, he contends—making particular reference to the way in which time is structured and perceived—the categories of thought are determined not by the givens of preexisting social structure, but rather by those of nature. Summarizing his argument, Bloch states:

> This lecture starts by considering the old problem of how to account for social change theoretically. . . . The source of this problem is traced to Durkheim's notion that cognition is socially determined. By contrast it is argued that those concepts which are moulded to social structure are not typical of knowledge but only found in ritual discourse, while the concepts using nonritual discourse are constrained by such factors as the requirements of human action on nature. This means that there are terms available to actors by which the social order can be criticised since not all terms are moulded by it.[6]

Thus, like Barthes, Bloch located a nonmystified and potentially revolutionary mode of thought and discourse within the experience of productive labor, and here, of course, they both follow Marx. This they dialectically oppose to another mode of thought and discourse that serves only to mystify and thereby perpetuate the sociopolitical status quo: This latter category they locate in myth (Barthes), ritual (Bloch), and ideology (Marx).[7] Notwithstanding the importance of the questions these authors have raised and the considerable interest their formulations hold, there are problems with their common line of analysis. Both Barthes and Bloch present the experience of productive labor in somewhat romanticized (one might even say mythologized) form, for it is hardly a sphere in which thought and discourse are conditioned solely by nature in the absence of society. Indeed, the very processes of production are themselves socially determined (e.g., by technology, division of labor, and patterns of access to, and ownership of, the means of production), as are the conceptual models through which laborers experience, reflect on, and discuss the givens of their work. It thus overstates things to posit an accurate and nonmystified "knowledge" existing within the sphere of productive labor, and it is preferable to argue that what one may find there is ideological systems that differ from those that dominate in other spheres of activity (myth and ritual included). Any criticism or struggle that ensues might then be described not as a case in which knowledge opposes mystification or science ideology, but one in which a hegemonic ideology is challenged by one of the many counterhegemonies that exist within any society.

This set of observations leads me to a second, more general point: To hold that thought is socially determined does not mean that all thought reflects, encodes, re-presents, or helps replicate the *established structures* of society, for society is far broader and more complex than its official structures and institutions alone. Rather, such a formulation rightly implies that all the tensions, contradictions, superficial stability, and potential fluidity of any given society *as a whole* are present within the full range of thought and discourse that circulates at any given moment. Change comes not when groups or individuals use "knowledge" to challenge ideological mystification, but rather when they employ thought and discourse, including even such modes as myth and ritual, as effective instruments of struggle.

Classification and Counterclassification

In truth, the very texts we are discussing may themselves be considered as counterhegemonic ideologies and instruments of struggle, for what both Barthes and Bloch developed, following Marx, is a system for the classification of thought and discourse that is based on two inversely correlated taxonomizing distinctions: mystification and labor. Thus, they argue that the discourse grounded in the experience of productive labor is nonmystificatory (and potentially demystificatory), whereas the discourse that is not so grounded is mystificatory. Moreover (as is true in general of taxonomies), this system does not simply and idly differentiate the phenomena being classified, but—what is more important—in classifying it also ranks them. Here the moral and, in the long run, historic superiority of that mode of discourse, which could be described as +Labor/—Mystification, is clearly asserted.

It is not enough to consider the taxonomic system advanced by these theoreticians in isolation, however, for it evolves largely in reaction to another classificatory system that is much more broadly influential and—as Marx and all since have realized—a cornerstone of modern industrial society. This system is classically known as the division of labor: In its first move of categorization, it differentiates work that is predominantly manual from that which is mental, with preferential status reserved for the latter. Viewed in their relation to this hegemonic system, the taxonomies proposed by Barthes and Bloch appear as counterhegemonic inversions, artfully and strategically designed to overturn (quite literally) the hierarchic relations that are established and encoded within the division of labor (see Fig. I.1).

For the most part taxonomies are regarded—and announce themselves—as systems of classifying the phenomenal world, systems through which otherwise indiscriminate data can be organized in a form wherein they become knowable. Knowers do not and cannot stand apart from the known, however, because they are objects as well as subjects of knowledge; consequently, they themselves come to be categorized within their own taxonomic systems. Taxonomy is thus not only an epistemological instrument (a means for organizing information), but it is also (as it comes to organize the organizers) an instru-

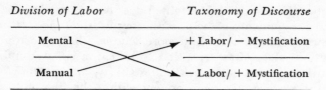

Division of Labor		Taxonomy of Discourse
Mental		+ Labor/ − Mystification
Manual		− Labor/ + Mystification

Figure I.1. Inversion of the hierarchy implicit within the division of labor, as effected by Barthes's analysis of myth, Bloch's analysis of ritual, and Marx's analysis of ideology.

ment for the construction of society. And to the extent that taxonomies are socially determined, hegemonic taxonomies will tend to reproduce the same hierarchic system of which they are themselves the product.[8] Within any society, nonetheless, there exist countertaxonomic discourses as well (inversions and others): Alternative models whereby members of subordinate strata and others marginalized under the existing social order are able to agitate for the deconstruction of that order and the reconstruction of society on a novel pattern.

Sentiment and Society

Whether such agitation can succeed in any given instance will depend on a great many factors, many of which are contingent to the specific situation. In general three factors must be taken into account. First, there is the question of whether a disruptive discourse can gain a hearing, that is, how widely and effectively it can be propagated; this largely depends on the ability of its propagators to gain access to and exploit the opportunities inherent within varied channels of communication—formal and informal, established and novel. Second, there is the question of whether the discourse is persuasive or not, which is only partially a function of its logical and ideological coherence. Although such factors, which are by nature internal to the discourse, have their importance, it must be stressed that persuasion does not reside within any discourse per se but is, rather, a measure of audiences' reaction to, and interaction with, the discourse. Although certain discourses may thus be said to have (or lack) persuasive potential as a result of their specific content, persuasion itself also depends on such factors as rhetoric, performance, timing, and the positioning of a given discourse vis-à-vis those others with which it is in active or potential competition.

Finally, there is the question of whether—and the extent to which—a discourse succeeds in calling forth a following; this ultimately depends on whether a discourse elicits those sentiments out of which new social formations can be constructed. For discourse is not only an instrument of persuasion, operating along rational (or pseudorational) and moral (or pseudomoral) lines, but it is also an instrument of sentiment evocation. Moreover,

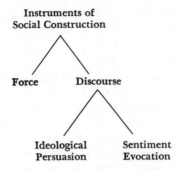

Figure I.2. Aspects of the instruments through which social formations are modified and maintained.

it is through these paired instrumentalities—ideological persuasion and sentiment evocation—that discourse holds the capacity to shape and reshape society itself (Fig. I.2).

In talking about society, it should be clear that I do not mean to focus primarily on political institutions: A state, a government, a system of laws, and the like, do not in and of themselves constitute society. Nor do I place primary emphasis on economic structures or those of kinship, although these, like politics, are a crucial part of any social entity and contribute powerfully to its stability and durability. Accordingly, consideration of these must inform any serious discussion. Often, however, analyses of social institutions or systems of social organization pass for the analysis of society itself, and it is worth recalling that the elusive and ill-defined entity that we call society (from the Latin verb *socio*, to join or unite together, to associate) is basically a grouping of people who feel bound together as a collectivity and, in corollary fashion, feel themselves separate from others who fall outside their group.

This state of affairs is often described by means of the metaphor of social borders, that is, those imaginary lines that distinguish one group of persons from another. Numerous and varied factors may help to mark and enforce such borders, for instance, differences in language, topography, diet, patterns of economic and marital exchange, habituated behaviors (customs), normative preferences (values in the moral sphere, aesthetics or taste in others), and so forth. However important such considerations may be to the parties involved, of infinitely greater analytic significance is the general pattern: That is, as groups and individuals note similarities and dissimilarities of whatever sort between themselves and others, they can employ these as instruments with which to evoke the specific sentiments out of which social borders are constructed. These I refer to as affinity and estrangement, meaning to include under the general rubric of these terms, on the one hand, all feelings of likeness, common belonging, mutual attachment, and solidarity—whatever their intensity, affective tone, and degree of consciousness—and, on

the other hand, those corresponding feelings of distance, separation, otherness, and alienation.[9] Although in practice the capacity of discourse to evoke
such sentiments is closely conjoined with its capacity to persuade, analytically the two are separate.

To cite a simplistic example, an inevitable part of any verbal discourse—
and one quite unrelated to ideological persuasion except as a precondition
for the latter—is the implicit statement "I speak language X." Ordinarily,
this level of communication goes unnoticed, but within a multilingual group
where X is not the language of choice, the introduction of a speech-act in X
will evoke some minimal (and probably ephemeral) sentiments of affinity between the speaker and other X speakers present and will simultaneously
evoke sentiments of estrangement between this group and that constituted
by nonspeakers of X. The same can happen in less dramatic fashion when a
particular idiom, accent, or patois is introduced into a conversation. In this
moment and by this process, an act of discourse thus reconstructs the social
field, catalyzing two previously latent groupings and (at least temporarily)
establishing a border between them. What is more, this process is unrelated
to the specific content of the catalyzing discourse: That is, ideological persuasion has nothing and sentiment evocation everything to do with it.

Because there are virtually infinite grounds on which individual and
group similarity/dissimilarity may be perceived and corresponding sentiments of affinity/estrangement evoked, the borders of society are never a
simple matter. In practice there always exist potential bases for associating
and for dissociating one's self and one's group from others, and the vast majority of social sentiments are ambivalent mixes in which potential sources
of affinity are (partially and perhaps temporarily) overlooked or suppressed
in the interests of establishing a clear social border or, conversely, potential
sources of estrangement are similarly treated in order to effect or preserve a
desired level of social integration and solidarity.

Several points follow from this way of seeing things. First, the metaphor
of social borders may be understood to describe those situations in which
sentiments of estrangement clearly and powerfully predominate over those
of affinity, so that groups of persons experience themselves as separate and
different from other groups with whom they might potentially be associated.
Second, such borders being neither natural, inevitable, nor immutable, affinity may in the course of events come to predominate over estrangement, with
the consequent emergence of a new social formation in which previously
separate social groups are mutually encompassed. Third, within any society
there exist what are commonly called (metaphorically again) cleavages, by
which is meant those situations in which strong sentiments of estrangement
persist between constituent subgroups of an encompassing social aggregate.
These subgroups are, thus, only imperfectly and precariously bound together
by the officially sanctioned sentiments of affinity that coexist with, and partially mask, the distintegrative and most often officially illicit sentiments of
estrangement.

Society is thus a synthesis, in the most literal sense of the term: something that is con-structed, put together (from the Greek compound verb *syn-tithēmi,* to put or place together). And like all synthetic entities, a society may either recombine with others to form syntheses larger still, or—a highly significant possibility ignored in most Hegelian and post-Hegelian dialectics—it may be split apart by the persisting tensions between those entities that conjoined in its formation, with the resultant formation of two or more smaller syntheses. That is to say that the formation of any synthesis (intellectual, social, political, etc.) is never a final step. Any synthetic entity, having its origin in a prior dialectic confrontation, bears within it the tensions that existed between the thesis and antithesis involved in its formation, and this residual tension remains ever capable of undoing the synthesis. Ultimately, that which either holds society together or takes it apart is sentiment, and the chief instrument with which such sentiment may be aroused, manipulated, and rendered dormant is discourse.

On the Writing of This Book

In these chapters I offer studies of those discursive modes that were mentioned earlier and that, given my initial training as a historian of religions, I feel best qualified to consider. Thus the first three chapters are devoted to myth, the next four to ritual, and the last three to classification. Specific examples are drawn from a number of disparate societies: ancient India, Iran, Greece, Ireland, Wales, and Rome; England and France in the early modern period; Spain, Iran, the United States, and parts of sub-Saharan Africa in the present century, with occasional excursuses elsewhere. Some of these data I gathered myself (all translations are original, unless noted), but more often I am indebted to others for them; I have tried to acknowledge my sources wherever appropriate, knowing full well how inadequately these citations serve as notice of my debt and my gratitude.

In truth, this book is itself something of a synthesis, held together more by an affinity of its constituent parts than by a single core thesis or predetermined plan. In part this is the result of the way in which it was written, as it evolved out of initially separate researches undertaken between 1980 and 1986, some of which saw publication in earlier stages of their development (see Acknowledgments). In many of these it is now clear to me that I was groping toward formulations that emerged only in the later pieces; this demanded a recasting of the earlier ones. Crucial changes in my style of analysis came during the winter of 1984–85 when I was fortunate enough to teach in the Institute of Anthropology and Folklore of the University of Siena. There, detached from all my normal obligations and social contacts, challenged by the need to explain my ideas entirely in a foreign language, and exhilarated by the extraordinary nature of my discussions with a splendid set of students and colleagues, I first brought together the materials and developed the major lines of theory and method that are presented in this book. Further revisions and refinements were made during 1986–87, after which this introduction and the concluding chapter were added, albeit at the expense of distorting a situation in which theory effectively coevolved with practice and remained always embedded therein.

There are many people to thank. Above all, I am immensely grateful to Louise Lincoln, whose suggestions and critical acumen have been invaluable; her support and encouragement equally so. Special debts, both intellectual and personal, are owed my Italian friends and colleagues, particularly Pier Giorgio Solinas, Pietro Clemente, Cristiano Grottanelli, Vittorio Lanternari, Luciano Li Causi, Maria Luisa Meoni, and to others, including John Archer, Françoise Bader, Kees Bolle, Barbara Diefendorf, Don Handelman, Hilda Kuper, Richard Leppert, William Malandra, John Middleton, Wendy O'Flaherty, Muhammad N'daou Saidou, James C. Scott, and Brian Smith, who generously read and commented on earlier versions of various chapters. Marlos Rudie and Monica Stumpf provided invaluable and much-appreciated assistance with the preparation of this manuscript. Financial support for various parts of the enterprise came from the National Endowment for the Humanities, the John Simon Guggenheim Memorial Foundation, the Università degli Studi di Siena, and the University of Minnesota—to all I am deeply grateful.

Part I

MYTH

1

Myth, Sentiment, and the Construction of Social Forms

The Putney Debates and the Power of the Past

As the English Civil War (1642–48) drew to a close, it was evident to all that, with the overthrow of Charles I, major changes were likely in the nature of politics and society alike. In October–November 1647, fully cognizant of the momentous nature of the occasion, members of the General Council of Cromwell's victorious New Model Army met at Putney Church to debate the shape in which English society would be remade. Specifically, the group, itself deeply divided on numerous issues, assembled to discuss a document, the *Agreement of the People,* that was nothing less than a draft of a sweeping new constitution proposed by leaders of the radical and populist Leveller faction, who then stood at the height of their power.

Among the central provisions of this document was the granting of suffrage to all adult males without regard to their social station or property holdings. Such an extension of the franchise had clear implications for the nature of politics in the post–Civil War era, and it was on this issue that debate—and a ferocious debate, at that—predictably centered. Failing to gain their desired ends, the Levellers lost their influence, their force, and their following; as a result England's revolution took a decisive turn to the right.

Against the Levellers stood the more conservative army grandees, led by Henry Ireton, commissary general of the army. Backed by Cromwell (who was not only his commander, but also his father-in-law), Ireton argued relentlessly for preservation of the existing electoral system, which restricted the franchise to those having "permanent fixed interest in the kingdom" by virtue of property holdings. The differing class interests, ideological positions, and rhetorical styles that so clearly divided the adversaries at Putney are highly instructive and have been subjected to close scrutiny, for we are fortunate enough to possess near-verbatim transcripts taken by the army council's secretary.

Of particular interest is an exchange that followed immediately upon the *Agreement*'s first formal presentation, when Ireton rose to speak against its First Article, in which the suffrage demands were put forth. Against those demands, he praised the delimitation of the franchise as established within the existing civil constitution, a constitution that—as he put it—"is original and fundamental, *and beyond which no memory of record does go.*" At that precise moment, however, as he sought to establish an absolute *terminus ante quem* to that past which might be considered as precedent, Ireton was challenged by a call from the floor: "Not before the Conquest."[1]

With these words, one Nicholas Cowling alluded to the popular belief that only with the Norman Conquest of 1066 were distinctions based on property and birth introduced, obliterating a paradisally egalitarian Anglo-Saxon society, a view which he amplified in later remarks, saying "In the time before the Conquest [all had a right of election], and since the Conquest the greatest part of the kingdom was in vassalage."[2] To meet this objection, which he clearly saw coming, Ireton was forced to cut his speech short, and to specify that whatever constitution may have existed before the Conquest was irrelevant, for "that hath been beyond memory."[3]

In the ensuing discussions, Ireton insisted time and again on the value of that historic precedent which he favored, while scorning the one invoked by Cowling and others. Witness, for instance, the following remarks:

> I am sure if we look upon *that which is the utmost (within [any] man's view) of what was originally the constitution of this kingdom, upon that which is most radical and fundamental,* and which if you take away, there is no man hath any land, any goods, [or] any civil interest, that is this: that those that choose the representers for the making of laws by which this state and kingdom are to be governed, are the persons who, taken together, do comprehend the local interest of this kingdom; that is, the persons in whom all land lies, and those in corporations in whom all trading lies. *This is the most fundamental constitution of this kingdom, and [that] which if you do not allow, you allow none at all.* This constitution hath limited and determined it, that only those shall have voices in elections.[4]

The debate over the extent of the franchise was thus encapsulated within a debate over the nature of English history, or—to put the issue in its starkest terms—over when relevant time began. For his part, Ireton portrayed the framing of the civil constitution as the absolute and authoritative point of departure for all rational discussion, and sought to consign accounts of all preceding time to the realm of fantasy and legend, just as he consigned the social patterns represented in these accounts to the realm of chaos and anarchy. In this he was aided by a consideration that remained implicit and subtextual: the prestige of written records. In contrast to the written constitution that Ireton championed, Leveller leaders could produce no comparable documentation for their beliefs regarding the period prior to imposition of "the Norman Yoke," and accordingly, were forced to relinquish them.[5] Faced with this dilemma, they attempted to restructure their arguments in other, more general terms. As the foremost historian of seventeenth-century England has put it, at Putney "bogus history was abandoned for political theory based on natural rights: it is a momentous transference."[6]

Perhaps. But was Ireton's "history" less "bogus" than that of the Levellers? And if the shift of the latter to "political theory based on natural rights" was such a profound advance, why is it that they lost both the debate and the broader struggle to adversaries who never faltered in their invocation of the past? In recent years there are those who have argued that the narrative presentation of the past is by its very nature a means of securing the replication of the past in the present, in which case one must conclude that poor Cowling was misguided in his intervention and should have left the past to Ireton and contested on some other, more promising grounds. I am inclined to believe that things are a good deal more complex, however, and that the sociopolitical instrumentality of the past is rather more varied than the adherents of such a position are prepared to admit.

Trotsky and the Spanish Revolution

Let me begin with a set of texts in which the problem of how to produce social change is treated as a practical, not a theoretical problem: the writings of Leon Trotsky regarding events in Spain under the Second Republic.[7] These documents are of particular interest because it was in Spain, just after his expulsion from the Soviet Union (1929), that Trotsky sought to guide others to a replication of the Bolsheviks' success of 1917. Toward this end his observations—particularly in the period between 1931 and 1933 when he maintained close relations with Andrés Nin (at that time a leading figure in the left opposition of the Spanish Communist party [PCE])—are a remarkable mixture of lucid analysis and grandiose fantasy. It is obvious that Trotsky was not always well informed. Furthermore, so anxious was he to vindicate his positions against those of Stalin that he deluded himself badly regarding the strength of the left opposition within the PCE and that of the latter vis-à-vis other Spanish parties.

The numerical weakness of his sympathizers in Spain was, in fact, one of the chief problems with which Trotsky wrestled. Wishing to transform this tiny group into the vanguard of a Spanish revolution, he counseled Nin and others on ways to build their popular support. Yet it is here that Trotsky seems most unrealistic of all: Stripped of all effective weapons—cadres, money, leadership positions, access to mass publications, and so on—he repeatedly impressed on his comrades the value of slogans as a means to accomplish great things. Witness, for instance, his advice on the eve of elections to the first Constituent Cortes of the Republic (18 June 1931):

> We have few forces. But the advantage of a revolutionary situation consists precisely in the fact that even a small group can become a great force in a brief space of time, provided that it gives a correct prognosis and raises the correct slogans in time.[8]

A few months earlier, when the fortunes of the left opposition seemed dim, in spite of the fact that other parties were making great gains and the fall of the monarchy seemed near, Trotsky wrote to Nin in a similar vein (15 February 1931):

> Unfortunately the communists were not the stars in the boycotters' performance. That is why they did not achieve any important victories in the campaign of the last two or three months. In periods of stormy revolutionary flux, the authority of the party grows rapidly, feverishly—if, in decisive turns, at new stages, the party immediately advances the necessary slogan, whose correctness is soon confirmed by the events.[9]

The apparent weakness of this advice notwithstanding, one does not dismiss a practitioner and theoretician of Trotsky's stature lightly, and it is worth considering why he put such confidence in the use of slogans. In the passages cited—to which others could easily be added—it is clear that he saw in slogans the means to catalyze a latent revolutionary movement. That is, by giving voice to the deeply felt but officially unacknowledged aspirations of those who are marginalized under existing social structures, even the tiniest party can mobilize a large, unified, and active following.

Three points require emphasis. First, although it is clear that the slogans Trotsky envisioned have a certain anticipatory quality to them (they depend on "correct prognosis" and are to be "confirmed by the events"), they are not a species of prophecy born of either divine inspiration or scientific analysis. Rather, it is only when a slogan—a call for a demonstration, strike, or boycott, for example—successfully rallies a following that it can be "confirmed by events." That is to say, the slogan is itself a contributing factor, necessary but not sufficient for its own fulfillment. Second, it is not the accomplishment of such projects per se that is of paramount importance; rather, the very formation of such a group as can be mobilized by these slogans is itself a revolutionary action. Indeed, it is *the* revolutionary action par excellence: It is nothing less than the embryonic appearance of a social formation arising in opposition to the established order. Third, Trotsky clearly felt that a "revolutionary situation" presents extraordinary possibilities for success by means of slogans. To put it differently, one may define as "revolutionary" those situations in which traditional, accepted, and customary social formations are in process of collapse, one aspect of this collapse being that the discursive instruments that had previously sustained those formations are in the process of losing their capacity to mobilize and persuade. At such moments dramatic change—that is to say, the emergence of new social formations—becomes possible, even through the agency of slogans.

Ancestral Invocations and Segmentary Lineages

Revolution and civil war offer instructive data: In such situations is revealed the potential fluidity of all social formations. Equally revealing are the segmentary lineage systems described in classic anthropological research,

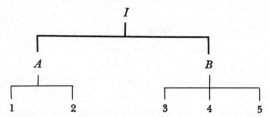

Figure 1.1. Fission and fusion of segmentary units.

where one can perceive not only fluidity, but also certain of the ways in which stability may be maintained in the midst of flux.[10]

Basic to the segmentary pattern is the principle of fission and fusion whereby the members of a total social field can recombine at different levels of integration to form aggregates of varying size. The situation is most easily conceived in diagrammatic form as in Figure 1.1, where the roman numeral one (*I*) represents the social whole (e.g., the *tribe*—using this term and those that follow only for the sake of convenience), capital letters represent the chief constituent subunits (*clans*), and arabic numerals represent sub-subunits (*lineages*).

Such a diagram as Figure 1.1—which could be extended both vertically (to encompass greater time depth) and horizontally (to encompass the synchronic interrelations of more subunits)—maps social organization in the form of a family tree. Indeed, it is often patterns of descent (real or fictive) that govern structures of social segmentation, for instance, when all members of a tribe (*I*) trace their family line to a primordial (often eponymous) ancestor, whom we may also call Ancestor *I*. Similarly, members of clans *A* and *B* descend from children of Ancestor *I* (Ancestors *A* and *B*), whereas members of the lineages (1, 2, etc.) trace their lines to the children of Ancestors *A* and *B*. It follows that the more remote a given ancestor, the larger will be the social group that is made up of his or her descendants. Further, because all individuals have multiple ancestors located at different generational depths, they simultaneously belong—in potential, at least—to multiple social groups, each of which takes a different apical ancestor as its point of origin. Moreover, these groups vary in size and nest comfortably one within another, like Russian dolls or Chinese boxes. At any given moment only one such level of social integration is active and evident, whereas the others exist as latent structural possibilities: alternate groups that may be mobilized under other circumstances.

One must also take note of the specific means whereby any given level of integration is mobilized and, as a consequence, all others are relegated to latency. In descent-based segmentary systems, it is not enough to observe blandly that the various groups and subgroups are defined by reference to apical ancestors: Rather, they are constructed, literally *called into being* by ancestral invocation—understanding within this term not only certain

formal and ceremonial speech acts, but all of the means whereby persons re-
mind themselves and others of the ancestral figures around whom their
groups take shape: allusions, gestures, narratives, displays of emblematic
objects or designs, and so forth.

Consider, for instance, what happens when individuals rally groups
around themselves in a situation of conflict. To take an arbitrary example,
when a man of lineage 1 struggles with a man of lineage 2, they invoke
Ancestors 1 and 2, respectively, that is, the apical ancestors from whom they
and all members of their lineages claim descent—but not more remote an-
tecedents nor others more proximate. When the time arrives to make peace,
however, they invoke Ancestor A together: the figure through whose recollection may be formed that social group in which they are reunited.

Here, we may perceive, first, how society is constructed from nothing so
much as from sentiments, as Durkheim and Mauss recognized.[11] These sentiments—above all those of internal affinity (affection, loyalty, mutual attachment, and solidarity) and external estrangement (detachment, alienation,
and hostility)—constitute the bonds and borders that we reify as society.
Second, the shape of society changes as these sentiments change. Within
segmentary systems, affinity in one set of circumstances can become estrangement in another, as when persons who had previously been encompassed
within a single social formation (e.g., *I*) redefine themselves as members of
smaller, differentiated, and competing groups (*A* and *B*). Third, the mechanism that accomplishes such redefinitions is the recollection of specific moments from the past—those associated with different apical ancestors. It is
when separate individuals recall their common descent from (and thus attachment to) a given ancestor that they reawaken their (latent) feelings of
affinity for, and attachment to, one another. In that very moment and by
that very act of memory, they (re-)define themselves as kin, that is, persons
who are joined together in the same familial group. In this way the past
shapes the present, *invocation* of an ancestor being simultaneously the *evocation* of a correlated social group. Conversely, the present also shapes the
past that is recollected, for specific ancestral invocations, being stimulated
by the needs of a present situation, must be appropriate to those needs: One
cannot rally tribal-sized groups for clan-level conflicts, or vice versa.

In practice, within a segmentary lineage system ancestral invocations
function very much as Trotsky expected slogans to function in a revolutionary situation, that is, given a relatively fluid social field, they are capable
of deconstructing established social forms and constructing new ones. A
significant difference, however, is that although the temporal orientation of
Trotsky's slogans tend to be toward the future, that of ancestral invocations
is to the past. Moreover, whereas with slogans it is possible to call into being radically novel social formations, it would appear that with ancestral
invocation one can only remobilize groups that existed previously but that
have more recently fallen into latency. The identity of the ancestors being
fixed by historic fact and collective memory, one can only call forth the
groups that are defined by those specific ancestors—unless, of course, one

tampers with the genealogy, a practice that is—to judge from the anthropological record and from the social register—not the least uncommon.[12]

Myth and the Construction of Social Borders

Such strategic tinkering with the past introduces the question of myth, a mode of discourse that may, I submit, be employed much in the manner of ancestral invocations or, alternatively, in that of revolutionary slogans. Here, I intend to explore the former possibility; in chapter 2, the latter. For the moment let us focus on a familiar example: The Myth of the First Cattle Raid as told among the Nuer, a people of the Nilotic Sudan for whom cattle are the primary means of production, measure of wealth, means of exchange, and the foremost prestige goods. The Nuer live in close proximity to, and maintain complex relations with, the Dinka people; although the two groups freely intermarry and Dinka are readily adopted into Nuer society, until colonial "pacification" the Nuer regularly raided their Dinka neighbors' cattle, often on a massive scale.[13] Within the rather limited corpus of Nuer myth, one story stands out as of cardinal importance. As recorded by E. E. Evans-Pritchard, it reads, "Nuer and Dinka are presented in this myth as two sons of God [sc. Kwoth], who promised his old cow to Dinka and its young calf to Nuer. Dinka came by night to God's byre and, imitating the voice of Nuer, obtained the calf. When God found that he had been tricked, he was angry and charged Nuer to avenge the injury by raiding Dinka's cattle to the end of time."[14]

Evans-Pritchard went on to assess the story as a "reflection of the political relations between the two peoples" and "a commentary on their characters." Indeed, Nuer have persistently raided the cattle of the Dinka, taking them by force of arms; in a successful adaptive response to the situation, Dinka have resorted to theft, relying on stealth and cunning to replenish their herds, which would otherwise have been long-since depleted. In proper functionalist fashion, one might say that the story charters and thereby perpetuates continuing patterns of intertribal relations: "And to this day," as one informant put it, "the Dinka has always lived by robbery, and the Nuer by war."[15] But one can go beyond functionalist formulations (and other simplistic models that treat discourse as purely superstructural to a socioeconomic base) to see that the telling of this story calls forth a familiar, if temporarily latent, level of social integration. Consider, for instance, the social dynamics evident in Evans-Pritchard's account of how Nuer men reacted to the sight of a Dinka driving a newly bought cow through their village shortly after colonial-imposed "pacification:" "The whole incident filled the Nuer with bitterness. To them it was grotesque. The cow by all that was right should not have been safe from them even in the heart of its owner's country and its passage through their own villages was certainly *contrary to what had been ordained by God.*"[16] No idle rhetorical flourish, this last phrase alludes to the myth we have been considering, recollection of which serves not only to legitimate Nuer claims to the possession of cattle, but also (and perhaps more important) to mobilize those sentiments of internal affinity and external estrangement that distinguish those groups and individuals who are able to identify themselves as descendants of Nuer and to separate them from those whom they identify as descendants of Dinka, while the latter group is defined, for the moment, as persons who hold cattle only by virtue of theft.

Details apart, stories that are similar to this one in their general narrative structure and social instrumentality are not difficult to find, and I offer two examples gathered informally during 1984–85 when I taught first at the University of Siena and then at the University of Uppsala. In both places colleagues and acquaintances tried to orient me (sometimes more and sometimes less self-consciously) by explaining themselves and their world. A striking feature of these conversations was that references to the historic past were quite conventionalized and thus, after a time, highly predictable. In practice a minuscule set of events drawn from the totality of past experience entered such discussions, although these signal events were themselves cited quite often. In Siena past-oriented discourse was dominated by the Battle of Montaperti (1260), the last and greatest defeat the Sienese inflicted on their Florentine archrivals. In the decades that followed, Florence eclipsed Siena permanently and became the dominant military, political, artistic, and commercial power in Tuscany. Yet in Siena to this day, any reference to Florence—a mention of the city's soccer team, for instance—is enough to prompt an allusion to the battle or even a richly embroidered account of the cowardice and humiliation of *i cani fiorentini* at Montaperti.[17]

In Sweden several stories from the past were recounted on occasion, yet that which was told most often, with greatest ceremony and greatest apparent enjoyment, was an incident that occurred toward the end of that period in which Sweden and Denmark were united under the Danish throne (1397–1523). This event, the Stockholm Bloodbath, involved the public decapitation of leading Swedish aristocrats in consequence of their opposition to Danish rule (1520). One leader of resistance to the Danes survived, however, the young Gustav Vasa. He had recently escaped from Danish captivity and, in the wake of these events, initiated the rising that made Sweden independent, with him as its king (1523).

For all their differences of narrative detail, these three stories bear a similar structure, as is shown in Figure 1.2.

These stories recount formative moments from the past: moments in which the enduring tensions that divide rival groups were dramatically at issue. Moreover, all three narratives construct social identity at a specific level of integration—civic (Sienese), tribal (Nuer), or national (Swedish)— whereas other potential social formations and sentiments of affinity (e.g., Nilotic, Tuscan, or Scandinavian unity) are deconstructed in the process.[18] Nor are these results exclusively a matter of the distant past. For whenever the story of Montaperti is told in a Sienese café, to take but one example, those present lose sight of their identity as members of the European continent, the Italian nation, the Tuscan region, or the wards (*contrade*) of Siena.

Narrative	No. 1	No. 2	No. 3
Primordial or potential level of unity	Nuer and Dinka are brothers	Tuscan region and language	Union of Sweden and Denmark (1397–1523)
Initial episode of rivalry	Dinka steals Nuer's calf	Sienese victory at Montaperti (1260)	Stockholm Blood-bath (1520)
Second episode of rivalry	Nuer authorized to raid Dinka cattle	Florentines gain ascendancy (late thirteenth century)	Rising of Gustav Vasa (1523)
Enduring social divisions	Nuer and Dinka	Siena and Florence	Sweden and Denmark

Figure 1.2. Common patterns in three narratives.

Rather, the story evokes certain stereotypical sentiments, to wit: (1) pride among Sienese, (2) shame, anger, annoyance, or bemused tolerance among Florentines, and (3) puzzlement or tedium among outsiders.[19] Moreover, although the sentiments experienced by given individuals vary according to their prior social identity, this bland and undialectical observation obscures more than clarifies the complex processes that are actually at work, for it is precisely through the repeated *evocation* of such sentiments via the *invocation* of select moments from the past that social identities are continually (re-)established and social formations (re-)constructed. Thus, it is not just because one *is* Sienese that one feels pride on hearing the story of Montaperti; rather, when one feels pride in this story, in that very moment one (re-)*becomes* Sienese, that is, a person who feels affinity for those others who also take pride in Montaperti and estrangement from those who do not. Individuals who feel attached to the same moment of the past—like those who share a common ancestor—can thereby be brought to feel attached to each other. And just as one can mobilize social groups of varying size and shape by invoking different ancestors, one can do so by recounting different episodes of the past, as when Sienese and Florentine identities are (temporarily and imperfectly) deconstructed in favor of Italian solidarity at the mention of Dante, Garibaldi, or Italian victories in World Cup soccer.

Toward a Redefinition of *History* and *Myth*

For all that I have stressed the similarity of these narratives, there persists an important difference among them. In the form in which I have presented them, this difference is signaled most obviously by the dates sprinkled through the Montaperti and Stockholm Bloodbath narratives but lacking in the Nuer and Dinka narrative: For the Battle of Montaperti and the Stockholm Bloodbath are *history* (given conventional definitions of this volatile term), whereas the first Nuer cattle raid is *myth* as the latter term is commonly (but misleadingly) used. The semantics of the term *myth* in common discourse is particularly revealing, for this word marks less the intrinsic truth-content of a narrative (i.e., *myth* = false story) than it serves to register the speaker's sense of estrangement from, and superiority to, the social group in which a given narrative normally circulates. For *myth* most precisely signifies, in its pejorative and condescending usage, a story that members of some other social group (or past era) regard(ed) as true and authoritative, but that the speaker and members of her or his group regard as false.

This is not the place to belabor either the logic or the self-serving nature of the Eurocentered taxonomy that grants a privileged position to history, that is, those past-oriented narratives that meet these criteria: (1) a numerically specified position in the sequence of elapsed time can be affixed to them; (2) written sources attest to them; and (3) their only significant actors are human. In general we are not inclined to accept the truth-claims of stories that fail on one or more of these counts, and for these we reserve a bewildering array of other designations: myth, legend, folktale, and the like. Yet a taxonomy that forces us to separate narratives so similar in form, structure, and effect as the three discussed earlier surely serves us ill as an analytic tool.[20] In its place I should like to suggest an alternative that is admittedly arbitrary in certain ways (and in this, it is only like all taxonomies) but that, nevertheless, has its advantages.

In my view we would do better to classify narratives not by their content but by the claims that are made by their narrators and the way in which those claims are received by their audience(s). Thus, some narratives make no truth-claims at all, but rather present themselves and are accepted as fictions pure and simple: These I propose to call Fable. Others, in differing styles and degrees, purport to offer accurate accounts of past events. But of the stories that make such truth-claims, only some have sufficient persuasive power to gain general acceptance, and the others—those that, in the opinion of their primary audience, lack credibility—I shall classify as Legend, calling those that do have credibility, History. And although these two categories are mutually exclusive (i.e., one cannot simultaneously accept and reject the truth-claims of a given story), reclassification of any individual narrative from one class to the other is always possible should the story either gain or lose credibility.[21] Beyond this, there is one further category, and that a crucial one: Myth—by which I designate that small class of stories that possess both credibility and *authority* (see Fig. 1.3).

Having offered such a definition of Myth, it is necessary, of course, to define *authority*, on which the definition of Myth hangs. In part I have in mind something similar to what Malinowski meant when he described myth as a form of social charter and what Clifford Geertz meant in his characterization of religion as being simultaneously a "model of" and a "model for" reality.[22] That is to say, a narrative possessed of authority is one for which successful claims are made not only to the status of truth, but what is more, to the status of *paradigmatic* truth. In this sense the authority of myth is somewhat akin to that of charters, models, templates, and blueprints, but one can go beyond this formulation and recognize that it is also (and perhaps

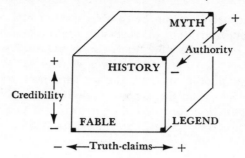

Figure 1.3. Classification of narratives.

	Truth-claims	Credibility	Authority
Fable	−	−	−
Legend	+	−	−
History	+	+	−
Myth	+	+	+

more important) akin to that of revolutionary slogans and ancestral invocations, in that through the recitation of myth one may effectively mobilize a social grouping. Thus, myth is not just a coding device in which important information is conveyed, on the basis of which actors *can then* construct society. It is also a discursive act through which actors evoke the sentiments out of which society is actively constructed.

In the cases we have examined thus far—Nuer, Sienese, Swedish—we have seen how the frequent repetition of the same authoritative story can help to maintain society in its regular and accustomed forms, the instrumentality of these familiar and traditional myths being quite similar to that of ancestral invocations. But other possibilities also exist, ones in which myths can be employed to construct new or unfamiliar social formations, much in the manner of revolutionary slogans. Among the ways in which those agitating for sociopolitical change can make use of myth, the following are some of the most common:

1. They can contest the authority or credibility of a given myth, reducing it to the status of history or legend and thereby deprive it of the capacity to continually reconstruct accustomed social forms.
2. They can attempt to invest a history, legend, or even a fable with authority and credibility, thus elevating it to the status of myth and thereby make of it an instrument with which to construct novel social forms.
3. They can advance novel lines of interpretation for an established myth or modify details in its narration and thereby change the nature of the sentiments (and the society) it evokes.

Obviously, these strategies can be combined, for instance, when a group seeks to deprive one narrative of authority while claiming authoritative status for another or when a new line of interpretation is advanced for a familiar story and is then used to justify a change in its status. Further, should any of these gambits succeed, the consequences are major and can amount to nothing less than the deconstruction of established social forms and the emergence of new formations. It is just such possibilities we shall pursue in chapter 2.

2

The Politics of Myth

The Instrumentality of the Past

In chapter 1 I indicated several ways in which myth could potentially be employed in attempts to change the nature of existing social formations. I suggested that, among other possibilities, one might struggle to deprive an established myth of its authority; one might agitate for the elevation of a lesser narrative to the status of myth; or one might modify the details in an accepted myth's standard narration or advance new lines of interpretation for it. The time has now come to put flesh on these bare bones and provide some examples.

Consider, for instance, a minor skirmish that took place in Swaziland during the middle 1930s as part of the ongoing struggle being waged at that time between British colonial authorities and the traditional leaders of the indigenous population:

> It happened that a high official spoke to Sobhuza [the Swazi king] about a landing site for planes. Near the Swazi National School was a level field, and Sobhuza either suggested or agreed that it would be suitable. When the people heard this they were resentful and asked—"Why Native Areas and not a European farm? Who would benefit from a 'fly-machine'? Why do white people always speak of generosity and yet take everything and give nothing?" The councillors thought of a way to prevent the transaction. The proposed ground was the site of an old royal village, marked by the shady tree under which the council of King Mbandzeni [the last independent Swazi king, r. 1872–89] had met in debate. To prepare the ground the tree would have to be removed. On their advice the King said that the ground could be used if the tree were not touched. There have since been negotiations to buy land from a European.[1]

Here, under the pressure of events, actors sought and found a story from the past that could serve their interests in the present. From Hilda Kuper's reporting of the event, it would appear that this story enjoyed some measure of credibility; but from the standpoint of theory, it would make no difference were it a total fabrication, although in strictly practical terms it is considerably more difficult to win authoritative status for a story that previously lacked credibility—a legend, or a fable, that is—than for one that already possessed the status of history. But whatever its source and prior status may have been, once this account had been re-collected by Sobhuza's councillors, they went on to claim an authoritative status for it, asserting that it exerted continuing demands and obligations on actors in the present moment. Insofar as these claims were accepted—by the Swazi and by the British—those who advanced them had succeeded in creating, at least temporarily, a new myth, one that resolved their initial problem by rendering the strategically located tree under which Mbandzeni met in council quite inviolable.

In its newly achieved status as myth, this story, previously little regarded—if known at all—proved an effective instrument of resistance and enabled the Swazi, most immediately, to keep the foreigners' airstrip off their land. More important, Sobhuza and his councillors were able to use this newly elevated myth as an effective slogan with which to mobilize a social formation—the traditional Swazi Nation—that was in danger of slipping into latency or even oblivion under colonial domination (see a further discussion in chap. 4). For in recounting this story of King Mbandzeni, they evoked strong sentiments of affinity among those who remembered and revered him, and these persons in that very moment reaffirmed their Swazi identity: That is, they re-became Swazi and, as such, experienced also sentiments of estrangement from those non-Swazi outsiders who would profane the sacred ground of their late monarch.

In many respects the dialectic interaction of past and present evidenced in this Swazi episode are similar to the way in which the Nuer Myth of the First Cattle Raid was seen to operate (described in chap. 1). In both instances a problematic situation in the present—the sight of a Dinka holding cattle or the request from a colonial officer that a piece of land be ceded—prompts an exploration of the past, a search for models and precedents that might be of help. In the Nuer case such a search entailed little difficulty and locating the desired story was virtually a reflex action, as the narrative was a familiar one that already enjoyed an unquestioned authoritative status. For the Swazi, however, the task was more demanding, and a story that would speak to the contingencies of the moment had to be either discovered or, failing that, fabricated afresh, after which claims for its authority had to be successfully advanced. This done, however, the Swazi could accomplish with their newly elevated myth what the Nuer could do with their more traditional one: That is, they could legitimate the actions and mobilize the social groupings that would enable them to deal with the initially problematic situation. Beginning in the present, they sought and appropriated that piece of the past—real or imagined, familiar or novel—that could best serve them as an instrument with which to confront and reshape their present moment (see Fig. 2.1).

	Nuer	*Swazi*
Problematic situation in the present	Dinka possession of cattle	Colonial request of land for airstrip
Stimulates search for a moment from the past	Myth of the First Cattle Raid	Mbandzeni's council meetings
That can serve to legitimate desired actions	Raiding Dinka cattle defined as recovery of stolen property	Refusal to cede land defined as reverence for sacred ground
And to stimulate sentiments from which social borders are (re-)constructed	Nuer solidarity and hostility to Dinka (re-)evoked	Swazi solidarity in resistance to colonial rule

Figure 2.1. Interaction of past and present and the instrumentality of myth.

Variation and Contestation

Whereas the Swazi use of stories about Mbandzeni's council was novel and ingenious, Nuer use of their Myth of the First Cattle Raid tends to be habituated and formulaic, the narrative being one of the chief instruments through which they maintain themselves separate from, hostile toward, and convinced of their moral and military superiority to their Dinka neighbors and "brothers." This is not to say, however, that this, the most frequently recounted of Nuer myths, is no more than an unproblematic charter through which well-established social forms are continually legitimated and reproduced. Rather, given its considerable import, this story has also been contested territory at times, the site of a struggle waged by those who would construct Nuer and Dinka society in rather different fashion from that which normally prevails. Their attempt, it appears, was not to discredit the myth—to rob it of its authority or credibility—but to reshape it in subtle ways that might open up new possibilities for Nuer–Dinka relations. This becomes evident when we consider a variant of the myth that differs markedly from the one obtained by Evans-Pritchard (quoted in chap. 1).[2] This version was collected by H. C. Jackson in the early 1920s:

> In the dim and distant past Deng Dit, the Great God of the Dinka, married a woman called Alyet in the Dinka language and Lit in that of the Nuer. While living in an aradeib tree Alyet gave birth to Akol, who married Garung, from whom are ultimately descended Deng and Nuer, the respective ancestors of the Dinka and Nuer tribes. . . . When Garung died he left behind him a cow and a calf, the former being bequeathed to Deng and the latter to Nuer. Deng, however, as can readily be believed by anyone with only the slightest acquaintance with the habits of this tribe, stole the calf of Nuer who was the younger brother and not able to retaliate. Nuer consequently left the family and, when he had grown to man's estate, returned with some friends and retook his calf. From that day to this the Nuer and Dinka are constantly raiding and counterraiding one another for cattle, the

original theft of the only calf in the tribe still being remembered with the bitterest of feelings.[3]

In contrast to that recorded by Evans-Pritchard, this varient is skewed in a number of details that render it considerably more sympathetic to Dinka interests. Most striking, of course, is the fact that here God—who is, after all, presented in this variant as a Dinka god—makes no judgment regarding Dinka's acts, and neither he nor anyone else authorizes Nuer to recover the stolen calf or to conduct future raids. Rather, Nuer undertakes these on his own initiative, acting only after some years have elapsed and with the (apparently necessary) help of allies. Other significant differences between the two variants also become apparent when one compares the genealogies that they give for Nuer and Dinka, as depicted in Figure 2.2.

Here one may note the differences:

1. The deity with whom the genealogy begins is the Nuer Kwoth in variant *A,* whereas in variant *B* he is the Dinka Deng Dit (Great Deng, Great Dinka), whose name is also taken by that grandson of his who becomes the eponymous ancestor of the Dinka people.
2. In variant *A* the deity appears as the father of Nuer and Dinka, but he appears as their mother's father in variant *B;* given patrilineal descent, the two youths are thus not of his lineage in *B.*
3. Although no birth order is specified in variant *A,* Deng (= Dinka) is said to be the elder in variant *B.*

Important differences in the narrative line also follow from these genealogical details. Both versions tell how Nuer was initially supposed to have received a calf and Dinka a cow from their father. However, in variant *A* this is the free gift of a sovereign deity; in variant *B* it is the last bequest of a deceased and decidedly human father. The deity plays no role in it and his relation to his daughter's sons remains distant throughout. In truth, it is somewhat unusual that Garung's cattle are distributed only after his death: The more normal procedure is that a man divide his holdings among his

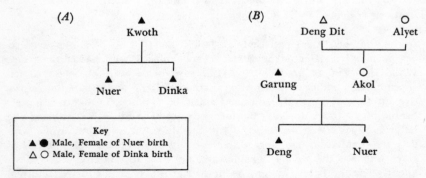

Figure 2.2. Differing genealogies for Nuer and Dinka in the mythic variants collected by Evans-Pritchard 1940 (*A*) and H. C. Jackson 1923 (*B*).

sons before his death in strict order of seniority so that the youths may marry in the order of their birth.[4] The favoritism shown to the second-born Nuer in this variant may be explained by a detail of familial practice, for when a Nuer man marries a Dinka woman, the latter returns to her natal home for the birth of a child and, what is more, her firstborn will often remain there until puberty in the care of his (or her) Dinka matri-kin.[5] Akol, being the daughter of Deng Dit, is a Dinka woman, and her first-born son, Deng is an interstitial figure of this type: a Nuer by birth who is in the process of becoming Dinka, a transformation that is finally and fully effected through the events recounted in this myth.

It is also worth noting certain facts regarding the collection of variant *B*. Jackson—a political officer of the Anglo-Egyptian Sudan—published the first systematic account of the Nuer, but he knew neither the Nuer nor the Dinka language. As a result his ability to collect data was quite restricted, and he was (as he confessed) totally dependent on a single individual who served as his chief informant and translator, "The chief Government Inter-preter at Malakal, one Tut Deng—or Bilal Said as he prefers to be called—a Dinka with an encyclopaedic knowledge of all that pertains to the Nuer *with whom he now chooses to identify himself.*"[6] Tut Deng (to give him back the ethnically significant name that he sought to erase) was then, one of the many Dinka who took up residence among the Nuer and was gradually assim-ilated into Nuer society. Regarding such persons, Evans-Pritchard observed:

> We have already described how Nuer scorn Dinka and persistently raid them, but they do not treat those Dinka who are permanent members of their community differently from its Nuer members, and we have seen that persons of Dinka descent form probably at least half the population of most [Nuer] tribes. These Dinka are either children of captives and immigrants who have been brought up as Nuer, or are themselves captives and immi-grants who are residing permanently among Nuer. They are *'Jaang-Nath,'* *'Dinka-Nuer,'* and it is said, *'caa Nath,'* 'they have become Nuer.' As we have explained, once their membership of a community is recognized, in most of Nuerland, their legal status is the same as that of a free-born Nuer, and it is only in relation to ritual and rules of exogamy that attention is drawn to their origin. In structural relations of a political kind they are undifferen-tiated members of a segment. Although in his domestic and kinship relations a Dinka has not so strong a position as a Nuer, because he has not the same range of kinship links, I have never observed that they suffer any serious dis-abilities, far less degradation.[7]

So Tut Deng was himself an interstitial person, a Dinka in the process of becoming Nuer, and thus in a position symmetrically opposite to that of the mythic Deng, son of Garung, but like the latter (and like a great many others), an individual whose social identity situated him squarely on the border of the categories Nuer and Dinka.[8] That the Myth of the First Cattle Raid as told by such a person was systematically skewed in its details—so as to minimize the crime of Dinka while deleting any hint of divine authoriza-tion for Nuer's retributive violence—can hardly be an accident but must be considered a serious and ingenious attempt to reconstruct authoritative stories and, through the agency of such modifications in myth, to reformulate social sentiments, borders, and, ultimately, society itself.

Myth, Countermyth, and the Iranian Revolution

In the myth of the First Cattle Raid as told to Jackson by Tut Deng and that of Mbandzeni's council as told by Sobhuza II and others, we can see how struggles about stories of the past may also be struggles over the proper shape of society in the present. Another example, more complex than either of these, may be found in Iran of the period leading up to the revolution of 1977–79.[9] Here we observe a situation in which two bitterly antagonistic segments of society both employed chosen moments from the past as instruments with which to pursue their struggle. Thus, it is clear that Muhammad Reza Shah Pahlavi (r. 1941–January 1979), cognizant of Iran's growing wealth and power in the late 1960s and early 1970s as a result of OPEC*-generated oil wealth and American military backing, sought out that moment from the national past that could best serve as a model and a slogan for the imperial society he hoped to create. This he found in the Achaemenian Empire of Cyrus the Great, Darius I, Xerxes I, and their descendants, which was, in truth, the first true world empire (c. 550–330 B.C.E.). Now, stories of this ancient Iranian dynasty were well-known and well respected, but seldom had they been taken to exert any call for replication in the present. In a series of highly publicized gestures, however, the shah made plain his intention to pattern himself and his realm on the Achaemenians, thereby attempting to elevate them from the level of history to that of myth. Among other examples, one may note the shah's 1969 self-coronation, in which he drew heavily on Achaemenian symbolism; the 1971 extravanganza he organized to celebrate the putative 2,500th anniversary of the founding of Achaemenian rule by Cyrus the Great; and his 1976 revision of the calendar so that time was no longer to be measured from Muhammad's hegira, but rather from Cyrus's accession.[10]

As the paradigmatic model that the shah repeatedly invoked, the Achaemenian Empire included a number of characteristics he sought to establish as prominent features of his own realm. Among the most important of these were: (1) projection of Iranian influence and military power on an international scale, (2) a cosmopolitan populace in which national and religious minorities were peacefully integrated, and (3) kingship as the central, indispensable, and divinely ordained institution for the unification and direction of the empire. Another, less obvious item might also be implied, inferred, or denied as the situation warranted: That is, an end to the privileged position of Islam, which did not enter Iran until nearly a millennium after the last Achaemenid. Although a careful ambiguity was preserved regarding

* Organization of Petroleum Exporting Countries.

this last point, it does not seem to have been lost on the Islamic clergy (*'ulama*) or on others, as is witnessed by the fact that in the late 1970s a significant (if improbable) rumor circulated to the effect that the shah would soon reveal himself a Zoroastrian and would proclaim Iran once more to be a Zoroastrian nation.[11]

The 'ulama had, in fact, long been among those most dissatisfied with Pahlavi rule. Since 1963 the shah had attacked them directly in a number of ways, depriving them of many traditional sources of income, undercutting their influence in education and culture, and driving some of their leaders into exile, most notably the Ayatollah Khomeini. In their discontent the 'ulama were hardly alone, however, although it was not until the late 1970s that opposition to the shah's regime became both widespread and vocal as a result of numerous factors. Among these were a pattern of corruption and nepotism within the government, excesses of the repressive apparatus, especially the secret police (SAVAK), and the uncritical imitation of Western mores in areas that violated Islamic law and offended the sensibilities of traditionalists (e.g., women going unveiled, public consumption of alcoholic beverages, etc.). Most important of all were the economic dislocations that resulted from fluctuations in oil revenue. Although oil prices quadrupled in 1973 as a result of policies implemented by OPEC at the shah's insistence, Iranian petrodollar profits remained concentrated in the upper strata of society and served only to exacerbate preexisting class antagonisms. Moreover, recession followed in 1977 as the conservation policies of oil-consuming nations took effect and oil sales declined.

Given the extremely restrictive government policies of censorship, the shah's critics had very few channels of discourse open to them through which they could voice their dissent and rally a movement of opposition. Among the most important of these was a story that has long been regarded as the most authoritative of all narratives by the vast majority of Iranians, that of Karbala: a story that recounts aspects of early Islamic history and has played an ongoing role in the construction of Iranian society through the centuries.

In order to appreciate the nature and importance of the Karbala myth, it is necessary to fill in some background regarding the struggles for succession to the office of caliph after the death of Muhammad in 632 C.E., struggles that have remained of enormous interest and importance to Muslims ever since (see Fig. 2.3). As Marshall Hodgson observed, "Later Muslims have identified themselves in terms of these events and the factions that grew out of them. They have interpreted the whole of history in symbolism derived from them, and have made the interpretation of those events and of the leading personalities in them the very test of religious allegiance."[12]

On Muhammad's death, political power and religious authority within the rapidly growing community of Islam passed at first to Abu Bakr (r. 632–34), the father of Muhammed's second (and favorite) wife, Ayesha, and one of the prophet's earliest converts; then it passed to another father-in-law, Umar (r. 634–644); and thirdly it passed to Muhammad's son-in-law, Uth-

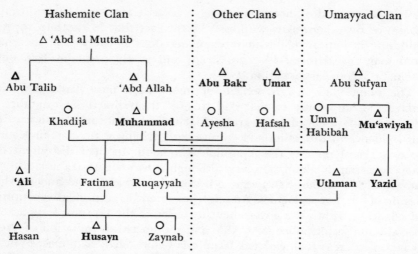

Figure 2.3. Genealogy of Muhammad and early leaders of the Muslim world (contenders for the caliphate appear in boldface).

man (r. 644–656). Each of the first three caliphs thus came from clans other than that of Muhammad (i.e., the Hashemite clan), as they were all related to him by marriage and not by birth, although all were members of the same tribe, that of Quraysh. At each succession, however, there were those who argued that the caliphate should rightly remain within the line of Muhammad's own clan and family, passing to 'Ali, his father's brother's son and his closest surviving male relative, who had further cemented his agnatic tie to the prophet by his marriage to Fatima, Muhammad's favorite daughter. Finally, when Uthman died by assassination, 'Ali fulfilled his ambitions and became the fourth caliph. His reign, however, was a turbulent one, and he was contested by Uthman's clansman Mu'awiyah, himself a brother-in-law of Muhammad. Their struggle ended in 'Ali's assassination, whereupon both Mu'awiyah and Hasan, 'Ali's elder son, were elected caliph by rival factions; but Mu'awiyah quickly induced his younger rival to withdraw his claim. Then, during his long and relatively successful reign (661–80), Mu'awiyah worked to transform the caliphate from an elective into a dynastic office, one he could pass to his son, Yazid and thus keep the caliphate, its power and authority, within the Umayyad clan. This was challenged, however, by 'Ali's younger son, Husayn, who cast himself as the rightful heir to the office and charisma of his grandfather, the prophet, and rallied a group of followers. Their rebellion ended, however, at Karbala, where Husayn and his adherents died in battle against the vastly superior forces of Yazid (10 Muharram 61 A.H. [680 C.E.]).

Husayn's martyrdom notwithstanding, the struggle did not end, but rather it assumed a different and enduring form. For within Islam there is one sect, or branch, that has continued to withhold recognition of Mu'awiyah, Yazid, and the Umayyad dynasty they founded. That sect maintains that by rights the caliphate should have passed to Husayn and through him to direct descendants of the prophet. This sect is known as the Shi'a, the party (*shi'a*) of 'Ali and Husayn. Holding themselves separate from the majority faction (the Sunni), Shi'is take the story of Husayn as their central mythic narrative, one they recount in elaborate detail, dwelling on the treachery of Yazid; the courage, determination, and righteousness of Husayn; and the suffering of Zaynab, Husayn's sister—all of whom provide mythic models for the actions and attitudes of Shi'is in the ongoing present. Bit by bit pieces of this master narrative are given ritual celebration over the course of each year, building toward the month of Muharram and the festival of 'Ashura, which commemorates Husayn's martyrdom at Karbala. At this time in particular, but more broadly, whenever the Karbala story is told, Shi'i society is reconstructed, as Shi'is recollect Husayn. In so doing they come to experience powerful sentiments of attachment both to Husayn and to one another along with complementary sentiments of estrangement from those other Muslims who perversely continue to accept the legitimacy of the archvillain Yazid. Furthermore, this myth has had an important role in the construction of national as well as sectarian borders and identities, for since the inauguration of the Safavid dynasty in 1501, Shi'a has been the official state religion of Iran, where Shi'is are in the vast majority, whereas Sunnis hold sway elsewhere, particularly within Arab nations. Invocation of the Husayn myth ever since has served, inter alia, to separate Shi'i from Sunni and Iranian from Arab, as is shown in Figure 2.4.

From the sixteenth century well into the twentieth, this myth was thus a useful instrument, one through which Iranian national identity could be continuously reconstructed along the same traditional pattern. Yet as many scholars have recognized, in the middle and late 1970s, the embattled Iranian 'ulama gave a radical new twist to the story as they identified the

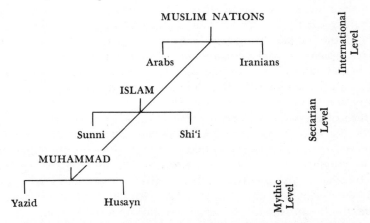

Figure 2.4. Sectarian and international divisions within the Islamic world as correlated with, and evoked by, the Karbala myth.

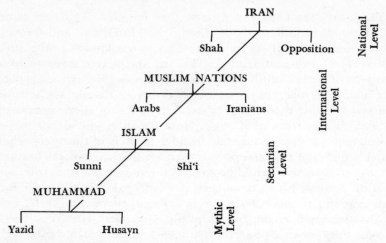

Figure 2.5. Sectarian, international, and internal Iranian divisions as evoked by the Karbala myth in its radical reinterpretation of the late 1970s.

shah—guardedly at first, then ever-more openly—with the quasi-demonic assassin and usurper Yazid. Thus interpreted, the Karbala myth no longer served primarily as the ancestral invocation through which Shi'i Iranians could define themselves in contradistinction to Sunni Arabs, but more important it became the revolutionary slogan through which the emerging movement of opposition to the shah was mobilized (Fig. 2.5).

Through skillful use of the Karbala myth, the previously fragmented members of this revolutionary coalition—some of whom were opposed to the shah on religious, some on political, and some on economic grounds—were welded together and came to view themselves collectively as the righteous descendants of Husayn confronting an evil and fundamentally alien ruler: a shah more Zoroastrian than Muslim, more Sunni than Shi'i, more Arab than Iranian, more Yazid than Husayn. Moreover, in the years of the revolution, the 'ulama within their preachings increasingly depicted Husayn as a paradigmatic model who demonstrated not the need to accept life's injustices and suffering (as he had usually been presented in preachings of the prerevolutionary period), but the need for fearless and militant opposition to tyranny.

In Iran of the 1970s two rival parties thus employed different moments from the past in their discourse as they struggled to construct very different kinds of society in the present. By means of the history of the Achaemenians, which he sought to elevate to the status of myth, the shah struggled to construct an imperial and non-Islamic Iran; with the myth of Karbala, to which they attached a radical new interpretation, the 'ulama sought precisely the opposite, that is, an Islamic and stridently anti-imperial nation.

In this struggle it was the 'ulama who proved successful. As Pahlavi power dwindled, it proved ever-more difficult to convert stories of the

Achaemenians from the status of history to that of myth. Although credible, such stories lacked authority, even in the best of times, and for all that the shah might invoke them, the Achaemenians remained ancestors to whom few Iranians felt deeply attached. Use of them as a slogan rallied no mass following and stirred little interest beyond the circle of those who were already favored by, and obligated to, the shah. In the final months of his reign, the shah was driven to rely almost entirely on force and the threat of force, having lost all capacity to rally or persuade the bulk of the Iranian populace through mythic or any other sort of discourse. At the same time the ability of his adversaries to mobilize a mass following grew rapidly, their lack of firepower notwithstanding. Significantly, the most potent and spectacular forms of their revolutionary agitation took the form of ritual dramas: re-presentations of Husayn's passion, in which participants emulated the latter and actively sought martyrdom, parading their defiance of the shah-*cum*-Yazid. Following the climactic marches of 'Ashura in December 1978, in which millions of Iranians took to the streets rallying simultaneously around Husayn and against the shah, Muhammad Reza Pahlavi was forced to abdicate. His attempts to construct an imperial Iran had come to an end and those of others to construct an Islamic republic were beginning, attempts in which—on one side as on the other—discourses focusing on the mythic past served as a primary instrument.[13]

3

Competing Uses of the Future
in the Present

The Flat Earth and Social Egalitarianism

Thus far, in considering the sociopolitical instrumentality of mythic discourse, we have limited ourselves to stories that are told in the past tense. Yet there are other myths, and extremely important ones, that are set not in the past but in the future, a mythic future that—like the mythic past—enters discourse in the present always and only for reasons of the present. What is more, such myths may well be (and have often been) contested territory as competing segments of society seek to appropriate them and turn them to their own interests, be those interests the preservation of the status quo or the reconstruction of society in some radically new form. As a case in point consider a common eschatological image that occurs, inter alia, in three Iranian accounts of the world's end. According to the first, "This also is said: 'The earth becomes flat, without a crown and without a seat. There are no mountain peaks or hollows, nor are *up* and *down* preserved'" (*Greater Bundahishn* 34.33).

The vision is a dramatic and picturesque one, but as we shall see, it is also possessed of considerable ideological import. In order to recognize this, it is necessary to consider the relation of this imminent cataclysmic moment to a corresponding moment from the primordial past, as recounted in this same text. For the *Bundahishn* also relates how at the beginning of time, the foremost Zoroastrian deity, Ohrmazd (literally, the Wise Lord), created seven perfect entities: sky, water, plants, earth, fire, the first ox, and the first man. Against these his archrival, Ahriman (the Evil Spirit), launched a ferocious assault and succeeded, not in destroying them, but in placing within each one a taint that will endure until the world's end. Thus, for instance, he placed salt in the water, smoke in the fire, and (of greatest interest to us in the present context) when he attacked the earth, the earth quaked in terror at his advance, causing mountains to erupt: mountains that corrupt and distort its primordial perfection (*Greater Bundahishn* 6C.1).

38

The eschatological leveling of mountains will thus reverse the results of Ahriman's assault and will restore the earth to its original pristine state. This is expected at the conclusion of a twelve thousand year cycle that began with Ohrmazd's act of creation, and it will end with the Renovation, or Making-wonderful (Middle Persian, *Frashagird*) of the universe when Ohrmazd will conclusively defeat Ahriman and return all existence to its original untainted state. At this time will occur such events as the resurrection of the dead, the last judgment, the bestowing of immortality, and the rout of demonic beings, but the final step in the world's renewal and the culminating sign of cosmic renovation according to the *Bundahishn* is nothing other than the restoration of the earth's level plain, which is described in rather elaborate fashion:

> Then fire . . . melts the metal which is in the mountains and hills, and it becomes like a river on the earth. Then all mortal beings pass through that molten metal and are made pure, and to righteous mortals this iron seems like nothing more than warm milk, but to the unrighteous it seems just like molten metal. . . . And the serpent Gochihr burns in that molten metal, and the metal flows into hell. The stench and the filth of hell are burnt up in that metal, and hell becomes pure. And the point of entry through which Ahriman launched his assault on the good creation is sealed up by that metal. Hell is thus recovered for the earth, and the Renovation comes about, and the world becomes undying forever and ever. This also is said: "The earth becomes flat, without a crown and without a seat. There are no mountain peaks or hollows, nor are 'up' and 'down' preserved (*Greater Bundahishn* 34.18–19, 31–33).

It is thus foreseen that the river of metal that will come into being out of the mountains at that time when they are finally leveled will itself have a number of important and beneficial effects. It will destroy a notorious monster, Gochihr (the celestial serpent said to be responsible for solar and lunar eclipses); it will seal off the hole through which Ahriman originally gained entry to Ohrmazd's good creation, thus preventing any renewal of the attack; and it will purify hell, a realm that becomes unnecessary after the raising and purification of the dead. Finally, it will provide the molten metal that is used for the last ordeal in which the souls of evildoers suffer for, and are purged of, their failings, whereas the souls of the righteous pass through unscathed. Thereafter, those differences that separated the righteous from the unrighteous—in life as in death—will be obliterated, as the totality of humankind is reunited in a state that is named and described as "the greatest love." The text continues:

> Then, all mortals arrive together in the greatest love: fathers and sons, brothers, and all friends. They ask one another: "Where have you been these many years? And what was the judgment on your soul? Were you righteous or unrighteous?" When first a soul sees a body it asks these questions and receives answers. Then all mortals come together in collaboration and bear high praise to Ohrmazd (*Greater Bundahishn* 34.20–21).

Similar images and themes recur in a related text, Plutarch's summary treatment of Iranian religion. This work, after describing the creation of gods by Ohrmazd, that of demons by Ahriman, and the ensuing struggle between them, goes on to state, "A time is destined in which Ahriman, bringer of plague and famine, must of necessity be wholly destroyed and made to disappear. And when the earth has come to be flat and level, then one life and one government come into being for all people, who are blessed and all speak the same tongue" (Plutarch, *Isis and Osiris* 47).

For all its brevity this passage shows considerable familiarity with the details of Iranian religion.[1] Particularly interesting is that it represents the leveling of the earth as the most important of eschatological events and, what is more, something that is directly and explicitly associated with the unity of humanity that will emerge at the time of Ahriman's fall when differences of political system and differences of language disappear and "one life" comes into being for all humanity.

Just how much is implied by the phrase "one life" (Greek, *ena bion*) is difficult to judge with any precision. It is possible, for instance, that Plutarch meant to describe a state in which the distinction between the righteous and the unrighteous disappears, as is specified in the *Bundahishn*. It may also be that differences in age were expected to vanish, just as the same source states that the adult dead will all be resurrected as forty years of age and all children as fifteen (*Greater Bundahishn* 34.8). It is also possible that an end to distinctions of social class is implied here, a point to which we shall return.

For the present, however, let us simply note that within human affairs in general, it is just such things as differences in language, politics, ethical standards, age, and class that produce, reproduce, and exacerbate those sentiments of estrangement that scholars (and others) reify in the form of social borders. Moreover, as described by both Plutarch and the *Bundahishn*, it is the eradication of such differences as these (but not, interestingly enough, differences of gender!) that will make possible the everlasting unity of humankind in love and harmony. Another Middle Persian text pursues these same themes of social unity, disunity, and the end of time:

> Human unity is caused by common love, and the separation of mortals from one another derives from the rupture of this love by the demons of Greed, Wrath, Envy, and Malice. . . . At the Renovation, however, the common love of all mortals becomes firm and immutable, and this causes despair among the demons, who recognize that their power is not eternal (*Dēnkart* 3.327).

The proper state of humanity—which is, of course, yet to come—is thus characterized as one of unity in love, a state that is blocked in the present by the continuing assault of demons created by Ahriman. Those demons, moreover, are nothing other than the quasi-personified disruptive sentiments (greed, wrath, envy, and malice) that undermine and inhibit the workings of such sentiments as trust, affection, harmony, and solidarity, out of which society is actively constructed. Finally, the power of these demonic beings is said to be of finite duration, for when a unified, loving humanity is finally reestablished, the demons are rendered powerless. Another passage from the same text pursues these ideas in ways that are now familiar to us, correlating an eschatological state to a primordial one:

> Now, since Ohrmazd created all creatures from a single substance, humans are all born of one father. And since all are of the same substance, they care for one another, and fix things for one another, and assist one another. And because of their common birth, they consider one another to be relatives, friendly brothers, and they do goodness to one another, and they carry evil away from one another (*Dēnkart* 3.246).

The opening phrase of this passage, "since Ohrmazd created all creatures from a single substance," alludes to another section of the cosmogonic myth, specifically the portion that describes Ohrmazd's creation and Ahriman's murder of the first man, Gayōmart (*Greater Bundahishn* 6F.1–10, 14.27–39). There it is told how although Ahriman killed Gayōmart, he did not succeed thereby in exterminating the human species as a whole: It is axiomatic within Zoroastrian theology that the Evil Spirit can never entirely destroy Ohrmazd's creations but can only corrupt or damage them. Thus, from the semen that fell from Gayōmart's dying body were born his children, who subsequently produced the nations and races of humankind in all their diversity.

This is why from its origin humankind is one, "created . . . from a single substance," that substance being Gayōmart's seed. In a quite literal and physiological sense all humans are kin, "born from one father," and accordingly, their proper attitude toward one another—called forth by this invocation of all peoples' primordial ancestor—ought be one of love and familial devotion. Two forms of corruption have entered humanity, however, as a result of Ahriman's assault. These are mortality at the level of the individual and disunity at that of the collective. However, at the end of time, when Ahriman is defeated and original perfection regained, these taints will be removed from human existence, just as salt disappears from the water and the mountains from the earth.

Other variants of Iranian cosmogonic myth also play on the theme of how from the sundered body of the first man, humanity was created in all its diversity. Moreover, in some of these it is specified that four hierarchized social classes came from different vertically ranked strata of his body: priests from his head, warriors from his hands and arms, herdsmen and pastoralists from his belly, and artisans from his feet.[2] Here, social classes may be viewed as the result of demonic assault, with the corollary expectation that the Renovation will bring an end to social stratification, so that the separate estates merge into an egalitarian social body congruent to the single physical body from which they all came.

By now it is clear why the apocalyptic image of the leveling of mountains should be associated with the ideal of a humanity united in love.

Mountains, plains, and hollows, like the social classes, are set apart on a vertical scale. Some are higher, loftier, and more distinguished; others lowlier and more degraded. Moreover, such distinctions—at least in the texts we have considered thus far—are perceived to be an injustice and a corruption of the primordial, perfect egalitarianism that preceded the demonic assault. Further, a key term in the passage with which we began clearly indicates that these images encode a critique of social class, for there it is stated that when the earth becomes flat, it will be "without a crown" (Middle Persian, *anabesar*), *crown* being in Iranian as in English a term and an image that refers simultaneously to the pinnacle of geologic and sociopolitical formations alike, and it appears as one of the chief emblems of royal power.

Mountains, Law, and Order

In addition to the Iranian texts cited, there exists a third text in which the image of the flat earth recurs, albeit with a dramatically different coloration. This is the *Oracles of Hystaspes,* a work of Iranian origin, famed and widely disseminated in late antiquity but now preserved only in fragmentary form within Greek and Roman sources, the most important of which is Lactantius's *Divine Institutions.*[3] The text is frankly apocalyptic and is highly charged politically: It contains ringing predictions of Rome's imminent fall and the subsequent return of kingship to Asia along with the punishment of the wicked and the triumph of righteousness, all as the result of God's direct intervention in history.

Such predictions are couched within the descriptions of revelatory dreams that are attributed to the legendary king Hystaspes (= Iranian Vishtāspa, who was wrongly understood to have been both the patron of Zoroaster and the father of Cyrus the Great). These dreams are presented quite vividly, and they abound in images of chaos, destruction, and devastation as well as the evils of the present age that are soon to be wiped away. Within such a context, in marked contrast to those sources we considered earlier, the *Oracles of Hystaspes* treats the leveling of mountains not as the culminating event in the work of cosmic renovation, but as one of the many woes characteristic of that period just prior to God's salvific action. Thus, it is said:

> The air will be defiled and corrupt, and will also be made pestilent by means of unfavorable rains and injurious drought; now by cold and now by excessive heat. And the earth will not give fruit to man, nor will field, tree, or vine bear fruit. But at the very time when they have given the greatest hope by their flowers, they will cheat with their fruit. . . . Then the year will be shortened, and the month diminished, and the day confined in a narrow space. Stars will fall repeatedly, so that the heavens appear dark and without any lights. *Also, the highest mountains will fall, and they are made level with the plains,* and the sea will be made unnavigable. . . . Men will lament,

groan, and grate their teeth. They will congratulate the dead and bewail the living. . . . That will be the time when justice is cast down and innocence hated, in which evil men plunder the good like an enemy. Neither law, nor order, nor military discipline will be preserved. No one will respect the aged, nor acknowledge the obligation of piety. Neither women nor children will be pitied. All will be confounded and mixed together, against what is right and against the laws of nature (Lactantius, *Divine Institutions*, 7.16.4, 7.16.10–12, and 7.17.9. Emphasis added).

The last sentence of this excerpt makes explicit the ideology that informs and structures the whole. The evils of the final age are characterized by nothing so much as by intermixture, that is the state in which categories fall together that ought (according to traditional norms and the text's viewpoint) be held apart. Good is thus contaminated by evil; pure, by impure. In the physical universe the air turns as rain and dry, hot and cold rebel against their proper place and order. Likewise, the very structure of time collapses as years become like months and months like days. Stars leave their proper place, and (what is of chief interest to us) the mountains and valleys become indistinguishable.

The literal con-fusion of categories that are ordinarily held separate also finds expression within the social as well as the natural order. Law and order crumble, and (a telling detail) their collapse is connected to that of military discipline. The point is a clear one: The social order, like that of an army, depends on the preservation of certain hierarchic and classificatory distinctions along with a full complement of behavioral rules through which these are made operational. But in the coming catastrophe, the aged will be treated like the young, women like men, soldiers like officers, foreigners like countrymen, the dead like the living, and servants like masters as the social order degenerates into chaos. On this point one must be perfectly clear: It is not the assault of some vague and amorphous evil that causes these categories to break down, rather, it is the breakdown of such categories that is itself the essence of evil.

This theme is a common one in Iranian thought, as others have rightly stressed.[4] Consider, for example, the following passage from the *Jāmāsp Nāmag*, a Middle Persian apocalypse that draws on the same body of tradition as does the *Oracles of Hystaspes:*

All Iran falls to the hand of the enemy, and Iranian and non-Iranian mix together such that non-Iranian-ness is indistinguishable from Iranian-ness, and Iranian becomes like non-Iranian. In this time, people consider the poor to be fortunate, but truly the poor are not fortunate. For the noble and the powerful, life is without savor. And for them death is as pleasant as the sight of a son is to a father, or a daughter's bridewealth is to a mother. The son strikes his father and mother, and during their life he takes authority over their household from them. The younger brother strikes his older brother, he takes his wealth from him, and for the sake of that wealth, he speaks falsehood. Women create souls deserving death. The lowly achieve visibility.
. . . The air is troubled: a cold wind and a hot wind blow. The fruits of the

plants become scarce, and not one fruit comes from the earth. Earthquakes become numerous and cause great desolation (*Jāmāsp Nāmag* 12–21, 26–28).

It is possible that the mention of earthquakes is meant to imply the collapse of mountains (cf. the earthquake with which they were created according to *Greater Bundahishn* 6C.1), but it is impossible to be certain. Other images closely parallel those found in the *Oracles of Hystaspes:* corruption of the air, intermixture of hot and cold, and the inability of the earth to bear fruit. Also common to the two texts is the observation that death is considered pleasant and life without savor, although the *Jāmāsp Nāmag* pointedly specifies that such is the case only "for the noble and the powerful" (Middle Persian, *āzādān ud wuzurgān*). Depiction of the disintegrating social order is intended to be graphic and shocking, particularly as evidenced in the perversion of intimate family relations. Thus, where Lactantius simply states, "No one will respect the aged," the Middle Persian passage shows sons striking parents and usurping their authority and in place of the bland assertion that evil men plunder the good, a younger son is shown defrauding the elder of his birthright.

One issue that is raised in the *Jāmāsp Nāmag*, but not (at least, not explicitly) in the *Oracles of Hystaspes,* is that of social class. In the former text, we are told first that in the apocalyptic age of woes, the poor are considered fortunate (if only in contrast to the wealthy) and second that "the lowly achieve visibility." Just as the fall of stars and of mountains are offered as images of downward motion that violates the established order of the cosmos, so the elevation of the lowly is an upward motion destructive of its social counterpart. Another related Middle Persian text develops this ideological line still further expressing the confusion of social classes through inversions of normative marital and authority relations:

> The little people take the daughters of the nobles, the powerful, and the Magi in marriage, and the nobles, the powerful, and the Magi go to poverty and servitude, while the little people achieve greatness, sovereignty, and foremost position. And the pronouncements of religious leaders, judges, and the righteous come to be regarded as mere rabble-rousing, while the pronouncements of the little people, slanderers, perverts, mockers, and liars come to be regarded as just and true (*Zand ī Vohuman Yasn* 4.35–37).

Clearly, alongside those who represented social distinctions as a demonic disruption of Ohrmazd's good creation, there existed others who gave expression to contrasting views by portraying any erosion of such categorical and hierarchic distinctions as those between parent and child, elder and younger, wealthy and poor, countryman and foreigner as the mark of a woefully fallen age. As for the leveling of mountains, within all ancient literature relevant to the pre-Islamic religions of Iran, this image occurs only in those three texts we have considered: the *Bundahishn*, Plutarch's *Isis and Osiris*, and the *Oracles of Hystaspes* as preserved by Lactantius. Yet as we have seen, for all that they share this common image, they treat it in strikingly different fashions. Whereas Plutarch and the *Bundahishn* make leveling the culminating act of the cosmic Renovation, the *Oracles of Hystaspes* groups it among the apocalyptic woes. What is more important, this variation is not random, but correlates to the texts' sociopolitical orientation. Thus, when social distinctions are denounced, the leveling of mountains is celebrated, but when social distinctions are celebrated, it is leveling that is condemned.

The Instrumentality of the Future

Outside of Iran, the image of the flat earth is quite widely attested, often with the same sort of sociopolitical content that we have observed.[5] Consider, for instance, a familiar passage from the New Testament: the opening of the sixth seal of the apocalyptic scroll, according to the *Revelation* of St. John:

> When he opened the sixth seal, I looked, and behold, there was a great earthquake; and the sun became black as sackcloth, the full moon became like blood, and the stars of the sky fell to the earth as the fig tree sheds its winter fruit when shaken by a gale; the sky vanished like a scroll that is rolled up, *and every mountain and island was removed from its place.* Then the kings of the earth and the great men and the generals and the rich and the strong, and every one, slave and free, hid in the caves and among the rocks of the mountains, calling to the mountains and rocks, "Fall on us and hide us from the face of him who is seated on the throne, and from the wrath of the Lamb; for the great day of their wrath has come, and who can stand before it?" (*Revelation* 6.12–17, Revised Standard Version).

Seven types of people are mentioned in this passage, in descending order of their social rank, with one exception, where the formulaic phrase "slave and free" (Greek, *doulos kai eleutheros*), follows a grammatical rule according to which the shorter noun precedes the longer. The list is as follows:

1. The kings of the earth
2. The great men
3. The generals
4. The rich
5. The strong
6–7. Every one, slave and free

Now, within the book of *Revelation,* as is well known, there is a recurrent pattern whereby seven items of any sort—seals, trumpets, bowls, cities, and so on—constitute a full and complete set. This list is one more such set, one in which the social hierarchy is mapped from top to bottom, kings to slaves. What is most noteworthy, however, is that the collapse of mountains at the end of time reduces all members of this carefully differentiated society to the very same state of abject fear and utter impotence in the face of divine wrath. Social stratification is thus obliterated, coincident with and dependent on the eschatological leveling of mountains.

For its part the Qu'rān makes the leveling of mountains a necessary precondition for the last judgment, stressing that on that day all shall stand equal and be judged on their deeds, not their social station. The full account of judgment occurs at Sūra 69.13–37, and leveling is mentioned almost immediately, at verse 14, whereas the social context is established later, in verses 28–29, when an evildoer laments, "Of no profit to me has been my wealth! My power has perished from me" (trans. Abdullah Yusuf Ali). Verse 34 goes on to specify that this individual's crime was a failure to show charity toward the poor. Elsewhere, yet another code is brought into correlation with those of geologic elevation and socioeconomic standing, it being stated that on the day of judgment all mortals will be naked when they gather on the level plain so that no ostentation or sign of rank may influence the judgment that will be passed upon them (Sūra 18.47–48).

In contrast to these stern images of divine wrath and impending judgment, Buddhist eschatology makes the leveling of mountains part of the paradisal realm of Maitreya, the Buddha yet to come. Once again, geophysical leveling is explicitly associated to a leveling of social distinctions, as in this passage from the *Maitreyavyākaraṇa Sūtra*:

> The Regions of the East [= China] shall become very flat and even, and as clear and bright as the face of a mirror. In the Regions of the East, grains and food shall flourish, having all kinds of wealth in profusion. . . . The people will all feel equal, and will be of one mind, mutually expressing pleasure upon meeting their fellows and in virtuous greetings. . . . And at this time all the people of the Regions of the East will be equal in all respects. And there it will be that men and women, upon wanting to relieve themselves, find that the earth will open a crack before them, and after they have finished it will close again.[6]

The physical world here mirrors the perfection of the social, wherein all disruptive sentiments disappear, rather like the excrements so tidily swallowed up by the earth. Furthermore, all privileges of wealth, position, and family fall, just like the mountains, as is signaled by the fact that the elaborate, hierarchically encoded Confucian system of obeisant salutations is replaced by "virtuous greetings" issued by happy people who "all feel equal." To the best of my knowledge, Confucian texts never make mention of a flat earth, but such an image recurs in the texts of those groups that challenged Confusian orthodoxy, as in the Taoist book of *Lieh-tzü*, which describes the paradisal kingdom of Utmost North as being "flat in all directions," and without the categories of deference characteristic of the Confucian state, "Old and young live as equals, and no one is ruler or subject; men and women mingle freely, without go-betweens and betrothal presents."[7]

In these visions of a perfect never-never land, the revolutionary (if not the critical) thrust of the flat earth is somewhat abated insofar as one may despair of ever establishing a Buddha-world or a kingdom of Utmost North in the here and now. Similarly, when the leveling of mountains is relegated to some distant or indeterminate judgment day, the effect may be to pre-serve present inequalities as the poor and oppressed are implicitly urged to rest easy and trust in God's final justice. But the image acquires an activist dimension whenever groups and individuals assert the possibility of them-selves establishing social equality and redressing past injustice rather than waiting patiently for divine intervention. Such is apparent, for instance, in the cry of those nineteenth-century Japanese rebels who styled their move-ment Yo-naoshi (World Renewal), and physically assaulted the wealthy and privileged, crying, "We are the people of World Renewal. We are the peas-ants who will level the earth!"[8]

The best known use of the leveling image within the history of the mod-ern West also provides a telling example of the multiple ways in which it may be employed. Thus, at the time of the English Civil War, those activ-ists we discussed briefly in chapter 1 who sought to attenuate class distinc-tions primarily by political means such as extending the franchise, won for themselves the title of Levellers, whereas those who focused on economic measures—redistribution of land and the like—came to be called True Levellers or Diggers. Other English radicals of the period also made liberal use of this image as, for example, in the following passage from Abiezer Coppe's wildly exuberant *Fiery Flying Roll*:

> Thus saith the Lord, *I inform you, that I overturn, overturn, overturn.* And as the Bishops, *Charles,* and the Lords have had their turn, overturn, so your turn shall be next (ye surviving great ones) by what Name or Title soever dignified or distinguished, who ever you are, that oppose me, the Eternall God, who am UNIVERSAL love, and whose service is perfect freedome, and pure Libertinisme. . . .
>
> And now thus saith the Lord:
>
> Though you can as little endure the word LEVELLING, as could the late slaine or dead Charles (your forerunner, who is gone before you) and had as lieve heare the Devill named, as heare of the Levellers (Man-Levellers) which is, and who (indeed) are but shadowes of most terrible, yet great and glorious good things to come.
>
> Behold, behold, behold, I the eternall God, the Lord of Hosts, who am that mighty Leveller, am coming (yea, even at the doores) to Levell in good earnest, to Levell to some purpose, to Levell with a witnesse, to Levell the Hills with the Valleyes, and to lay the Mountaines low.
>
> High Mountaines! lofty Cedars! its high time for you to enter into the Rocks, and to hide you in the dust, for feare of the Lord, and for the glory of his Majesty. For the lofty looks of men shall be humbled, and the haughtiness of men shall be bowed downe, and the Lord ALONE shall be exalted in that day.[9]

Writing in 1649, shortly after the trial and execution of Charles 1 (which occurred in January of that year), Coppe—who is usually as a Ranter, that is, an extreme libertarian and revolutionary—sensed a new world in the

making and expressed his egalitarian hopes in this flamboyant discourse
that drew both on biblical and contemporary rhetoric of leveling. Others,
however, were able to employ the same image as a means to advance other
positions. Thus, for example, just a few years earlier, at a time when the
king and his cause were still very much alive, Cavalier wags mocked the
pretentions of their adversaries in a satiric verse known as "The Levellers'
Rant":

> 'Tis we will pull down what e'er is above us,
> And make them to fear us, that never did love us;
> We'll level the proud, and make every degree
> To our royalty bow the knee;
> 'Tis no less than treason
> 'Gainst freedom and reason
> For our brethren to be higher than we.[10]

The image is the same as Coppe, but a few subtle shifts produce a tone
of contemptuous mockery in place of Coppe's fervent advocacy. All mention of divine agency disappears, as does the prophetic voice, which is replaced by that of an apparently impudent and overconfident lout. Consistent with this shift, leveling appears not as the means to establish
"UNIVERSAL love," but as a terroristic device whereby the subordinate orders
can settle old scores ("'Tis we will pull down what e'er is above us, / And
make them to fear us, that never did love us"). Along these lines, it is further suggested that the aim of all self-styled levelers is not so much the
eradication of social hierarchy per se, but the inversion of an existing
hierarchy to their own benefit and enrichment ("We'll level the proud,
and make every degree / To our royalty bow the knee"), something that is
to be scornfully rejected.[11]

Most significant, these seventeenth-century English data exhibit the
same correlations and distributions as do the ancient Iranian sources. In
both instances we find several texts that address the same themes and make
use of the same images, but to very different purposes. Thus, one strain of
tradition in England as in Iran denounces mountains and hierarchy while
embracing the apocalyptic vision of an egalitarian society on a flat earth;
conversely, a second strain rallies to mountains and social differentiation
while denouncing social and geophysical leveling alike (see Fig. 3.1). Un-
fortunately, we possess little independent information regarding the social
identity and political allegiance of those who produced, propagated, and
were influenced by these conflicting discourses in Iran, nor do we know
much about the circumstances in which they were active. Regarding the
English materials, however, we are more fortunate, and it surely comes as
no shock to learn that the positions advanced in the various texts were fully
congruent with the class interests and consciousness of those connected to
them.

In England of the 1640s, as in ancient Iran, contending parties em-

		Attitude Expressed Toward:			
		Mountains	*Hierarchy*	*Leveling*	*Egalitarianism*
Iran	Bundahishn & Plutarch	−	−	+	+
	Oracles of Hystaspes	+	+	−	−
England	Fiery Flying Roll (Ranter)	−	−	+	+
	Levellers' Rant (Cavalier)	+	+	−	−

Figure 3.1. Orientations of five texts in which the flat earth is at issue.

ployed the same mythic image as a means to promote their own favored positions, while simultaneously countering those of their adversaries. Far from being a stereotypical and vague piece of apocalyptic bricolage, within their usage the leveling of mountains encoded—clearly and precisely—a vision of social egalitarianism and a world stripped of high and low. Certain groups and individuals tended to embrace that image, whereas others recoiled at it, but the image itself belonged to none. Rather, it was an instrument of agitation that could be appropriated and employed with equal facility by a wide variety of actors who differed markedly in their ideological positions, social identities, and practical goals.

From these data we may also suggest some broader conclusions, for similar observations may now be advanced regarding those authoritative narratives (myths) that draw the future into the present as were earlier made regarding those narratives that do the same for the past. That is to say, myth—whatever its temporal point of reference—is a mode of discourse, the instrumentality of which is not restricted to the reproduction of those social relations of which it is itself the product. That it is frequently—and effectively—employed to this end is beyond question, yet there is no innate necessity that makes it so, and there are sufficiently compelling counterexamples that may be cited to discredit any neat and simplistic formulation that would reduce myth to a tool of the right and the right only.

That myth has been used more often and more effectively by those who seek to mystify and preserve exploitative patterns of social relations than it has by those who would reform or radically restructure such relations is not something I would ever contest. What I do contest, however, is the claim that this state of affairs results from some intrinsic, invariant, and categoric property of myth per se. Rather, if one may paraphrase the single most frequently cited sentence from Marx and Engels's *The German Ideology,* it seems best to observe that the dominant discourse—including mythic discourse—in any age is the discourse of the dominant class. This does not mean that other groups are without their discourses and without their myths, nor that they are incapable of appropriating the myths and discourse of the dominant class, which they may also refashion and employ to telling advantage. In this, moreover, there is nothing primitive or archaic, nor is it something that is necessarily ineffective. Even Marx himself had recourse to myth at times, as when he spoke of "primitive communism" and the classless society yet to come: stories that, in truth, differ not so greatly from Iranian accounts of the flat earth.

Part II

RITUAL

4

Ritual, Rebellion, Resistance: Rethinking the Swazi Ncwala

On Ritual and Social Stability

Like myth, ritual is best understood as an authoritative mode of symbolic discourse and a powerful instrument for the evocation of those sentiments (affinity and estrangement) out of which society is constructed. The differences between the two, although hardly negligible, are in large measure a matter of genre, ritual discourse being primarily gestural and dramatic; mythic discourse, verbal and narrative. I hope I have shown that the politics of myth are considerably more complex than is generally recognized; now the time has come to turn our attention to ritual.[1]

That ritual performances can contribute powerfully to the maintenance of society—a crucial insight of functionalist and structural-functionalist theoreticians—remains an accepted truism, and others who write from a Marxist position have advanced powerful arguments in support of the view that ritual is both intrinsically and categorically conservative in nature. Among the most influential discussions in this general vein, of course, is Max Gluckman's famed Frazer lecture of 1952 on "Rituals of Rebellion in South and South-east Africa," in which he attempted to demonstrate that when sociopolitical tensions and conflicts of a potentially violent and disintegrative nature are set within ritual discourse, they are thereby rendered harmless and result only in continuation of the status quo.[2] Yet before passing judgment on such formulations, it is worth reconsidering Gluckman's central example: the Swazi Ncwala ceremony as it was meticulously reported by Hilda Kuper.[3]

The Ncwala Summarized

It is a formidable task to describe the events of the Ncwala briefly. In truth, Kuper's dense twenty-nine pages seem a model of concision and precision alike, detailing a spectacular celebration that unfolds over several weeks and involves scores of ritual sequences that cumulatively are expected to renew the powers of the Swazi king, kingship, nation, and land. Yet in a general fashion there are certain points that might be stressed. Celebrated annually, the Ncwala is timed to commence shortly before the summer (i.e., December) solstice and to end afterward: It thus straddles the turning point of the year. Further, each Ncwala consists of two distinct phases: The Little Ncwala, which begins on the new moon, and the Great Ncwala, which begins fourteen days later, that is, on the first full moon following the solstice. The ritual thus marks a transition from lack to plenty, as marked by the absence or presence of moonlight. This lunar code is both reinforced and extended to the sociopolitical sphere by carefully choreographed changes in the military formations adopted by the king's regiments, which shift from a crescent pattern to a circle at climactic moments of the Little Ncwala when the strength of the king is forcefully reasserted. One must also note that the month in which the ritual begins is called To Swallow the Pickings of the Teeth, food being scarcest and labor most demanding just before the harvest. In contrast, the month in which the Ncwala ends is the time of first fruits and bears the name Everyone Is Satisfied.

These contrasts—marked in lunar, calendric, agricultural, and other codes—are thematically central to the Ncwala: contrasts between darkness and light, exhaustion and energy, dearth and abundance, impotence and power. Nor does the ritual simply pose these contrasts in some symbolic game; rather, in performing the Ncwala, the participants take action to transform a preexisting empty or negative state into its positive counterpart.

The Little Ncwala lasts two days, in both of which the same general processes and sequences are evident. Thus, songs are sung, the lyrics of which voice hatred of the king, but these give way to songs of triumph and praise as the warriors shift to their full moon formation.[4] Moreover, these dramatic changes come at that precise moment when the king spits certain powerful medicines to the east, then to the west in order to "stab" the new year, that is, to commence and consecrate it. Before he can undertake this task, however, he must be secured against all his enemies—active and potential—who are driven from the ritual arena to the general cry, "Out, foreigners!"

After a hiatus of twelve days, the Great Ncwala phase commences and lasts six days more. The first three of these are given to preparations, particularly the gathering of waters and plants from all parts of the Swazi realm, which will be used in medicines to strengthen the king. The fourth day, known as the Great Day, is the ritual's dramatic climax. Before dawn, songs are heard. Young boys sing a sacred lullaby for the revitalization of king and nation. Adults sing the *Simemo,* which Kuper translates as:

> Shi shi ishi ishi—you hate him,
> ishi ishi ishi—mother, the enemies are the people.
> ishi ishi ishi—you hate him,
> Mother—the people are wizards.
> Admit the treason of Mabedla [a nineteenth-century rebel]

ishi ishi ishi—you hate him,
you have wronged,
ishi ishi—bend great neck.
those and those they hate him,
ishi ishi—they hate the king.[5]

And as a refrain, the people add, speaking directly to the king:

Jjiya oh o o King, alas for your fate
Jjiya oh o o King, they reject thee
Jjiya oh o o King, they hate thee.[6]

While this song is sung, the king is within the *Kabayethe* (the National Shrine located inside the queen mother's compound) being bathed by his *tinsila*, two close ritual attendants whom we will have reason to consider later. Meanwhile, outside the people form themselves into two lines between the *Kabayethe* and the White *Sigodlo*, the hut of his first ritual queen. When all is ready, the king emerges from the *Kabayethe* naked, save for an ivory penis cap. Flanked by priests, he walks through the people as they sing the *Simemo* and the women weep.

Once the king has entered the White *Sigodlo*, his councillors enforce silence on the crowd. The king then spits medicines east and west once more, and the people acclaim him: "Eh eh! He stabs [the year]!" Again he spits and then bites the first fruits of the new harvest, the food that signifies passage from hunger to satiety. Only after he has bitten may other Swazi eat, and then only in the precise order of their position within the social hierarchy. These sequences transpire on the morning of the Great Day. There follows a pause and during the colonial period there was at this point a brief visit (usually for not more than an hour) from the resident commissioner for Swaziland, the chief colonial authority in the immediate area, and his party.

Late in the afternoon begin the most dramatic sequences of the Ncwala. At that time the princes of the Dlamini clan—who are simultaneously the half brothers, the subordinate administrators, and the potential rivals of the king—press against him frantically, singing a song thus far unheard within the ceremony. Warrior regiments join the princes, throwing themselves against the king and driving him back inside the *Nhlambelo* (the hut at the head of the National Cattle Byre, where all are gathered). Their song is wild; the singers rhythmically stamp the ground, the women cry. Everywhere this song is heard:

We shall leave them with their country,
Whose travellers are like distant thunder,
Do you hear, Dlambula [a royal title], do you hear?

The women sing:

Do you hear?
Let us go, let us go.

The princes now throw themselves against the door of the *Nhlambelo* and beg the king to come forth, "Come from your sanctuary. The sun is leaving you, you the High One. Dlambula." Then the song continues:

> Come, come, king of kings,
> Come, father, come,
> Come, king, oh come here king.

Once the princes and the warriors have driven the king into the *Nhlambelo*, they withdraw a bit, but the atmosphere remains one of extreme tension. Finally the king returns—but not as the same man who entered the hut. Rather, he is dressed as *Silo*, the "monster of legends," and he dances madly, out of control. There follows a back-and-forth choreography of king and people: The former alternately advances into the crowd and withdraws to his hut, from which the others beseech him to emerge.

Gradually, the action builds to a climax, signaled by the entrance of young, "pure" warriors into the ritual arena. As they advance to face the king, the song changes to a triumphal chorus:

> Thunder deep,
> That they hear the thundrous beat
> Dji, eh, eh.[7]

Back and forth they dance with the king until the cry is heard once more, "Out, foreigners!" At this, all those whose loyalty may be suspect—aliens, Dlamini princes, and women pregnant by Dlamini men—are forced to leave, while the king withdraws to the *Nhlambelo* one last time. When they have departed, he comes forth again carrying in his hand a green gourd. This gourd is an emblem of the past by virtue of its spatial and temporal origin, for it was gathered during the Ncwala of the preceding year in the ancestral homeland of the Swazi, the land they left to enter the present Swaziland. As the king casts this away, the dance and the drama of the Great Day come to an end. The regiments retire to a nearby river and wash while the king is treated with powerful medicines. When they return to the National Cattle Byre, they find him enthroned, with the emblem of the full moon painted on both cheeks.

The following day is characterized by prohibitions: a gradual withdrawal from the power of the Great Day. The final day (i.e., the sixth of the Great Ncwala and the twentieth of the full ceremony) is one of celebration: much food, much beer, and much sexual activity. Ritual paraphernalia are burned in a fire considered to be both a purgation of the past year's pollutions and an offering that will secure rain. In all, the expectation is evident that through the Ncwala—above all, through the passion of the king—the well-being of the earth, the harvest, and the Swazi nation have been secured for another year.

Scholarly Approaches to the Ncwala

Since its publication, Kuper's account has become a classic, and the Ncwala stands alongside the Kwakiutl potlatch, Vedic sacrifice, and a few other privileged examples that serve as touchstones for students of ritual. But the discussion that remains most influential is that of Max Gluckman mentioned earlier.[8]

What Gluckman saw in the Ncwala was a stunning example of how the ritual dramatization of social tensions and conflict can result—in a fashion only superficially paradoxical—in increased group cohesion and attendant stability. Accordingly, he called attention to the cleavages within the traditional social structure of the Swazi Nation, in which the king stands apart from and superordinate to other members of the (royal) Dlamini clan, who, in turn, stand above members of other (commoner) Swazi clans, with whom the king usually enjoys good relations. One might well represent such relations as in Figure 4.1:

Tensions between the king and the Dlamini princes are constant and structurally predictable. For on the death of a king, one of his many sons (usually among the youngest, but born of a distinguished mother and with no full brothers) is named successor, whereas his older half brothers, many of whom had themselves hoped to rule, are relegated to subordinate positions. To protect the new king from their jealousies, these princes are regularly assigned their own centers of administrative power, spatially removed from the royal capitals. There they pose a less-immediate threat to the monarch but, nonetheless, are able to attract adherents and to build up rival power centers, even centers of rebellion. Such rebellions, in fact, have been relatively frequent in Swazi history,[9] but as Gluckman stressed, these were rebellions, not revolutions—that is, they were challenges to individual kings, not to king*ship* nor to any traditional structures of Swazi society: The rebels sought only to depose the incumbents and make themselves king.

It is these tensions and conflicts that Gluckman took to be dramatized in the Ncwala, particularly in (1) its songs, (2) the assault of the Dlamini

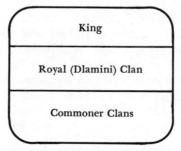

Figure 4.1. Cleavages within the Swazi Nation.

princes against the king on the afternoon of the Great Day, and (3) their subsequent expulsion from the ritual ground. Such a symbolic enactment of sociopolitical roles and oppositions, in Gluckman's view—and here he followed Aristotle, not only in the latter's distinction of rebellion from revolution (in the *Politics*), but also his theory of catharsis and dramatic purgation (in the *Poetics*)—served to discharge (but only temporarily and partially) the antagonisms between the king and his rivals, while also involving them in affirmations of the kingship for which they struggled, thus contributing to the stability of the Swazi Nation and the continuation of its sociopolitical structures and institutions.

These views have been criticized on occasion, most fully by T. O. Beidelman, who argued that Gluckman paid too much attention to the latent sociopolitical functions of the Ncwala and not enough to either the indigenous system of symbolism and belief or to the underlying psychophysiological processes that inform this ritual.[10] Consideration of such dimensions of Swazi thought and practice led Beidelman to argue that far from being a ritual of rebellion or expressing resentment of the king, the Ncwala is "a ritual separation of the king so that he may take on certain supernatural attributes which provide him with power."[11]

Beidelman's article, which has itself been highly influential, had an aggressive, even polemic, tone to it, and one can sense in its pages the confidence of symbolic and structuralist anthropology in its struggle against functionalism (though Gluckman was hardly a typical functionalist, nor Beidelman a typical structuralist). Subsequent students of the Ncwala have been inclined to grant points to both antagonists, striving for some synthesis of their insights while avoiding their more procrustean interpretations. For my part, I find Beidelman's critique at best a minor corrective, providing a more refined understanding of those ideological mystifications that take the form of Swazi cosmology, while generally ignoring the social processes that are masked by such mystifications. What Beidelman's style of analysis can afford us is an appreciation of the subtlety, coherence, and persuasive power of religious ideology as enacted in ritual. All this is to the good, but it can only complement and never replace inquiry into the sociopolitical and socioeconomic effects of ritual performances as championed by Gluckman, for all his failings.

Failings, indeed, there are. I intend to show, first, that in his study of the Ncwala, Gluckman—like Kuper before him and like most students of the Ncwala since—failed to set the data in their proper historic context, mistaking the performance of the ceremony in 1934, 1935, and 1936 (when Kuper observed the proceedings and on which she based her description) for the Ncwala per se; second, that this led Gluckman to misconstrue the social field in which the ceremony was operative; and third, that this caused him to misunderstand its sociopolitical intent and effect in considerable measure.[12]

The first of these points is the easiest to establish, given some of the more recent literature. It is now clear that the Ncwala has changed over time, that of the colonial period being different from its precolonial and postcolonial counterparts. Thus, on the one hand, Philip Bonner has shown how the Ncwala was consciously restructured by the great Swazi king Mswati (r. 1839?–65) following a revolt led by his half brother Fokoti. After suppression of this rising, Mswati, together with the queen mother, Thandile (daughter of Zwide the Ndwandwe king) drew upon traditional Swazi and Ndwandwe symbolism to shape a ceremony wherein the king's central position, capacity for economic expropriation, and ideological hegemony were annually reaffirmed and all potential rivals were forced to acknowledge his preeminence. Prior to this the Ncwala had been above all a first fruits ceremony; afterward—and for the duration of the precolonial period—it was an effective instrument of royal domination.[13]

At the other end of the temporal spectrum, Hilda Kuper returned to Swaziland in 1966 to observe the Ncwala as it was celebrated on the eve of independence. In her reports of this ceremony, she noted quite a different political emphasis from that present in the Ncwala of the colonial era: that is, an intensified nationalism that manifested itself, inter alia, in a heightened demand for participation and for traditional dress as signs of Swazi identity and allegiance.[14] Moreover, Kuper detailed the skillful ways in which King Sobhuza II (1899–1982) at that time used the Ncwala as an instrument for asserting his independence of the British and for defeating the modernizing (and, thus, antimonarchic) Swazi political parties.[15]

It is thus apparent that there were different sociopolitical dimensions and implications to the Ncwala as performed in precolonial, colonial, and postcolonial periods: Indeed, there were surely subtle differences from one year's celebration to the next. Sensitivity to such differences—at least the broader ones—should help us refine our views of "the" Ncwala.

The Problem of the Right-hand *Insila*

As one example of how treating the Ncwala of the mid-1930s as if it were the Ncwala *tout court* has resulted in errors both of reporting and interpretation, consider a statement Kuper made regarding the two senior *tinsila*, the ritual assistants of the Swazi king mentioned earlier. These officials are the king's closest attendants, both within the Ncwala and without. Chosen when the young king reaches puberty, they leave their familial homes to live with him; being of commoner clans, they are bound to the king through a ritual exchange of blood, after which they and they alone may eat from the same dish as the king, wear his clothes, or touch his body. But the king may establish such relations only twice in his life: the first time, to the man who becomes his right-hand *insila* (pl. *tinsila*), and the second to his left-hand counterpart. Under no circumstances may these officials be replaced, for while there are junior *tinsila*, who assist the assistants as it were, these latter "will not have the strength" to serve the king properly, having neither received his blood nor passed the formative experiences of youth together with him.[16]

Given this background information, we may now recognize a minor error in Kuper's account: At two different points she stated that in the Ncwala, the left-hand *insila* plays a more active and important role than does the right-hand *insila*, something that would be most interesting, given the complex codes often attached to the categories of right and left.[17] But there exists a better explanation for this datum than any attempt to connect it to sweeping (and ahistorical) categories of thought and symbolism, for Kuper also informs us in a different context, that Shwapa Mdluli, the right-hand *insila* of Sobhuza II, had died many years prior to 1934. It being forbidden to acknowledge publicly the death of a senior *insila*—such a death being "a greater menace to the king than the death of a full brother or any other subject"—during the Ncwala a convenient fiction was employed, whereby a junior *insila* played the role (but only partially and temporarily) of Sobhuza's long-dead right-hand man.[18] One may thus correctly say that the role of the left-hand *insila* was more important in the Ncwala as performed after the death of Shwapa Mdluli, but not necessarily that it always was and will be so in "the" Ncwala.

This minor correction to Kuper's report opens up a long series of questions about the *tinsila*, specifically regarding the nature of their services to the king and the significance of their deaths. Some of their duties are administrative: They keep watch over the Dlamini princes, reporting any potentially treasonous activity, and they also serve as arbitrators and peacemakers on occasion. But most important is their magico-religious service, whereby—as a result of the ritual exchange of blood—they protect the king against sorcery and aggression. Kuper explains:

> The tinsila act as "shields" of the king, warding off evil directed against him. The blood, believed to remain in psycho-physical contact with the person from which it is drawn, enables the tinsila to "feel" when harm threatens the king. Witchcraft directed against him is intercepted without conscious effort by the tinsila, and their own lives are endangered in his defence. Ngolotsheni Motsa [the surviving left-hand *insila* of Sobhuza II] is always ailing, and he attributes his ill health to his position, pointing out that he is never so ill as when near to Sobhuza. He is also subject to terrible nightmares, which he interprets as witchcraft directed against both Sobhuza and himself by men who are jealous of his power and contact with the king.[19]

A delicate system of checks and balances existed within the Swazi polity. Witchcraft constituted not only a major weapon that could be (and was) employed against the king by his Dlamini rivals, but it was also the foremost check against his excessive or arbitrary use of royal power because any discontented Swazi could take recourse to witchcraft as well. Against such magical assault, the king's chief defense lay in his two "shields," the *tinsila*.

In 1934 when Kuper first visited Swaziland, Sobhuza's right-hand *insila* was dead and his left-hand *insila* ailing. Was his throne (and his life) then in jeopardy? Just how powerful (or powerless) was this Swazi king?

The King's Powers of Execution

When considering the importance of the *tinsila* (as in other instances), it is instructive to contrast the nature of Swazi kingship prior to colonial domination with its nature in the colonial period (Boer protectorate 1894–99; British 1902–68). For until the late nineteenth century, Swazi kings were less dependent on their *tinsila* for protection because they possessed at that time a much more formidable system of defense: the right to kill those suspected of practicing magic against the throne. Every king used this power during his life and after a king's death—such deaths always being considered the result of sorcery—the councillors of the deceased ruler took mass vengeance against all suspects. Moreover, these practices were considered essential to the safety of kings, kingship, and the nation itself.

One can well understand that the right of summary execution served as a powerful tool for restraining would-be rebels, and it was jealously guarded by Swazi kings. Ironically, this traditional power came to be a major weakness for those Swazi kings who confronted rivals of a different sort: the Boers and the British who made royal executions a prominent item in their campaign to undermine independent Swazi rule. Several historical documents make this clear.

The first of these is a letter sent in December 1888 by the Swazi king, Mbandzeni (r. 1872–89), to the British governor at Natal at a time when Swazi independence had been severely eroded by disastrous concessions granted European business interests and by the pressures (implicit and explicit) exerted by European governments and their military forces. In his letter Mbandzeni announced that he had discovered a conspiracy led by his half brother Nkopolo and a senior counselor (formerly regent) Sandlane Zwane, who together plotted to kill him at the Ncwala ceremony. When word of the king's suspicions leaked, Nkopolo fled, but Sandlane Zwane and others were caught and clubbed to death. It is this execution Mbandzeni defended in his letter:

> For the protection of my people, my country, my children, and my throne, I was compelled to take severe and decisive action. From the time of my forefathers to the present, the law of my country has allowed and allows but one punishment for convicted rebels and traitors, and that punishment is death. . . . So, unprejudiced by any strictly personal motives, and acting as I sincerely believed for the safety and welfare of my people, *the security of the many interests vested in my country by white people,* and for the prevention of eternal war, sentence of death was passed upon the ringleaders, the majority of whom were executed.[20]

From Mbandzeni's defensive tone, it is clear that he felt himself and the powers of his office to be under attack, not only by internal enemies (this much is obvious), but also by foreign powers, whose possible displeasure concerned him and to whom he felt obliged to justify his actions. To this end the king stressed two points. First, there was the obvious line of argument: that is, Swazi tradition authorized him to execute his (internal) enemies. Beyond that, Mbandzeni added a second, more subtle and more revealing justification, alleging that his actions were designed in part to protect white business interests in Swaziland. Hardly the statement of a confident and independent monarch, this was a calculated attempt to placate the whites, whose displeasure he expected. Although there are reports of growing "revulsion" over these executions, Mbandzeni did not live to see major repercussions, for he became seriously ill shortly thereafter and died the following October, stating on his deathbed, "Swazi kingship dies with me."[21]

As was standard in such cases, Mbandzeni's councillors took his death (at the age of 34) to be the result of witchcraft, and they sought vengeance against his (and their) enemies. The European powers intervened, however, announcing ominously that "action would be taken" should executions occur. In response to this statement—which the Swazi correctly took as interference in their internal affairs—members of the national council protested strenuously. The words of one senior councillor, Jokova, are recorded, "We thank you for the words that have been said, but you talk about the independence of the Swazi nation. We do not see that unless you allow us to rule in our own way there is any independence at all. Our way of ruling is to kill each other, and what shall be the rule if we are not allowed to kill?"[22]

Mbandzeni's mother pleaded for permission "for just one day" of vengeance against those who had destroyed her son by sorcery. But the Europeans were firm: There would be no executions. As a result, a young and inexperienced son of Mbandzeni, Bhunu (r. 1889–99), ascended to the throne in an atmosphere of menace and confusion; the European press gave prominent and propagandistic coverage to all signs of disorder in Swaziland, presumably as a means to prepare public opinion for direct intervention.

Never was it possible for Bhunu to secure his reign adequately under these circumstances. In 1898 things moved toward a crisis when Bhunu charged that his foremost councillor, Mbaba Sibandze—of whose influence Bhunu was bitterly jealous—had betrayed him by giving magical assistance to a group of hostile Sotho. Like his father, Bhunu asserted the traditional prerogative of Swazi kings and ordered his councillor's death, thereby giving the Republic of South Africa an excuse to move against him and against Swazi independence. Thus, directly following the excution, the Boer government ordered that Bhunu stand trial, acting under a clause of the Third Swaziland Convention concluded by Great Britain and the republic in 1894 (without Swazi participation and over Swazi objections), which made Swaziland a "protected dependency" of the latter power. Eager to assert its power, the republic sent troops to arrest the king, whereupon he fled, seeking protection from the British administration in Natal. On arrival, Bhunu announced, "I have fled my country because Boers are invading it, and bringing arms to kill me. I have seen their troops with my own eyes. I have stolen no sheep and shed no white man's blood."[23]

Bhunu's strategy at this critical moment was to exploit the growing rivalry between the European powers in order to save himself, and in some measure he succeeded. It is now evident from the documentary records of the ensuing negotiations that the republic intended to exploit this incident fully and to abolish Swazi kingship altogether. The British, although wishing to reduce Swazi power, were reluctant to create a vacuum into which the Boers could move. Ultimately, a compromise was reached whereby Bhunu retained his throne but was forced to stand trial, the republic having given assurances that he would not be "judged too harshly" for a crime that, although regrettable, was but "the act of a young uncivilized chief of a barbaric people." This trial was held, Bhunu convicted of "allowing public violence without trying to prevent it," fined £500, and a Boer–British protocol was concluded that significantly reduced Bhunu's powers, particularly in the area of criminal jurisdiction.[24]

In the following year there were further developments. Rivalry between the British and the republic culminated in the Boer War (1899–1902), which ended in British victory and dominion ("protectorate") over Swaziland. Further, Bhunu collapsed and died during celebration of the Ncwala (December 1899), being then but twenty-three years old. After a brief period of debate and maneuvering, his five-month-old son, Mona—who was given the royal name Sobhuza II—was chosen as his heir. Finally, taking advantage of the fact that the Boers had withdrawn from Swaziland during the war, Bhunu's councillors took vengeance in traditional fashion.

Aspects of the Reign of Sobhuza II

After the war, among many other changes, it quickly became clear that neither Sobhuza nor his councillors and regents would ever again be able to order the execution of enemies. Stripped of many traditional powers under British rule, particularly those that permitted him to defend himself against internal rivals (actual and potential), there was every reason to believe that Sobhuza would be a weak king, a situation that could only help the British in their consolidation of political and economic power. During the period of Sobhuza's minority (December 1899–December 1921), the power of the colonial administration increased dramatically, all firearms in the hands of Swazi were confiscated, the collection of taxes was expanded and regularized, the legality of crassly exploitative concessions (often granted under false pretences) was ratified, and the land question was "settled" by a ruling that assigned a full two-thirds of Swaziland to white interests. Moreover, during this same period, the Ncwala—the most important ritual for the fortification of king, kingship, and the Swazi Nation—was not celebrated, for the ceremony was considered too powerful for a young king to bear.

In December 1921, however, Sobhuza achieved majority and celebrated the Ncwala for the first time. Loyal Swazi flocked to the royal capital at Lobamba "to show the strength of kingship," even though this first Ncwala was but a reduced version of the full ceremony, with many of the most powerful sequences being held in abeyance. Every year thereafter, more of these sequences were added as the Ncwala grew toward maturity with its chief celebrant. This notwithstanding, celebration of a king's first Ncwala traditionally granted him command over the regiments and the right to launch attacks against enemies, military action during the king's minority being limited to defensive operations only. These new powers Sobhuza used immediately, but in unprecedented ways, for the attack he launched against the British was legal rather than military. He petitioned the local authorities for withdrawal of the legislation establishing colonial control over Swazi land and, when this petition was unsuccessful, he sought and won permission to go to London where he personally put the case before King George V in January 1923.

Not surprisingly, this mission and the lawsuits that followed ended in failure. In the years 1922–34, however, Sobhuza and the Ncwala matured together. And in the very year that Hilda Kuper first observed the ritual (1934), it was judged by Sobhuza's councillors that he had reached the full height of his powers.

Sobhuza's position was a dangerous and difficult one. A traditional king who had lost many of his most important powers, he occupied an office that was riddled with ambiguities and contradictions, being understood—indeed, constructed—quite differently by the British and the Swazi. The former regarded Sobhuza as Paramount Chief, a title that signified his loss of autonomous authority, and they sought to use him to implement numerous aspects of their policy, offering him significant support and benefits in return. In contrast, the Swazi saw him as their King (*Nkosi*) and Lion (*Ngwenyama*), the bulwark of tradition and their chief protection against colonial rule.[25] These competing definitions are highlighted in a historic document of signal importance: the letter written on the day after Sobhuza celebrated his first Ncwala (22 December 1921) by the queen regent, Gwamile Mdluli, in which she formally introduced the new Swazi ruler to the resident commissioner. Here with the greatest of care neither to challenge the British openly nor to cede them any ground, she presented her grandson as "Sobhuza II, the Paramount Chief of Swaziland and King of the Swazi Nation."[26]

What Gwamile signaled—with real sociological precision—was a fact ignored by Gluckman and virtually all other students of the Ncwala: There existed two different, contradictory and antagonistic levels of sociopolitical integration present within the same geographic and historic locus, one of which was encapsulated within the other.[27] Of these, the smaller and older was the Swazi Nation, composed of 150,000 Swazi and ruled over by their

	Sociopolitical Configuration No. 1	Sociopolitical Configuration No. 2
Formal name	Swaziland Protectorate	Swazi Nation
Dominant stratum	European colonists	Dlamini clan
Chief official	Resident Commissioner	King (*Nkosi*)
Sobhuza's title	Paramount Chief	King or Lion (*Ngwenyama*)

Figure 4.2. Competing levels of sociopolitical integration in Swaziland during the colonial period.

king, Sobhuza II. Superimposed on this (with only partial success) was a unit officially known as The High Protectorate of Swaziland, a British colony in which the Swazi were subordinate to some 2,740 Europeans and in which Sobhuza was relegated to the position of paramount chief, subordinate to the resident commissioner. These relations may be represented as in Figure 4.2.

We should also note that different patterns of cleavage mark these two different levels of integration. Earlier, we considered the cleavages of king-Dlamini-commoners internal to the Swazi Nation. For the record it should be noted that there were also certain cleavages within the European population of Swaziland, above all that between Boers and Britons. These faded into relative insignificance, however, at the level of the Swaziland Protectorate, just as within that larger context, all Swazi rallied around their embattled king. These relations may be shown as in Figure 4.3.

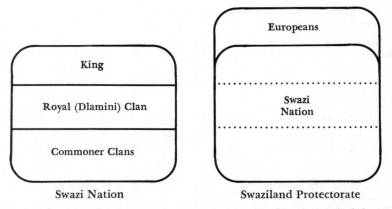

Figure 4.3. Lines of cleavage within different levels of sociopolitical integration during the colonial period.

It is, then, only at the level of the Swazi Nation that the king faced potential problems with the Dlamini princes, and in the precolonial period (i.e., when the Swaziland Protectorate did not yet exist) the Ncwala was consciously constructed as an instrument to solidify the king's position at the expense of his Dlamini rivals, employing sequences of ritual rebellion to accomplish this aim.

Under colonialism, however, things were different: cleavages internal to the Swazi Nation became much less important as Swazi of all subgroupings confronted foreign rule. One notes, for example, that in stark contrast to the experience of his predecessors, Sobhuza never once faced a serious challenge from any Dlamini rival over the course of his remarkable seventy-year reign. Real (i.e., nonritual) rebellion, so common in the precolonial period, virtually disappeared thereafter, in spite of the fact that the king had lost his power to order executions. Rather, Sobhuza was able to represent his personal interest in preserving the kingship as an integral part of the much broader interest, which he shared with all Swazi, in preserving their nation in the face of colonial rule. In this endeavor, the Ncwala served as a multifaceted and highly effective instrument of struggle.

The Afternoon of the Great Day

At no time was this instrumentality of the ritual more evident than on the afternoon of the Great Day, the dramatic culmination of the Ncwala and, what is more, the time at which relations with the British were most openly called into focus. This occurred in a sequence performed only during the colonial period, which has regrettably received little attention, presumably being viewed as an episode that falls outside of the ritual proper. Kuper reported:

> It has become customary for the Resident Commissioner or his representative to come to the afternoon of the Great Day and look around. Sobhuza and his bodyguard, all in full Ncwala clothes, lead the members of the European government past the men as they stand and sing in the cattle byre, and then the Europeans sit and watch from the tent specially sent down and erected by native police in the morning. Quite a few other Europeans also come to look on, and near them hover a number of native men in European clothes. The presence of the Europeans in no way interferes with the ceremony, and they leave before the climax.[28]

The information provided in this passage is invaluable, but Kuper's analytic comments, elsewhere so astute, here seem uncharacteristically naive, colored perhaps by her own conflicting obligations and loyalties.[29] It is hardly credible, for instance, that the presence of such significant spectators as these "in no way" interfered with the proceedings, for (as Werner Heisenberg taught us) even in subatomic reactions, the presence of an observer alters the nature of the processes under observation. At the very least one must note that Sobhuza was obliged to take time out from his other ceremonial duties in order to deal with the members of the official delegation. What is more, those dealings—held in full public view—were conducted with the greatest of care to preserve a convenient ambiguity whereby it was possible for different actors and spectators to view the Swazi ruler as the host, guide, or servant of (also superior, subordinate, or equal to) the colonial officer.

Also handled with extreme care was the delicate matter of the resident commissioner's departure after a stay of about an hour—but always in advance of that sequence in which the Dlamini princes besiege the king, only to be ordered from the ritual ground. For it is not only the Dlamini who are expelled at that moment to the cry "Out, foreigners!" but all those who are not a loyal part of the Swazi Nation. Were they still present at this moment, the colonial authorities would have had to decide whether to leave (thus giving the appearance of retreating under pressure) or to stay (thus risking confrontation). Both alternatives being unacceptable, the commissioner and his party withdrew early in a manner both tactful and ostentatious: by limousine, seeking thereby to assert that they departed of their own free will.

It is also worth reconsidering the much-discussed sequence of the princes' "rebellion" against the king, for important details have been overlooked by Gluckman and by others. In particular note the song the princes sing at this dramatic moment:

> We shall leave them with their country
> Whose travellers are like distant thunder,
> Do you hear, Dlambula, do you hear?

It is regrettable that no student of the Ncwala to date has considered these words in detail, although they are of considerable import. In Kuper's translation, certain difficulties are evident, but a reasonably secure interpretation may be ventured nevertheless. Surely the first line is clear: The singers ["we" includes the Dlamini and any who will join them in their proposed project, above all, they hope to include the king in this "we"] suggest a line of action—the abandonment of Swaziland to unnamed others ["them," it being "their country"], who may either be taken as the (post-Swazi) colonizers, or the (pre-Swazi) autochthons. Armed resistance to the former being impossible, and submission equally so, the princes counsel withdrawal: migration or flight.[30]

The second line of this song is more difficult to interpret than the first, but—if I am right—it recalls the Swazi migrations of the eighteenth and nineteenth centuries that brought them to their present home. Given this history, the princes argue that the relation of the Swazi Nation to Swaziland is only that of travelers to the terrain through which they journey [I take the "whose" of the second line to refer back to "country" in the first, although given my ignorance of siSwati, I can offer this only as speculation]. Further, they compare their presence in Swaziland to the passage of a storm, for having moved through the country and shaken it for a time, they expect to pass further on, becoming "like distant thunder" in relation to the land:

powerful still, but powerful somewhere else. Having concluded this analysis of their situation, they call to their king for his assent to their proposal, "Do you hear, Dlambula, do you hear?" At this, the women join them, adding a plea in support of the princes' counsel:

> Do you hear?
> Let us go, let us go

There exists strong evidence to support such a line of analysis: Kuper obtained two interpretations of this song, which she considered to be mutually exclusive. The first of these was, "The Malangeni [People of the Sun, a title of the Dlamini] want to migrate again. They want their king to come with them, they want to leave the people whom they distrust in the country where they stayed a little while." The second, "The Malangeni show their hatred of the king. They denounce him and force him from their midst." Of these, Kuper initially rejected the first outright, believing that "the next act seems to support the second version."[31] Yet it is hard to see why this is so. The next act of the Ncwala drama comes after the princes have driven the king into his sanctuary. There, beating against the doorway and imploring him to come forth, they resume their song with a new verse:

> Come, come, king of kings,
> Come, father, come,
> Come king, oh come here king.

Gluckman took issue with Kuper in her dismissal of the first interpretation, this being the sole point on which the two were in open disagreement. In his view the two testimonies could be reconciled, although he offered no suggestions on how this might be done, and—in practice—he nowhere gave serious consideration to the song as a counsel of flight.[32] Moreover, in recent years, Kuper has reversed her position, having been persuaded in this by members of the advisory committee of eminent Swazi who supervised her work on the official biography of Sobhuza II. At their urging she now sees this song as "expressing the desire of the royal Dlamini clan to leave the country to non-Dlamini inhabitants."[33] Such a view is also consistent with the ambiguous nature of relations between the king and the Dlamini princes. For the latter are not only the king's rivals and potential rebels against his reign, but serve also as his lieutenants and core members of his advisory council. When the Dlamini pressed against Sobhuza on the afternoon of the Great Day, these ambiguities were fully evident: The policy they urged as councillors also implied a strong, even seditious criticism. For implicitly they advised their king that, being insufficiently powerful to resist the British, only through flight could he avoid the permanent absorption of the Swazi Nation into the Swaziland Protectorate, and permanent reduction of the Swazi kingship to a paramount chieftancy.

The question of how serious the Dlamini were in advocating flight must be left open for lack of adequate information. No doubt there was some variation from year to year and from prince to prince. Yet in large measure, I

am inclined to see their counsel as having been offered *pro forma* for dialectic or contrapuntal reasons. The dialectic structure here, as in certain
other ritual inversions (on which, see chap. 9), is not that of the familiar
Hegelian variety, but one in which a weak thesis—which here might be presented as (diminished) kingly power—confronts an antithesis deliberately
constructed *in order to be rejected:* here, the charge of kingly weakness. The
result of such a dialectic is no synthesis in the ordinary sense, but rather a
reaffirmation and reinforcement of the original thesis: kingly power reasserted and—in some measure—restored. The normal course of a Swazi council is open debate while the king remains silent, followed by his pronounce-
ments, which are met with applause and formalized praise. Although one
ought not press the comparison too far, the next sequence of the Ncwala
may be viewed as Sobhuza's response to the princes' counsel. This is his appearance as a monster. Kuper's description is unforgettable:

> There emerges a figure weird as a monster of legends. He is *Silo,* a name-
> less creature. On his head is a cap of black plumes that cover his face and
> blow about his shoulders, and underneath the feathers is glimpsed a head-
> band of a lion's skin. His body is covered in bright green grass and ever-
> green shoots that trail on the ground. In his left hand he holds a shield
> smeared with fat of the sacred herd, the *mfukwane.*[34] His right hand is empty
> and as he moves it gleams with lines of dark medicine. The fatty tissue of
> the *umdvutshulwa* [a bull beaten to death by young warriors on the preced-
> ing day] is tied crosswise on his chest and its blown up gall bladder lies on
> the costume. Round his loins is a belt of silver monkey skin. . . .
>
> In this powerful costume the king appears reluctant to return to the na-
> tion. He executes a crazy, elusive dance with knees flexed and swaying body.
> The movements are an intuitive response to the rhythm and situation, a
> dance that no ordinary man knows and that the king was never taught. The
> old teachers who trained him in all his duties explained: "We do not know
> it; we are not kings; it will come to you at the time." Suddenly he crouches
> low and disappears into his hole, and the tinsila follow close behind picking
> up any bits that drop off the sacred costume, lest they be used by enemies
> to ruin the nation. The princes spring forward crying: "Come out, king of
> kings." They draw back, pause, sway forward. At last he responds. At his
> approach they return, enticing him to follow, but after a few steps he turns
> back and they close behind him again. Everyone is urged to dance. The
> *tindvuna* [royal assistants drawn from the commoner clans] bring down their
> batons and shout: "Beat your shields." The people dance with vigour; here
> more than at any other stage they keep their king alive and healthy by their
> own movements. The mime goes on with increasing tension, each appearance
> of the king making a sudden startling and unforgettable impact. His eyes
> shine through the feathers as he tosses his head, his face is dark with black
> medicine, dripping down his legs and arms are black streaks—he is terrifying,
> and as the knife-edged grass cuts into his skin, he tosses his body furiously
> in pain and rage.[35]

In this spectacular image of king-as-monster, there is nothing arbitrary
or done simply for effect. Rather, every element of the costume and dance is

significant, revealing some aspect of the inner nature of kingship, for as the
remarks of the royal instructors reveal, the king's frenzied performance is
nothing less than the spontaneous self-expression of the kingship within
him. Regarding the physical appearance of *Silo* (Powerful Creature, a royal
title), we do well to follow the lead of Victor Turner, who observed that in
such figures the component parts "are so radically ill-assorted that they
stand out and can be thought about. The monstrosity of the configuration
throws its elements into relief."[36] Thus, we may note that the belt of silver
monkey skin connotes the eternity of kingship: It is said that no one has
ever seen this animal die, and (accordingly) it is only those children expected to be king who are carried in slings made of its skin. Similarly, the
evergreen shoots (species unspecified) connote abundant life force and ever-
recurrent fertility; and the razor-sharp *umuzi* grass expresses not only the
double-edged powers of kingship (the king himself is cut by them as he
dances), but also its continuity, for the mats kept in the National Shrine (the
Kabayethe) from one reign to another are always made of this same grass.

Most prominent, however, are items drawn from animals of great physical strength: bulls and lions, the names of which figure prominently as royal
titles as well as in the *Lihubo*, the Swazi national anthem:

> Here is the Inexplicable,
> Our Bull! Lion! Descend.
> Descend, Being of Heaven
> Unconquerable.

Similarly unconquerable is the lion–bull–monster–king who comes forth
from the *Nhlambelo* and dances wildly in the face of the Dlamini, forcing
them to withdraw at his advance. Challenged and under pressure, he re-
sponds awesomely, intimidating his enemies and overpowering them, revealing in his frenzy that Swazi kings at all times possess the potential for horrific, even monstrous, displays of force. Moreover, within the sequences on
the afternoon of the Great Day, the king's anger is provoked, precisely in order that he may display the unbridled power of kingship.

Such was Sobhuza's response to the Dlamini princes' counsel of flight. In
an epiphany of raw, untamed force, he served notice that colonial restrictions and pressures notwithstanding, the Swazi kingship retained awesome
resources of energy and power, which the Swazi king stood ready to use
against those who challenged him from within or without. This display was
staged, it should be noted, at a time when all those who might be suspected
of either disloyalty or open enmity—that is, Dlamini princes and foreign visitors alike (but not the official party, who had already chosen to absent
themselves)—were still present, for it was desired that they see, appreciate,
and report to others the might of the Swazi king. Once this was accomplished, the presence of such persons was no longer tolerated, and directly
they were ordered from the ritual ground. Their expulsion, moreover, must
itself be considered an important part of the Ncwala, and not some bit of
stage management preparatory to the next ritual sequence proper. For with

the cry, "Out, foreigners!" Swazi unity was not merely reaffirmed, but actively reconstructed.

When only loyal Swazi remained, the king made his final gesture, solemnly discarding the gourd, "the powerful vessel symbolizing the past," as Kuper put it, although others have argued that more precisely this gourd signifies the accumulated pollution of the year past.[37] Beyond this it is tempting to see the gourd that King Sobhuza II cast away in the Ncwala of the 1930s as representing most immediately the defeats and indignities inflicted on the Swazi Nation by colonialism. It was this he hurled down in the fullness of his powers while reaffirming his ability to resist, dismissing any counsel of flight, and looking forward to the day in which he might cast away colonial rule itself.[38]

Domination, Resistance and the Politics of the Colonial Ncwala

The preceding observations suggest the limitations of Gluckman's analysis of *the* Ncwala as a "ritual of rebellion." In my opinion, this characterization has considerable validity and merit, but only within the carefully delimited context of the Swazi Nation. In the precolonial period, of course, this was the only relevant context, but with the establishment of colonial rule and the encapsulation of the Swazi Nation within the Swaziland Protectorate, another, broader sociopolitical context was added, and the Ncwala assumed an additional significance, becoming also (and much more importantly) a "ritual of resistance" against British domination.

In order to appreciate Gluckman's contribution and to place it in proper perspective, it is important to recognize that he was active during that period when the analysis of social segmentation and the correlated fission-fusion model of social integration, which we touched on briefly in chapter 1, was at the forefront of anthropological research. But more than any of his colleagues, Gluckman—a Marxist who grew up in, and was trained in, South Africa—stressed the conflict, tension, and contradictions internal to any society, his greatest single contribution being the Frazer lecture on "Rituals of Rebellion," a piece that fully merits its place as a classic of social and political anthropology and one that has enduring value, its flaws and limitations notwithstanding. Here, Gluckman was able to synthesize his own interest in conflict with the dominant interest (ultimately derived from Émile Durkheim) in issues of integration, showing how conflict at one level of social organization can foster cohesion and stability at a higher level as competing parties reaffirm in the course of their conflict those institutions, values, loyalties, and sentiments they hold in common and that ultimately bind them together. In this line of analysis, the Swazi Ncwala—where ritually dramatized conflict between king and Dlamini yielded a broader Swazi solidarity—served as a key example.

For all that Gluckman may have differed from others of his generation in his close attention to issues of conflict, he did, nonetheless, share with them a rather dubious inheritance from Durkheim, transmitted through Malinowski and A. R. Radcliffe-Brown. This was a relatively uncritical view of social integration as a fundamental good, and a consequent blindness to the fact that social fusion (i.e., the construction of social aggregates out of groups that retain some measure of independent identity as segments within the larger unit) often depends on and results from the subordination of some groups to others, from whom they were independent at lower levels of integration.

Such issues are particularly relevant to the colonial situation that neither Gluckman nor any of his contemporaries ever treated satisfactorily, for all that they had ample opportunity to do so.[39] Indeed, analytically it is possible—and quite instructive—to treat colonialism as a specialized case of social fusion whereby colonizer and colonized are integrated within the sociopolitical aggregate that is the colony.[40] In the case at hand, this is seen in the formation of the Swaziland Protectorate by means of fusion of the Europeans resident in Swaziland and the Swazi Nation, as illustrated in a segmentation diagram (Fig. 4.4) such as we considered in chapter 1.

Certainly, we have seen how the establishment of the highest level of integration (i.e., the Swaziland Protectorate) was directly beneficial to one group (the Europeans) at the expense of the others subsumed therein. Thus, for instance, political institutions were reorganized in the protectorate so that the foremost authority of group *B* (= the Swazi king) was officially reduced in stature and subordinated to the chief authority of group *A* (the British resident commissioner). Similarly, the legal institutions of group *A* were established as supreme so that, for instance, disputes between Europeans and Swazi over land and mineral rights were heard in British courts, with predictable results.

Colonial situations are particularly revealing, moreover, of the tensions and contradictions that exist within other societies as well. Whereas fusion

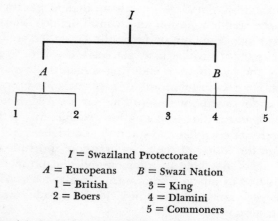

I = Swaziland Protectorate
A = Europeans   *B* = Swazi Nation
 1 = British   3 = King
 2 = Boers   4 = Dlamini
                       5 = Commoners

Figure 4.4. Social segmentation in the Swaziland Protectorate.

may initially result from the exercise or threat of coercive force, the aggregate formed thereby cannot be maintained indefinitely by such means. Rather, if a new level of integration is to achieve any lasting stability, this will happen only when its members come to accept its legitimacy, experience a sense of their own proper belonging within it, and share sentiments of affinity with other members of the unit, whatever their initial group identity might have been. When such sentiments are weak or lacking among the members of one or more segments, there will remain a line of cleavage along which conflict and fission can readily occur. In truth, one might well define cleavage as the situation that obtains when subgroups of a given society are imperfectly integrated within the larger aggregate, so that their primary sentiments of affinity remain lodged at the subgroup level while they retain correspondingly strong sentiments of estrangement from, or antipathy toward, other subgroups.

Such considerations permit us to offer an analysis of domination and resistance as evidenced within colonialism (and in other contexts as well), making use of the fission-fusion model. Thus, domination may be defined as the attempt (never entirely successful) of a given group (A) to absorb other groups (B, C, etc.) within a higher level of social integration (I) in which the members of A occupy a position of hierarchic, material, and sociopolitical supremacy. Domination is thus the imposition of an unwanted and exploitative fusion on groups that are converted into subordinate segments of the new social aggregate.

Conversely, resistance is the (sustained, but never fully successful) refusal of a given group (such as B) to accept absorption into a higher level of integration, the politico-economic realities and dominant ideology of which are imposed by an initially alien group (A) that seeks to establish itself as the ruling stratum of the new aggregate. Resistance—which may take material, political, cultural, ritual, or countless other forms[41]—is thus continued fissionary pressure against an unwanted and exploitative fusion imposed from outside.

Such a stance of resistance depends on—or better yet, amounts to—the continued mobilization of powerful sentiments of affinity, solidarity, and corporate identity at a lower level of integration than that championed by the would-be dominant group, toward whom corollary sentiments of estrangement and hostility are maintained. Moreover, anything that evokes or perpetuates such sentiments may be used as an effective instrument of resistance. Among those instruments commonly so employed are "tradition," myth, and ritual.

As we have seen, the Ncwala of the colonial period served as such an instrument whereby the Swazi Nation was rallied, its political institutions reaffirmed, and those who threatened it—either with fission (i.e., the Dlamini princes) or an unwanted fusion—were triumphantly expelled from the ritual ground. At that moment society itself was disarticulated and rearticulated, literally, taken apart and put back together, as two different groups—that some sought to merge—were dramatically separated in space and in sentiment: those who were considered and in that very moment defined themselves as loyal Swazi and those whose sentiments of loyalty to the Swazi king being suspect were accordingly labeled alien (foreigners).

Careful attention ought to be given the statement of a Swazi informant, who spoke to Hilda Kuper in the 1930s of the Ncwala's effects: "We see we are all Swazi; we are joined against outside foes."[42] Of all grammatical forms, I know of none more subtle and problematic in their sociopolitical implications than pronouns of the first person plural that, when skillfully employed, permit speakers to construct groups in which they join with unnamed others and stand apart from others still: others who fall outside this "we." Under colonialism, the Ncwala was a pointed and a potent exercise in the framing of just such a "we": a Swazi "we" that existed before the Europeans came and that (it was rightly hoped) would exist again after they departed. During the colonial era, that "we" was embattled and it was preserved, above all in celebrations of the Ncwala. To be sure, this may be described as the ritual maintenance of established (if temporarily eclipsed) social patterns, but even should one adopt this grudgingly minimalist view, it must still be acknowledged that the maintenance in question is hardly something simple, passive, or reactionary. Indeed, the Ncwala affords us an instructive example of just how dynamic maintenance can be, involving as it does the active, continuous, and ongoing re-evocation and reconstruction of established social norms, forms, and sentiments.

5

Banquets and Brawls:
Aspects of Ceremonial Meals

The Royal Feast at Tara

Although it was once fashionable to differentiate the communicative from the technical-instrumental dimension of human activity and to view ritual as more a mode of speech than one of action, such formulations, like other attempts to treat ritual as mere symbolism, have been rendered obsolete by more recent, subtle, and sophisticated studies of the interrelations between discourse and practice.[1] For over the course of the last two decades, it has gradually become clear that ritual, etiquette, and other strongly habituated forms of practical discourse and discursive practice do not just encode and transmit messages, but they play an active and important role in the construction, maintenance, and modification of the borders, structures, and hierarchic relations that characterize and constitute society itself.

This may be seen—to take an apparently, if misleadingly simple example—in the patterns in which people are seated on high state occasions. Consider, for example, the seating arrangements for the Feast of Tara (*Feis Temró*), one of the most important of traditional Irish ritual celebrations, which took the form of an all-encompassing banquet held at regular intervals in the great castle of Tara, the royal and ceremonial center of medieval Ireland.[2] Regarding this feast, we are particularly fortunate as a schematic drawing of the banquet hall at Tara survives in two variants, one in the twelfth-century *Book of Leinster* and the other in the slightly later *Yellow Book of Lecan*. Interpretation of these documents is not unproblematic, for the language in which they are couched is archaic and sometimes obscure. Moreover, whereas one text (the *Book of Leinster*) is more reliable on matters of detail, the other better preserves the general structure in which those details were organized. Ultimately, however, careful comparison of these two sources and related materials permits us to reconstruct a prototype from which both variants apparently derived (Fig. 5.1).[3]

A wealth of information is contained in this figure, a complex diagram that fuses multiple levels of signification. First, it obviously gives a floor

	A	B		C	D
1	To horsemen a *cuinn*	To carvers a head	To butlers a head	To stewards a head	To charioteers a *cuinn*
2	To harpists a pig's shoulder	To pipers a shank	FIRE	To chessplayers a shank	To champions a pig's shoulder
3	To judges a tenderloin	To scholars a rump steak	FIRE	To cupbearers a rump steak	To *Aire forgill* 1st-rank nobles a tenderloin
4a b	To literati a tenderloin To 2d-rank literati a rump steak	To artisans a lower shank		To braziers a lower shank	To the king a tenderloin To the queen a rump steak
5a b	To Ollam filed 1st-rank poets a haunch To Anroth 2d-rank poets a knee	To smiths a front shoulder	FIRE	To physicians a front shoulder	To *Aire ard* 2d-rank nobles a haunch To *Cli* 3d-rank poets a knee
6a b	To hostelers and ? a haunch	To armorers a *milgetan*	VAT	To pilots a *milgetan*	To *Aire túise* 3d-rank nobles and historians a haunch
7a b	To expert a *roichnech* To 2d-rank craftsmen a knee	To chariot- makers -a knee	CANDLE	To pirates a knee	To *Aire échta* 4th-rank nobles a *roichnech* To *Cano* 4th-rank poets a knee
8a b	To diviners, sorcerers, and *Commilid* a shank	To jugglers a shank		To buffoons a shank	To *Aire déso* 5th-rank nobles and *Doss* 5th-rank poets a shank
9a b	To plasterers and carpenters a lower shank	To satirists the thick part of the shoulder	LAMP	To clowns the thick part of the shoulder	To *Mac fuirmid* 6th-rank poets and *Fochloc* 7th-rank poets a lower shank
10	To trumpeters and hornplayers an outpouring of mead		COMMON HALL		To cooks an outpouring of mead
11	To engravers and ringmakers a *milgetan*				To fort builders and *oblaire* a *milgetan*
12	To shoemakers and turners the thick part of the shoulder	To the royal doorkeepers the coccyx	DOOR	To the royal jesters the ribs	To wallmakers and ditchdiggers the thick part of the shoulder

Figure 5.1. Seating arrangements and distribution of meat at the Royal Feast of Tara.

plan for Tara's banquet hall. Thus, beginning at the center and top of the diagram, we find a kitchen area (positions B/1 and C/1; the letter refers to a vertical column, the number to a horizontal row) that—as prose descriptions tell us—stood at the western end of the hall. Then, as one moves further into the hall, the center area (i.e., the space between columns B and C in rows 2–9) is given over to space in which servants circulated, warming food at fires and drawing mead from vats, carrying cups and plates to those seated on either side of two long tables, one on the hall's southern side (between columns A and B), and the other to the north (between columns C and D). Where these tables ended, the hall gave onto a large common space (rows 10–12), at the western end of which was the doorway to the hall (between columns B and C at row 12).

Superimposed on this floor plan, and no less obvious, is a seating diagram in which locations are specified for all those involved in the feast. Thus, in the kitchen area we find carvers, butlers, and stewards (B/1 and C/1), with servants of a loftier character, horsemen (A/1) and charioteers (D/1), standing to either side. Rows 2–9 map seating arrangements at the two tables: Column A represents the outer, or southern, side of the southern table, where harpists (A/2), judges (A/3), literati (A/4a), and the like, were to be found; column B represents the inside of that same table, where pipers (B/2) and scholars (B/3) down to satirists (B/9) were seated. Column C shows the inner, or southern, side of the northern table, with its chessplayers (C/2), cupbearers (C/3), and bronze workers (C/4), and column D shows the northern, or outer, side of the northern table, where champions (D/2), nobles of the foremost rank (D/3), and others joined the king (D/4a).

The king's position, as we shall see, is the pivot on which all turns, but before pursuing this further, let us simply note that within the Common Hall area (rows 10–12), no tables or seats were provided. There were found trumpeters and hornplayers (A/10), cooks (D/10), wallmakers and ditchdiggers (D/12), and others, including the royal jesters (C/12) and doorkeepers (B/12), who stood to either side of the entryway.

Returning now to the king, we note that he sat in the fourth position on the northern side of the northern table (D/4a), with one quarter of the hall to his right (rows 1–3) and three quarters to his left (rows 4b–12). This is the paramount position, and others were placed near or far from it in order of their honor and status. To his right were the foremost nobles (*Aire forgill*, seated at D/3), followed by the champion, or foremost hero in battle (D/2). On the king's immediate left sat his queen (D/4b), the only woman admitted to the feast; members of the lower noble grades were placed everfurther to her left as they descended in rank.

Now, five different grades of nobility were recognized within Old Irish legal texts (not including kings, who were also subcategorized in graded rank), and to each of these was assigned a specific honorprice. This figure not only measured the extent to which persons could enter into relations of patronage and clientship, give legal testimony, make pledges, and recover damages, but also served more broadly as a quantified index of social standing. Beyond honorprice, legal texts also specified other means whereby the different grades of the nobility were to be distinguished, including the size of the retinue they could command, the payments due them annually by retainers, and even the size of their houses and outhouses.[4] Implementation of this legal system, thus, not only encoded, but actively constituted the differential ranks of the nobility, as it rendered the relative status of each rank visible in a variety of forms, each of which could be measured against like representations of other ranks, something that also occurred every time the nobles took their assigned seats at the Feast of Tara (Fig. 5.2).

Seated on the opposite side of the banquet hall from the nobles—that is, on the southern, or outer, side of the southern table (col. A)—were grouped the foremost members of that social category known as the men-of-crafts (Irish, *áes dána*). These included persons distinguished for their works of intellect and their mastery of speech: men-of-letters (A/4a and A/4b, opposite the king and queen), judges (A/3, opposite the first-rank nobles), harpists (A/2, opposite the champions), and poets of the first and second rank (A/5a and A/5b, opposite nobles of the second rank and poets of the third rank), all of whom were assigned sizable honorprices—up to 21 chattels for a top-rank poet or man-of-letters.

As in the case of nobles, an elaborate system of classification organized poets into differential strata based on their years of training, the number of stories they had committed to memory, the meters they were permitted to employ, and the fees they could command.[5] And again, this hierarchic system was given tangible representation in the Feast of Tara when the various grades of poets were seated in descending order from west to east, the first- and second-rank poets being placed at the fifth row on the southern side of the southern table (A/5a and A/5b), and the others in lower positions on the northern side of the northern table (D/5b–D/9b), as is shown in Figure 5.3.

Middle ranking men-of-crafts—those freemen who worked with their hands and were assigned modest honorprices (3–7 chattels)—were generally given seats on the inner side of both tables (cols. B and C, rows 2–9, where are found smiths, bronze workers, armorers, etc.) or toward the bottom

Rank	Title	Feast Seat	Honor-price	Clients	House Size	Outhouse
1	*Aire forgill*	D/3	30 chattels	40 men	30 ft.	20 ft.
2	*Aire ard*	D/5a	20 chattels	27 men	?	19 ft.
3	*Aire túise*	D/6a	15 chattels	20 men	29 ft.	?
4	*Aire échta*	D/7a	10 chattels	[15 men?]	[28 ft.?]	?
5	*Aire déso*	D/8a	7 chattels	10 men	27 ft.	"as proper"

Figure 5.2. Classification of the noble ranks according to Old Irish legal texts and seating arrangements for the Royal Feast of Tara.

Rank	Title	Feast Seat	Training	Retinue	Fee	Honor-Price
1	*Ollam filed*	A/5a	12 years	24 men	10 milk cows	21 chattels
2	*Anroth*	A/5b	6 years	12 men	5 milk cows	20 chattels
3	*Clí*	D/5b	5 years	8 men	4 milk cows	10 chattels
4	*Cano*	D/7b	4 years	6 men	2 milk cows	7 chattels
5	*Doss*	D/8b	3 years	5 men	1 milk cow	5 chattels
6	*Mac fuirmid*	D/9a	2 years	3 men	1 pregnant cow	3 chattels
7	*Fochloc*	D/9b	1 year	2 men	1 heifer	1 chattel

Figure 5.3. Classification of the poets' ranks according to Old Irish legal texts, manuals of poetry and seating arrangement for the Royal Feast of Tara.

on the southern side of the southern table (col. A, rows 7a–9b). Others, for whom only the most minimal honorprice was assigned (e.g., shoemakers and turners [A/12], whose honorprice was 1 chattel) or who had no independent honorprice at all (e.g., trumpeters and hornplayers [A/10], whose evaluation depended on that of their lord) were generally grouped in the Common Hall and were given no seat.[6]

The map of the hall is thus also a map of society, in which persons of different rank and standing were assigned to different loci along a north–south axis. The northern side of the northern table (col. D) was thus reserved chiefly for nobles, the southern side of the southern table (col. A) for those who were distinguished but nonnoble (i.e., the high-ranking men-of-crafts), and the intermediate zone (cols. B and C) plus the Common Hall (rows 10–12) for those who were free, but neither noble nor distinguished. Nonfree persons and women other than the queen had no place whatever in the banquet hall. Rank was also encoded in finer-grained divisions within each of these general categories by means of distance on an east–west axis from the fourth row, where the king was seated, and the farther one fell to the king's left or right (east and west, respectively), the lesser was one's status. In all instances spatial relations within the hall mirrored hierarchic relations within society.

Did this diagram simply establish a relation between seats and stations, that alone would be of considerable interest, but yet a third set of data is brought into the correlations: the portions of meat assigned guests at the feast. Beginning again with the king, we see that he is given a tenderloin (Irish, *lón-chrochit*), or chine, that is, one of the long strips of meat taken from either side of the spinal column. Similar portions are given to those persons spatially and structurally closest to the king: literati of the first rank, who sat opposite him at A/4a, nobles of the first rank, seated to his immediate right (D/3), and jurists, across from those nobles (A/3). None of those who were placed on the inner side of either table received such a cut of meat, which, being taken from the spine, came from the topmost bodily part of the animal.

Another portion of meat that is mentioned only in columns A and D is the haunch (Irish, *loarc*) assigned to first-rank poets (A/5a), second- and third-rank nobles (D/5a and D/6a), hostelers (A/6a), and historians (D/6b). In a corresponding row, however, one finds a portion unique to columns B and C: the front shoulder (Irish, *maél*)[7] assigned to smiths (B/5) and physicians (C/5). The contrast is revealing, for not only is it clear from the social identity of those who receive these portions that the haunch is a noble cut and the front shoulder nonnoble, but one can further conclude that those seated on the outer sides of either table received cuts from the thicker, longer, and meatier hind legs of animals, whereas the men of lower rank, seated on the inner sides, took pieces from the less desirable front legs.

Our diagram is thus not only a floor plan, a seating arrangement, and a map of society, but also a butcher's chart, in which the cuts from an animal's hind legs appear in columns A and D (which are perfectly symmetric), whereas those from the forelegs are similarly treated in columns B and C (which differ from cols. A and D, but are symmetric with each other). If, for the sake of simplicity, we trace the pattern in column D alone, we thus find that starting with the tenderloin assigned to the king in D/4a, portions descend gradually from the top of the animal's back to the rump (i.e., the portion just above the beginning of the limb proper), which is assigned to the queen in D/4b; the haunch or upper part of the limb, cuts from which were assigned to the second- and third-rank nobles and the historians in D/5a, D/6a, and D/6b, respectively; the unexplained *roichnech* (perhaps the lower part of the thigh?) assigned to fourth-rank nobles in D/7a; the knee, assigned to third- and fourth-rank poets in D/5b and D/7b; the shank or portion just below the knee, assigned to fifth-rank nobles and poets in D/8a and D/8b; and finally the bottom end of the shank, assigned to sixth- and seventh-rank poets in D/9a and D/9b. At this point the tables of the hall, the limbs of the beast, and the polite ranks of society give out. In the next position (D/10) one finds those for whom no seat and no meat were provided: the cooks, who may well have prepared the feast, but still had to content themselves with no more than "an outpouring of mead."

One last point might be ventured regarding the butcher's chart aspect of the diagram. Given the fact that the animal's head is placed at the top of the diagram (B/1 and C/1) and its coccyx at the bottom (B/12), we may further infer that columns B and C represent the right foreleg and hind leg, respectively whereas columns A and B do similar service for the left. Moreover, given the spatial contrast between the top of the diagram/head of the animal/kitchen area, on the one hand, and the bottom of the diagram/coccyx of the animal/doorway, on the other, it does not seem too farfetched to suggest that a trip from one end of the hall to the other might well be associated to a similar (and not unrelated) passage through the alimentary canal.

Battles over the Champion's Portion

Insofar as the Feast of Tara conformed to the patterns of this diagram, the previously existing—if temporarily latent—social hierarchy was thereby reactualized through seating arrangements and the distribution of differentially graded pieces of meat. If such banquets might serve to catalyze, confirm, celebrate, and thereby perpetuate the established order, there existed other possibilities as well: By rendering the social order visible, these same exercises also opened it up for possible contestation.

Consider, for instance, the celebrated "Story of Mac Datho's Pig," the action of which transpires during a banquet at which the leading men of two rival kingdoms, Ulster and Connacht, were both in attendance, and in which a dispute arose over who would carve the pig of the title. Now, for all that a quarrel over carving may strike a modern audience as something trivial, its seriousness becomes apparent when we recall that in medieval Ireland, as in many other places, the apportioning of meat was tantamount to the distribution of honor.[8] As becomes clear in the course of the story, while it was normal to do this in such a way as to replicate the established honorific patterns of the status quo, one could also carve in such a way as to *re*-distribute honor and thereby reconstruct the social order in rather pointed ways.

Thus, we are told that Conall Cernach of Ulster, having finally won the right to carve, "gave the pig's two front legs to the men of Connacht, and this seemed a small portion indeed to them. So they jumped up, and then the Ulstermen jumped up, and each one hit the other." To make sense out of this, one must begin with the recognition that by assigning to the heroes of Connacht the animal's forelegs—a distinctly and categorically non-noble portion, as we have seen—Conall announced and effected their literal de-gradation from the ranks of nobility to those of the men-of-crafts. To such a provocation, they could only respond with violent, if ultimately ineffective protest, for in the ensuing brawl the Connachtmen were routed.

Another Old Irish tale, "Bricriu's Feast," pursues similar themes, telling how the well-known trickster Bricriu Poison-tongue built a replica of Tara's banquet hall and invited King Conchobar and the heroes of Ulster to feast there, all the while plotting to undo them by stratagems that played on seating arrangements, the distribution of meat, and the role of women. In the first place, although the seat reserved for Conchobar seemed highest of all, Bricriu had a seat of equal height built for himself and hidden in a secret annex overlooking the hall. Further, he separately incited each of Ulster's three greatest warriors—Loegaire Buadach, Conall Cernach, and Cu Chulainn—to claim the champion's portion (Irish, *caurathmir*), which at this epic feast included not merly a choice cut of meat, but an entire boar, a bull, a hundred honey cakes and a vat of wine.

This part of the scheme Bricriu set in motion as he withdrew from the

feast (Conchobar having insisted on this as a condition of his own attendance), announcing that the champion's portion should go to that warrior
who was judged best. At this, the three heroes laid claim to the honor and
took up weapons to make good on the claim. There followed a battle so
furious that "half of the palace was an atmosphere of fire from swords and
spears, the other half a white sheet from their shields' enamel," which ended
only with the intervention of Conchobar and others, who proposed that on
this occasion, the champion's portion would be divided among all the Ulstermen. This being accepted, the full company reorganized themselves to
sit in a circle around the fire.

Peace, however, was short-lived; Bricriu, observing these developments,
sought out Fedelm of the Fresh Heart, Lendabair, and Emer of the Fair
Hair, the wives of Loegaire, Conall, and Cu Chulainn, respectively. Flatter-
ing each in turn, he urged these women to insist on entering the banquet
hall before any of the others, which, as he told them, would secure them
"the enduring sovereignty of queenship." Thus incited, they raced to the
hall together with their ladies-in-waiting and, finding its doors barred to
them, they flew at each other with words, much as their husbands had just
done with arms. Hearing this, their husbands flew into a rage: Conall and
Loegaire broke open the walls to let their wives enter; Cu Chulainn, for his
part, hoisted the entire hall aloft. In doing this he managed to knock down
the secret chamber in which Bricriu was seated, with the result that the latter—who had schemed to sit level with the king—clattered to earth, where he
rolled amid the dogs. Finally, with the hall once more restored to its foundations, the feast resumed, with yet another change of seating such that the
men were placed on one side, clustered around Conchobar, and all the
women, now admitted, were placed on the other side, round Mugain, his
queen.

Later portions of the tale tell how the competition among Loegaire,
Conall, and Cu Chulainn was renewed, with victory going to the last, but
this concerns us less than the more immediate outcome of Bricriu's feast.
For there, a hierarchic seating plan, an honorific distribution of meat, and
the exclusion of women were used, not as instruments for replication of the
preexisting and normative social order, but rather for its disruption. And
for all that poor Bricriu's schemes failed to secure his own elevation, still
they resulted in the emergence of new and unexpected social and ritual
forms: a banquet in which all men shared in the champion's portion and sat
in a circle (i.e., an antihierarchic formation with neither head nor foot), followed by a continuation of that same banquet in which all women who
sought one were granted a place.

Competition over a champion's portion is well attested for the Celts, not
only in these works of Old Irish literature, but also in several Greek accounts of the continental Celtic populations. Thus, quoting from a lost
work of the early first century B.C.E., Athenaeus reports:

Posidonius, in the twenty-third book of his *Histories,* says: "The Celts sometimes engage in single combat during meals. For gathered together in arms,

they engage in shadow-fighting and struggle with one another at arm's length, and at times they even inflict wounds. Being roused to anger by this, if those present do not restrain them, they go so far as to kill." Of old, he says, when hind legs were served up, the most powerful man took the thigh, and if someone else claimed it, they met in single combat, even unto the death (*Deipnosophistae* 4.154ab).[9]

The scene resembles closely that of Bricriu's feast, as many authors have noted: In both we find the same manner of claims, challenges, brawls, and duels that threaten to turn lethal if others do not intervene. All of this follows, moreover, from the custom of awarding an honorific portion of meat to that man who is judged best (Irish, *dech*) or most powerful (Greek, *kratistos*) and who might be called on to defend his position and privilege through the test of combat. The same practices are described in Diodorus Siculus's account of Celtic meals:

They all dine sitting not on chairs, but upon the ground, making use of the strewn skins of wolves or dogs, and they are served by the youngest children, male and female. Close by lie their fiery hearths, with cauldrons on them and spits full of meat in whole limbs, and they reward noble warriors with the fairest portions of meat, just as the poet [sc. Homer] introduces Ajax being honored by the chiefs when, having fought Hektor in single combat, he was victorious:

> "He gave to Ajax as a portion of honor the whole,
> undivided tenderloin." [*Iliad* 7.321]

They ask strangers to their feasts, and only after the meal do they inquire who they are and what they need. It is their custom during a meal to dispute those little things which happen, and to challenge each other to do single combat, without regard for their lives, for the teaching of Pythagoras prevails among them that human souls are immortal (5.28.4–5).

Similarities in wording suggest that Diodorus, like Athenaeus, took Posidonius's account as the source of his information.[10] And although we learn a number of things about the feasting behavior of the continental Celts—for example, their youthful servants, lack of tables, and practice of hospitality—on the specific question of the champion's portion, Diodorus provides us with little information that is novel, save his attempt to locate a Greek analogue for such practices. This he finds in a scene from Book 7 of the *Iliad*, where Ajax is greeted with sacrifice and feasting after having prevailed in a duel against Hector. The full passage runs:

> And when they came upon the huts of Atreus's son,
> Agamemnon, lord of men, sacrificed a head of cattle for
>   them:
> A five year old bull, to Zeus, foremost in power.
> This they flayed and prepared, and dismembered it all.
> And they cut it into pieces knowledgeably, and spitted
>   them on forks,

> Then they roasted them carefully, and took all the pieces
>   off the spits.
> But when they ceased from their labors and prepared the
>   feast,
> They feasted, and no spirit was lacking in the equal
>   feast.[11]
> And the heroic son of Atreus, wide-ruling Agamemnon,
> *Gave to Ajax as a portion of honor the whole, undivided*
>   *tenderloin (Iliad 7.313–22).*

Here again one finds honor bestowed on a champion who has proven himself in single combat by means of a presentation of meat. Although there is some variation evident in the texts we have considered regarding which specific portions are used to convey such honor, in general they are consistently those that are both large and originate high up on an animal's body: the tenderloin, haunch, thigh or shoulder, which might be served undivided (*diēnekeessi* [*Iliad* 7.321]) or in whole limbs (*holomerōn* [Diodorus Siculus 5.28.4]).[12] By virtue of their size and "lofty" nature, these pieces stand in contrast to others that are smaller, lowlier, and are awarded to persons who have been judged—but who also, in the very moment that they receive these portions, are *made*—to be lesser than those to whom the prize cuts are awarded. It is through just such micropractices as these that hierarchy is actively constructed.

Their strong similarities notwithstanding, significant differences also separate the Homeric from the Celtic data. Of these, the most important is the question of who fought whom and why. Ajax, for his part, did battle against a Trojan (i.e., a non-Greek), and in this he was understood to be defending his people and their collective honor against others from whom they felt radically estranged. Cu Chulainn, in contrast, fought against other Ulstermen, and the point of such combat, itself a form of potentially lethal competition over scarce resources (meat, prestige, and position), was to establish distinctions of honor and merit (i.e., internal borders within Ulster society) through which he would be set apart from, and above, the others.

Beef and Liberty

If the specific arrangements of festal meals have often served as instruments for the construction of social hierarchy, examples may also be found in which they have been put to opposite uses. In "Bricriu's Feast," we saw novel seating patterns and modes of distribution emerge that smacked of egalitarianism, and in Arthur's famed Table Round we may view yet another. Nor is this a literary theme only, for in certain quasi-sacrificial celebrations of modern Greek villages, to take one example, it has been shown how all meat is cut into small pieces and boiled in a stew, so that the portions distributed may all be equal.[13]

Egalitarianism, however, is never a simple matter, there being a multitude of ways in which hierarchy may be reasserted, the most egalitarian of claims and intentions notwithstanding. Thus, when a king sits at a round table, preexisting social evaluations are superimposed on the table's geometry to establish an unmistakable head for the supposedly headless table.[14] Similarly, for all that portions of stew may be scrupulously equal, still someone is always served first and someone else last.

An instructive case study for many of these issues that is a bit closer to our own age than the materials we have been considering may be found in the workings of a London club, the Sublime Society of Beef Steaks—most celebrated, perhaps, as the birthplace of the sandwich, which was made from some of its beef and named for one of its members.[15] Founded in 1735, the Beefsteak Society endured until 1866, consisting always of twenty-four elected members who assembled for dinner every Saturday between November and June for ceremonial meals, in which, as the group's bylaws put it, "Beef Steaks shall be the only meat for dinner."[16]

Now, a preliminary examination of the seating arrangement in the society's dining hall (Fig. 5.4) conveys the impression of clear hierarchy, as one chair, the president's, not only is placed at the table's head, but is also nearly twice the size of all the others. Moreover, this seat stands opposite the kitchen, a realm separated from the diners by "an enormous grating in the form of a gridiron, through which the fire was seen and the steaks handed . . . from cook to serving man."[17]

Although this iron, reminiscent of a gate and a cage as much as a grill, marked the external and absolute border between members of the society and those beyond, the president's chair marked an internal border between that officer and the others. But one ought not make too much of the latter border, for the position of president, we are told, held no power and no privileges. On the contrary, this office—like others in the society—circulated at each meeting, and the chief duty of officers was to serve as the butt for a wide variety of verbal and practical jokes that were a mainstay of club activity. Rather than a place of honor, the president's chair was thus, in effect, a sort of dunce's seat.

To appreciate aspects of the group's structure, it is helpful to trace its history. Although it had its beginnings among artists and theatrical people, by the end of the eighteenth century the Beefsteak Society had become a fashionable meeting place for male members of the upper social strata. Of the one hundred fifty-three members elected after 1770, forty-four were of the nobility, twenty-two members of Parliament, and twelve high-ranking military officers. Yet among this company there continued to be found painters, merchants, and theatrical managers as well.[18] It was thus a group in which men (and men only) of different external stations gathered to eat together. But it is of particular interest that within the spatial and temporal confines of their ritualized meetings, members claimed to be equals, and the workings of the group were designed to foster a spirit of egalitarianism among them. Thus, members always called one another "Brother" and dressed in

Figure 5.4. The dining room of the Sublime Society of Beefsteaks, from a sketch by James Hallett. (Reproduced in Arnold, *Life and Death*, p. 1.)

uniform, complete with rings and buttons emblazoned with the image of the gridiron and inscribed with the society's rallying slogan, "Beef and liberty." Offices, as we have seen, carried with them not prestige, but ridicule; rules and customs existed in such complexity and profusion that members might be judged guilty of an infraction at any moment, whereupon they were subjected to a ritual of public humiliation and comic rebuke. As one visitor to the club commented, "It is a club in which nae man can ken whether he is doing right or wrong; the kindest action may be counted an offence; but always the more outré a man's behaviour is, the better."[19]

All of these mechanisms—uniform costume, pseudofamiliar address, status inversions, and joking behavior—are well-known means of obliterating differential status and creating a spirit of common belonging.[20] As Brother Walter Arnold—to whom we owe the chief surviving account of the Beefsteak Society—nostalgically put it, "the friendly equality that existed among the members of the Sublime Society of Beef Steaks, tempered always by good breeding, constituted one of its principal charms."[21]

This egalitarian spirit, to which Arnold returns time and again, was nowhere better expressed than in the Beefsteak Society's menu, which was central to the group's self-understanding, as evidenced by its very name. Two factors must here be stressed. First, by insisting on expensive steaks as their *sole* fare (consumed in obscene abundance, six or more to each diner), members defined themselves as an elite.[22] Second, by insisting on steaks as their *common* fare, they defined themselves as social equals. Not only did they eat together, but all partook of the same, equally valued dishes.

That this exercise in egalitarianism was imperfect, however, is clearly announced in Arnold's contradictory qualification that "friendly equality" was "tempered . . . by good breeding," a qualification amplified elsewhere in his account. Consider, for instance, "the charge" given to new members on induction to the group:

> "The charge" was then delivered by the Recorder [sc. one of the club's officers]. In it he dwelt on the solemnity of the obligations the new member was about to take on himself. He was made to understand in tones alternately serious and gay, the true Brotherly spirit of the Sublime Society of Beef Steaks; *that while a perfect equality existed among the Brethren, such equality never should be permitted to degenerate into undue familiarity,* that while badinage was encouraged in the freest sense of the word, such badinage must never approach to a personality; and that good fellowship must be united with good breeding.[23]

In practice, deference was always shown to titled and prestigious members. Joking songs, for instance, display a consistent structure, in which members are sequentially named and mocked, yet the sequence always somehow culminates with those members drawn from the upper nobility, who are lauded instead of lampooned.[24] Again, visitors were always introduced to the society's titled members first, and when Arnold attempts to explain the group's demise, the very first thing he mentions is their loss of the royal family with the retirement of H.R.H. the duke of Sussex in 1839, observing: "It is needless to say that the presence of Royalty enhanced [the Beefsteak Society's] celebrity, and the absence of so distinguished an element affected its prosperity."[25]

Most striking of all is to find the egalitarian title "Brother" ludicrously conjoined to hierarchic titles, as in Arnold's slavish references to "Brother the Duke of York," "Brother the Duke of Leinster," or even "Brother H.R.H. the Prince of Wales, afterwards George IV." Evidently the Beefsteak Society sought to trade on both its egalitarian spirit *and* the distinction of certain members without ever acknowledging or resolving this inherent contradiction. For one hundred thirty-two years members officially denied that there was any difference in their statuses, while unofficially acknowledging, enacting, and thereby reconstructing such differences in countless ways. Finally, when the upper crust ceased to join, other members ceased to attend, and in its last years the society stood empty, egalitarianism in the absence of a covert hierarchy apparently being unbearable or—at the very least—no fun.[26]

By way of conclusion, I would simply observe that of all human behaviors, there is none more conducive to the integration of society than the ritual sharing of food. For commensality facilitates the formation of *societas* by establishing bonds of sentiment and obligation among those who share a meal while also drawing a rigid boundary such as that marked by the doors at the hall of Tara or the Beefsteak Society's grate, between them and those outsiders with whom they do not or emphatically will not eat.

There is more to society, however, than the simple distinction between insiders and outsiders. In addition there is also a system of semipermeable borders that establishes separate subcategories among the insiders and organizes their dealings with one another: That is to say, society is characterized by hierarchy as much as by solidarity. Such hierarchies not only find expression through, but are actively constructed and regularly reconstructed in, mealtime rituals by means of particularities of menu, portion, seating arrangements, order of service, and the like. Although such rituals most often (and perhaps most importantly) serve as effective instruments of social replication, we have seen that there exist other possibilities as well, for instance, when individuals work through them to secure their own upward mobility (witness the Celtic battles over the champion's portion) or on those rare, contradictory, and sometimes even laughable occasions when meals serve as the instruments with which alternatives are posed to the established order, as with Arthur's Table Round, Bricriu's Feast, or the Sublime Society of Beef Steaks.

6

Festivals and Massacres:
Reflections on St. Bartholomew's Day

Ritual and the Deconstruction of Social Forms

As has been long recognized, any society, even the smallest, is a complex amalgam of multiple subunits—clans, lineages, socioeconomic classes, political factions, age groups, genders, and so on that are only imperfectly bonded together to form the total social unit. Such integration, which is necessary for the smooth and harmonious functioning of society, is regularly sought and accomplished through numerous overlapping systems and mechanisms—among them law, pedagogy, etiquette, aesthetics, and ideology, particularly religious ideology. It is, in fact, the particular competence of religion for achieving broad social integration that led Durkheim to consecrate his masterwork, *The Elementary Forms of the Religious Life,* to the study of religion, and the Durkheimian tradition—which has been so influential in sociological, anthropological, and historical scholarship—has enriched our understanding of the means whereby religion powerfully promotes social cohesion and sentiments of common belonging.[1]

Among the many aspects of religion that promote social integration perhaps none is more powerful and important than ritual, although it must be noted that not all ritual is necessarily religious.[2] It should immediately be stressed, however, that for all its power and efficacy, ritual is never able either to eradicate cleavages or to resolve tensions between groups in competition for scarce resources of a material and nonmaterial nature. Rather, what ritual is competent to do—as Max Gluckman rightly observed—is to "cloak the fundamental conflicts,"[3] thereby permitting groups and individuals to forget them for a time (or at least to take them less seriously) so that some temporary measure of good will, common spirit, and stability may emerge.

There now exists a spendid tradition of studies demonstrating how rituals of one sort and another "cloak" the issues that might otherwise force cleavages between subunits to erupt. But what has been given considerably less thorough attention are ritualistic responses to situations of crisis when the normal techniques of integration and social maintenance are inadequate to their weighty task: What happens when the tensions between competing groups cannot be controlled by ritual means?

One work in which this important topic was addressed is Emmanuel Le Roy Ladurie's justly celebrated *Carnival in Romans,* in which he describes how growing friction and resentment between the lower social orders (chiefly artisans and peasants) and their traditional superiors (*notables* and bourgeoisie) in a small city of Dauphiné came to a head during carnival week of 1580.[4] The setting was an appropriate one, for carnival is normally a time of "ritual rebellion" (in Gluckman's sense), where norms and hierarchies temporarily dissolve in symbolic inversions, moral license, and generalized antistructure, only to be reestablished when carnival is over.[5] But in this year, the disorder threatened to spill beyond its accustomed limits, as the lower classes staged ever-more aggressive shows of force, all within the ritual discourse of masquerades, processions, and dances, through which they voiced and enacted their determination to force a permanent reordering of power and privilege within the city. Acutely sensitive to this threat, the upper orders responded with a premeditated and brutal massacre of the popular party on Mardi Gras Day. That is, when the ritual appeared capable of reconstructing society along lines different from its traditional hierarchic order, extreme measures were employed by those who were determined that this should not transpire. In place of the normal ritual celebration, we find agitation followed by massacre.

Within the Carnival of Romans is revealed the simple fact, more apparent to Marxists than to Durkheimians, that social integration benefits some segments of society considerably more than others and is always won at the expense of the lower orders. Ladurie's data further make plain that where ritual and other forms of discourse fail to effect integration, coercion may quickly follow. But let us move to another example, separated from Ladurie's by only eight years: the St. Bartholomew's Day Massacre, the single most dramatic event of the French Wars of Religion.[6]

Background to a Massacre

As with any such incident, one must begin by considering the nature of the total social aggregate and the chief cleavages within it. Here, as is often the case, what appears simple at first, proves more complex on closer study. Although the struggle that rent France during the latter half of the sixteenth century is conventionally called the Wars of Religion, more was at issue than a straightforward confrontation of Catholics and Huguenots. To be sure, religious differences were of tremendous importance to both parties, but other factors also figured prominently.[7]

To begin, the Huguenot/Catholic cleavage had an important socioeconomic dimension to it, Protestants in general being more urban and more prosperous than Catholics, although such data that are available do not permit any precise measurement of these differences. Of particular note is the concentration of Huguenots in certain sectors of the legal and financial professions, at the master level within the artisanry, and in such prestigious trades as goldsmithing, jewelry, and printing.[8] Moreover, the Huguenot party met with considerable success in converting a large section of the upper class (the *notables*) and other *notables* still were quite sympathetic to their cause without actively committing themselves to it.[9]

Geographic distributions were also significant. Protestants enjoyed numerical superiority only in the center-west of France and in the south—Languedoc, Dauphiné, Provence, Béarn, and the Garonne valley—Catholics predominated elsewhere. Significant Protestant communities existed in Paris, Rouen, Orléans, Lyon, and Meaux where, however, they were surrounded by a hostile Catholic majority. A difference in political ideology also became apparent in the years after St. Bartholomew's, for as Michael Walzer has shown, such prominent Huguenot authors as Francis Hotman, Theodore Beza, and Philip de Mornay at that time and partly in consequence of the St. Bartholomew's events, sought to estabilsh a set of justifications for resistance to royal authority.[10]

Finally, the cleavage found expression in contrasting cultural styles: *différences des moeurs*. The sobriety, zeal, and fervor of the Protestants effectively constituted a direct challenge to the traditional values and behaviors of the more relaxed, self-indulgent Catholics, and the Protestants' general demeanor, as well as many of their distinctive practices were taken as an affront by their adversaries in this conflict of cultural styles. Janine Estèbe describes this situation vividly:

> The daily habits of the Huguenot were not those of a Catholic: the Huguenot did not fast, neither on Friday nor during Lent, and on these days the aroma of roasts which issued from Calvinist kitchens was as the stench of a funeral pyre. In their clothing and their external demeanor, the Protestants affected a great austerity: somber and decent clothes, and neither vertiginous décolletage nor flowing dresses for the women. Again the Calvinists voluntarily cut themselves off from the popular milieu by not participating in the usual pastimes: they did not frequent the cabarets, play cards or dice, and above all they did not dance. And dance in the 16th century was the diversion *par excellence*.[11]

Religious differences were thus compounded by differences in income level, social standing, geographic distribution, political orientation as well as in patterns of dress, demeanor, and recreation. These last considerations, far from being the least important aspects of the cleavage, were extremely weighty, for through such *différences des moeurs*, the Huguenots estranged themselves from the rest of French society. To quote Estèbe again, "The Protestants had put themselves, by their religious choice on the margin of the urban or village community whose rites, feasts, and games they no longer accepted. . . . [They] were already outside traditional society, even though they continued to share its language and its conditions of life."[12] As with the Swaziland Protectorate, at issue is the question of whether there was one (somewhat fragile) society having two segments or two societies co-existing uneasily under the cover of a superficial integration. But it is sense-less to consider this in purely synchronic fashion: Over the course of several decades, the first state of affairs degenerated into the second, and St. Barthol-omew's is an important turning point in this process.[13]

In the years leading up to St. Bartholomew's, violence mounted through-out France.[14] Between 1562 and 1570, three wars of religion were fought in which many Catholics understood themselves to be defending not only their religion, but their traditional way of life against the threat posed by the Huguenots (April 1562–March 1563, September 1567–March 1568, and Au-gust 1568–August 1570). Each war was inconclusive, with neither side being able to force the other into submission. In the last of these conflicts, despite significant victories won by the Catholics under the duc d'Anjou at Jarnac (13 March 1569) and Moncontour (3 October 1569), the Protestants success-fully regrouped, and the Edict of Saint-Germain (signed 8 August 1570) brought the war to an end on terms considered by Catholics to be extremely generous.

What the young king Charles IX sought in this treaty—his policy here, as elsewhere, being guided by his mother (and former regent) Catherine de Medici—was a reconciliation of Catholic and Protestant France under the auspices and to the ultimate benefit of the royal family, whose power had been considerably eroded by the recurrent civil wars. This treaty was only part of a much broader set of compromises, in which the Catholics agreed to greater tolerance toward the Huguenots and accepted the eleva-tion of their chief leader, Admiral Gaspard de Coligny, to a position as se-nior advisor at court. Foreign policy as envisioned by Coligny—and incon-sistently implemented by the king—had as its chief features alliance with (Protestant) England, support for the (Calvinist) rebels in the Netherlands, and ultimately war with (Catholic) Spain: the goal being to unite all France in a war against an encircling power and traditional rival. Protestants, for their part, agreed to a royal wedding, in which the cleavage within the na-tion would find symbolic redress in the union to be consummated between the foremost Huguenot prince, Henri de Navarre (later Henri IV), and the king's own sister, Marguerite de Valois.

One by one, the elements of this policy encountered difficulties. First, Cath-olics were not reconciled to Protestants, but they resented the favorable treat-ment accorded to the latter under the Edict of Saint-Germain, feeling that what the heretics could not win in war had been granted in an incomprehensi-ble peace. Second, diplomatic and military reverses, particularly Spanish vic-tories against the Turks at Lepanto (7 October 1571) and against the rebels in the Netherlands at Mons (17 July 1572), rendered Coligny's foreign policy much less feasible, but rather than reformulate it he clung to his plans more tenaciously than ever, threatening that if there were not war with Spain there would be war at home. Such a stance brought him ever more into conflict with Catherine de Medici, with whom he wrestled for the king's favor. Although it is easy to personalize this last struggle (as historians have often done), it is something of a fallacy to do so: the fallacy of misplaced concreteness, for this was not so much a personal struggle as it was a personal expression (one among many) of a broader social struggle. The attitudes and actions of the admiral and the queen mother, like those of all individuals, resulted from and represented forces that were inscribed on their individual consciousness and personal predispositions by society at large. Catherine and Coligny could not be reconciled primarily because they were the representatives and products of broad social groupings, Catholic and Huguenot, respectively. And so long as the sentiments of estrangement that divided these groups were too strong and their sentiments of affinity too weak to permit any lasting peace, so also would their representatives experience jealousies, rivalries, misunderstandings, mistrusts, arguments, and other manifestations of personal estrangement in their dealings with one another. The tensions inherent in the broader social situation thus generated and found expression in conflict between individuals, not only within the royal court, but at all levels of society, and no simple personalistic solution could reunite the separate segments of French society: neither the attempt to bring Coligny and Catherine together in council, nor that to join in marriage the royal houses of Catholic Valois and Huguenot Navarre.

A Royal Wedding:
The Failed Ritual of Social Integration

After the enormous success of Claude Lévi-Strauss's *Structures élémentaires de la parenté,* anthropologists regularly treat marriage as that means whereby men forge bonds of affinity (in the technical, as well as the more general sense) between their respective social groups through the carefully regulated exchange of women.[15] Although this view may be subject to debate and modification in many instances, there is perhaps no body of evidence for which it is so adequate and accurate a description than the system of royal marriages within the great European monarchies. And among all those adept in the use of marriage as an instrument of foreign policy, few surpassed Catherine de Medici, who arranged for her only daughter the first official marriage between a Catholic and a Huguenot, celebrated Monday, 18 August 1572 at Notre Dame de Paris between Henri de Navarre and Marguerite de Valois, six days before the St. Bartholomew's Day Massacre (Fig. 6.1).

That this marriage was no union of two happy individuals is abundantly clear. The bride stated plainly that she did not love the groom (she was reputed to favor the duc de Guise, the most militant champion of the Catholic cause) and agreed to the union only under duress, her mother having insisted that it was necessary for the welfare of France. On the groom's side, there was also hesitation, as Henri's mother, Jeanne d'Albret signed the marriage contract with profound misgivings. Her letters show her as bitter and recriminating, deeply disturbed by the frivolity of the royal court, Marguerite's coldness toward Henri, and above all the refusal of the

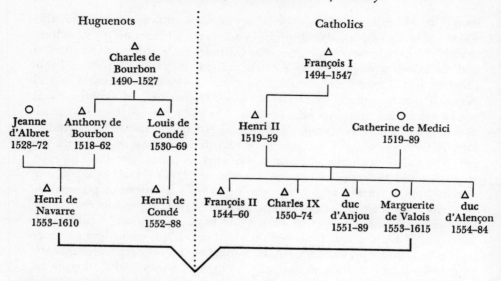

Figure 6.1. Royal marriage as an instrument of social integration: Religious and familial connections of the chief actors in the wedding of Henri de Navarre and Marguerite de Valois, 18 August 1572.

bride to accept the religion of her husband-to-be, something that would ordinarily have been expected of her.[16] The wedding itself dramatized the same misgivings and latent hostilities evident in the prenuptial negotiations. Far from being a celebration of unity and harmonious integration, the ceremony was in large measure a ritual dramatization of the gulf that separated the two major segments of the French nation. Several ominous shadows lay over the wedding, chiefly resulting from, and giving voice to, Catholic resistance. Among these was the fact that the expected papal dispensation failed to arrive, which could invalidate the wedding. Further, two influential Parisian preachers—Sorbin and Vigor—delivered violent sermons in the days before the ceremony, inveighing against it, promising divine anger, torrents of blood, and comparing the king to Esau, who would lose his birthright to Jacob (an obvious reference to the duc d'Anjou [later Henri III], hero of Jarnac and Moncontour) if he permitted the union, and stating pointblank, "God will not tolerate this execrable mating (*Dieu ne souffira pas cet exécrable accouplement*)."[17]

If dress and demeanor normally served as indexes of Catholic–Protestant estrangement, they did so emphatically on the day of the wedding. Whereas the Huguenots chose to wear their normal black attire for the most part, the royal family seized the opportunity to parade their most brilliant fineries. Charles came *"en soleil,"* Anjou in pale yellow satin covered with silver and pearls, Marguerite in a *robe d'or* and a cloak of blue velvet. Even Catherine abandoned her habitual mourning and appeared bedecked in diamonds. A competition was thus encoded in the contrasting styles of dress, and each group strove not only to express something of their values and position through the medium of clothing, but also to cast shame upon their rivals: the Huguenots for their lack of elegance; the Catholics for their frivolity. Predictably, each side considered itself victorious in this competition. Yet the pride displayed by the Huguenots on this occasion was taken as an affront by the predominantly Catholic Parisian crowds, who resented their hauteur and "hypocrisy." A contemporary source speaks of the animus felt toward the strutting of the Protestants, "thinking themselves to be fortified by the marriage of the King of Navarre to *Madame*."[18]

Madame herself—that is, Marguerite de Valois—was not without her misgivings, as we have seen. Once again, it would be a mistake to overly personalize her reluctance to marry the Huguenot prince. And for all that it may be that she "simply didn't love him," the ultimate sources of her actions and sentiments must be sought not in romantic chemistry or personalistic psychology, but within the social, political, and historic context in which she was formed and in which she found herself a significant actor. For if the forces seeking the integration of French society drove her toward the historic marriage, sentiments of estrangement prevailed over those of affinity at this crucial juncture—in her as in the nation at large. At the crucial moment, when Marguerite was called on for the final *"oui"* that would join her lawfully to Henri de Navarre, she hesitated, unwilling to speak, and it is told that King Charles himself placed his hand on her head and physically forced her nod of assent.

What followed the wedding was equally revealing: There ensued a series of nocturnal *fêtes*, including dramatic spectacles that were arranged by the duc d'Anjou with the deliberate intention of humiliating the Protestant party. Thus, on the evening of Wednesday 20 August at the Hôtel de Bourbon was staged the *Mystère des trois mondes*, in which a troop of *chevaliers* led by the Huguenot princes Navarre and Henri de Condé sought entrance to a Paradise filled with nymphs. Their way into this heavenly grove being blocked by a set of angelic *chevaliers*—played by the king, Anjou, and their younger brother, the duc d'Alençon—a struggle ensued in which the would-be assailants of Paradise were defeated and cast into Hell, where they were encaged by a group of devils. Although a song in honor of love and a nymphic ballet were followed by the Huguenots' release, never were the latter united with the nymphs of their desire.

It takes no particular sensitivity or expertise to interpret such crude and deliberate symbolic discourse. The same struggle that had rent France for more than a decade and that was apparent in the contrasting apparel at Monday's wedding again found graphic expression in Wednesday's masque. The dénouement—a resounding victory of the Catholic party—must be seen as part wish and part (accurate) prophecy. The only mystery in the *Mystère* is the question of what was signified by the nymphs in Paradise: nymphs sought by the Huguenots, but ultimately denied them. At the most obvious level of signification, they clearly represent Marguerite and, beyond that,

Catholic women in general. In this light the masque forms a counterpoint to the wedding of two days prior, for here intermarriage—all intermarriage— is firmly and conclusively rejected as an impious affront that leads to death and damnation for those male Huguenots who would seek it. At a deeper level, however, the celestial nymphs signify the same thing as did Marguerite herself, for there is no indication she was an object of any personal desire. Rather, she—like the nymphs in paradise—signified that which is sought in any marriage: peaceful union, harmony, and social integration. It is this that the Protestant *chevaliers* hoped to win and that the Catholic *chevaliers,* who cast themselves as defenders of heaven (i.e., of the true faith), violently denied them.

On the next night, the same points were reiterated when Anjou staged a *course de bague* in which Navarre and his companions were defeated in mimed joust by the king and his brothers, the former party dressed as Turks and the latter as Amazons. What was here staged, in effect, was an elaborate inversion of the royal wedding: a denial and an undoing of its effects. For in place of a union effected between the sexes was battle between them and in place of the joining of two social groups was the conclusive victory of one over the other. One must also pay close attention to the sexual and religious codes employed, for the groom's party were presented as heathens and effeminate males (complete with great floppy turbans), whereas the bride's party appeared as martial females and defenders of civilization. With this ominous display, the wedding festivities celebrating the union of Catholic Valois and Protestant Navarre officially came to an end.[19]

On the following day, Friday, 22 August, an attempt was made on the life of Gaspard de Coligny, admiral of France, chief adviser to the king, and leader of the Huguenot party.

A Ritual Massacre:
The Feast of St. Bartholomew, 1572

From the moment of this unsuccessful attempt on the admiral's life, all Paris was galvanized. Among the Protestants debate raged as to the most appropriate response. Some urged flight, fearing they had been lured to a hostile city for slaughter, the royal wedding having been bait in the trap. Others urged an attack on their enemies, particularly the forces of the duc de Guise. Still others—and their counsel prevailed—demanded justice from the king, issuing dire (but foolhardy) threats should such justice not be forthcoming.

On the Catholic side, too, there was confusion and maneuvering. Contemporary sources are both lacunary and at points contradictory, particularly in their attempts to assign responsibility for the attempted assassination: Most incriminate the duc de Guise, who owned the house from which the shots were fired; others implicate Catherine, Anjou, and prominent members of the king's council.[20] What is clear is that the king began an investigation and himself called on the wounded Coligny on Saturday, 23 August, with members of the court and royal family in attendance. Coligny, however, insisted on speaking to the king in private, at which time he urged him to pursue the war in Flanders against Spain, and (according to some) to repudiate the influence of Catherine and Anjou.

There followed a critical series of meetings and discussions within the court, culminating in a royal council held on the evening of August 23, in which Charles was brought to support the elimination of the Huguenot leaders. A purge list was rapidly prepared, although not within certain disagreements,[21] and the assault on Coligny's quarters (where most of the Protestant leaders were to be found) was entrusted to the duc de Guise. During that night the latter gathered his forces, instrucitng them, "Now is the hour in which, by the grace of the king, we must avenge ourselves on the race of the enemies of God" (*Voici l'heure que par le volonté du roi, il se faut vanger de la race ennemie de Dieu*).[22] Meanwhile, in the streets, rumors circulated wildly as workers—freed from their labors for the vigil of the feast day—milled about. Catholic preachers also used the approaching feast to stir up popular emotion against the Huguenots, and the Huguenots made matters worse by publicly hurling threats at the family of Guise, who were particularly loved by the Parisian crowd.

An hour before dawn on Sunday, 24 August, the holy Feast of St. Bartholomew, the tocsin was rung at Catherine's order as a signal for the massacre to begin. Coligny's guard was overpowered, numerous Huguenot leaders were killed, and the admiral himself, announcing "I am ready for death," was murdered, defenestrated, and his body abused. By dawn, the official proscription was complete, with approximately two hundred victims.

At this point the Parisian people took over. Assembling first at the Hôtel de Ville toward daybreak, a mob, which included not only the rootless poor, but also a high percentage of artisans, moved on Huguenots throughout the city. Three days of riot, murder, and pillage followed, despite sporadic attempts to restore order. Not until Saturday, 30 August, was the city calm, by which time a bare minimum of two thousand Huguenots lay dead. Throughout August, September, and into early October rioting and massacre spread into the provinces, as far north as Rouen, south to Toulouse, east to Lyon, and west to Angers. Total casualties are estimated in the neighborhood of ten thousand.

Numbers alone cannot possibly convey the horrors of St. Bartholomew's, for in addition to death the victims were subjected to fearful degradation. Repeatedly, corpses were stripped naked, dragged through the streets, pelted with dung, and flung into rivers. The most extreme case was the treatment of Coligny's body: Having been defenestrated, kicked, and cursed by Guise, it fell to the mob, who decapitated and castrated it, dragged it through Paris, and consigned it to the Seine. Thereafter, the cadaver was fished out, paraded through the streets, and hung by its heels over a fire which, being ineptly constructed, failed to consume it. Such actions as these recurred throughout all cities in which there was rioting.

Also noteworthy is the Miracle of the Hawthorn, reported on the afternoon of 25 August, when the killing had continued for nearly a day and a half. At that moment, when it appeared there might be a lull in the carnage, a withered hawthorn tree, dead many years, is said to have turned green and burst into flower before an image of the Virgin. This occurred, fittingly enough, at the *Cimetière des Innocents,* located at a center of considerable slaughter. Church authorities took this as a sign of God's favor and interpreted the miracle as conveying divine authorization for the massacre to continue, the restoration of the tree representing the renewal of France through sacrifice.

On Tuesday, 26 August, yet another form of legitimation was added. Holding a *lit de justice,* Charles declared that he had ordered the massacre in order to thwart a Huguenot plot against the royal family. As the killing continued, a solemn Jubilee was staged, complete with a procession in which clergy and royal family marched in a show of unity, strength, and remorse-free celebration. This Parisian Jubilee was mirrored in another: On receiving reports of the massacre, Pope Gregory XIII announced a Jubilee to be held in Rome on 11 September 1572 and every year thereafter in commemoration of the event. Medallions struck for the occasion show Gregory on one side and the Exterminating Angel on the other, the latter wielding a sword against the Protestants. The legend reads, "Slaughter of the Huguenots" (Latin, *Ugnotorum strages*).

Analysis of a Socioritual Drama

In the events of St. Bartholomew's Day, French society was effectively deconstructed: A previously established level of integration came apart, bloodily and dramatically. Basic to the history of the latter half of the sixteenth century is the fact that two segments of society became gradually ever-more estranged from one another, given their religious, political, economic, geographic, moral, aesthetic, and cultural differences. Unity was sought through military, political, diplomatic, legal, and ritual means. None succeeded.

When the normal instruments for achieving or maintaining social integration fail, the likelihood of an open breach becomes great. One form that such breaches may take is schism: the formal separation of two (or more) irreconcilable parties that had earlier been contending segments within one encompassing society.[23] St. Bartholomew's Day and the Carnival in Romans as well as such similar incidents as the Sicilian Vespers and the Nazi *Kristallnacht* present another possible means to deal with an irresolvable cleavage: massacre or even genocide.[24]

Analytically, schism and massacre have much in common. Both are instances of social deconstruction, involving the radical redrawing of social borders along lines more restrictive than those that had previously obtained. Where schism and massacre differ, however, is in the rather fundamental question of whether the members of all segments of the original aggregate will be left alive when the process is completed. Horrific though it may seem, these important social processes may be represented in quasialgebraic equations, in which A and B represent segments of society and parentheses represent social borders within which sufficiently powerful sentiments of affinity prevail to maintain some reasonable degree of unity, harmony, and integration (Fig. 6.2):

$$
\begin{aligned}
\text{Integrated Society} &= (A + B) \\
\text{Schism} &= (A + B) \rightarrow (A) + (B) \\
\text{Massacre} &= (A + B) - B \rightarrow (A)
\end{aligned}
$$

Figure 6.2. Processes of social deconstruction (I).

Similar processes may also be observed within relatively small-scale groups and events. Thus, for instance, when an individual has been branded as a dangerous deviant for one reason or another, society excludes him or her from its midst. This exclusion can take such forms as ostracism, imprisonment, enslavement, ghettoization, or banishment—to name a few. But in certain cases, stronger measures are sought, and the offender is executed. Again, that minimal social unit composed of two persons and ordinarily known as marriage may be dissolved either through divorce (including under this rubric such variants as annulment, desertion, and separation); alternatively, one partner may murder the other. An analogy between these various forms might be posited as in Figure 6.3.

In each instance, the first alternative is a relatively bloodless means for dealing with situations in which integration cannot be maintained. The latter is the most sanguinary of options.

Given the relation between schism and massacre, it is worth asking what factors lead toward the exercise of massacre as an option. Among such factors may be noted first, the transformation of sentiments of simple estrangement into those of pronounced animosity along the line of cleavage where division will occur, and second, a pattern whereby in the minds and rhetoric of one or both of the rival segments, the other is characterized as less than human. Third, when the larger society in which the segments are encompassed takes the form of a nation-state effectively controlled by one of the segments, this increases the probability of violence insofar as the dominant party, striving to preserve its territory and authority intact, may tend to

	Pacific	*Violent*
Individual level	Exclusion	Execution
Marital level	Divorce	Uxoricide
Social level	Schism	Massacre

Figure 6.3. Processes of social deconstruction (II).

characterize schism as secession and dissidents as traitors. Finally, there is the question of legitimation. If actors can be persuaded that mass killings are a rightful—or even a religious—act, such killings become more likely.

All of these points have relevance for the case at hand. Thus, with regard to the St. Bartholomew's Day Massacre, it is clear that Catholic clergy and crown alike exercised their full authority to legitimate it through their sermons, proclamations, and exploitation of the Miracle of the Hawthorn. Further, it must be acknowledged that the massacre itself, in important ways, was nothing less than a ritual performance: a celebration of the holy feast of St. Bartholomew, a day that was doubly sacred for falling on a Sunday in 1572. Such a provocative and profoundly disquieting line of interpretation does not, it should be stressed, originate with scholars who sit at a comfortable distance from the events. Rather, contemporary witnesses themselves regularly described the degradations perpetrated on victims of sectarian violence throughout the latter half of the sixteenth century as acts of ritual purification. Regarding St. Bartholomew's specifically, they emphasized the way in which Huguenot corpses were ritually, if abusively, treated with the four classic elements: earth (pelted with dung), air (stripped naked to the winds), fire (burnt), and water (flung into rivers). The attempt was thus not merely to kill enemies, but to eradicate a pollution and to cleanse society of an infesting evil.

The characteristic term used by militant Catholics for the Huguenots in the sixteenth century—others have since become more fashionable—was *vermin,* by which Protestants were discursively reduced to the level of a subhuman annoyance, a source of disease fit only for extermination.[25] Consider, for example, an anonymous poem published in the wake of the massacre:

> O joyous victory! To you alone, Lord—
> Not to us—is the signal honor
> Of having with a single blow torn them out root and
>   branch:
> The ground is strewn with heretic vermin.
> Vermin who that night were caught in the snares.[26]

For all that we may find it shocking in a moral or aesthetic sense, there are strong reasons to take the contemporary testimonies most seriously and to consider the St. Bartholomew's Day Massacre as a ritual while remaining aware of the fact that it was other things as well.[27] Many of the chief hallmarks of ritual are patently evident: Thus, within moments set dramatically apart from those of normal, profane time, there transpired a discourse of highly stylized and symbolic (as well as materially effective) gestures and actions that were understood by their perpetrators to be divinely ordained and religiously legitimated. It is instructive, moreover, to juxtapose this ritual with another: the royal wedding of 18 August, which preceded it by less than a week. In that wedding, as we have seen, an attempt was made to effect ritual integration of the total French social body: to call forth sentiments of affinity and diminish those of estrangement through celebration of an unprecedented union between two individuals who acted as the focal representatives of the contending segments encompassed within France. That attempt failed, and six days later the consequences of its failure became all too apparent.

I do not think it goes too far to insist on the close relation that exists between the royal wedding—a failed ritual of social integration—and the massacre that followed, an all-too-successful ritual purge. Yet it would be wholly inaccurate to describe the relation between these two events as one of simple cause and effect. For it is hardly the case that *because* the wedding miscarried, *therefore* the massacre occurred. Rather, the same forces that made it impossible for the wedding to succeed *also* rendered further bloodletting all but inevitable. Moreover, those same forces gave shape to, and found expression in, the full range of individual actions and attitudes that culminated in the massacre: the strategic manipulations of Catherine de Medici, the reluctance of Marguerite de Valois, the militance of the ducs d'Anjou and de Guise, the inflexibility of Coligny, the willingness of the Parisian populace to kill and that of the Huguenots to die.[28] In the simplest terms, those forces may be understood as the sentiments of estrangement—radical otherness—that came to prevail over sentiments of affinity between Catholics and Protestants during the latter half of the sixteenth century, producing that state of affairs that, following sociological parlance, we tend to call cleavage.

When normal rituals fail, other rituals of an extraordinary nature may be improvised in order to achieve the desired results, as is seen, for instance, in ceremonies for rain or success in the hunt.[29] Thus, for example, in San Salvador during the entire year of 1894 no rain fell, and the town council responded to this crisis with a resolution stipulating that if rain did not come within eight days, no one would go to mass or say their prayers. After another eight days, all churches would be burned, all missals and rosaries destroyed; were there still no rain after a third eight days, all priests and nuns would be beheaded. Further, it was stated, "For the present permission is given for the commission of all sorts of sin, in order that the Supreme Creator may understand with whom He has to deal."[30] Here, we see a solemn moment, in which the normative moral and ritual order were symbolically deconstructed as a means of redressing the cosmic disorder evidenced in the failure of rain. And for all that the specifics may seem untoward or outlandish, the underlying logic is straightforward, even elegant. Thus, normal ritual being intended to maintain the cosmos in its familiar, established order, when such rituals prove counterproductive (i.e., yielding the opposite of their desired effects), the solution lies in the performance of extraordinary rituals that symbolically and materially undo the discredited normal rituals: rosaries are broken, priests beheaded, and so forth.

A similar line of analysis may be advanced with regard to the normal rituals through which social integration is maintained or—to put it more actively—continually reconstructed in its familiar established order. When weddings, gift exchanges, banquets, and the like, are no longer sufficient to bind a given social aggregate together in relative harmony and goodwill,[31] rituals of an extraordinary type may be improvised, rituals in which the preexisting socioritual order is effectively deconstructed and sentiments of estrangement are celebrated rather than those of affinity. Banishment, divorce, and formally proclaimed schism (e.g., the celebrations staged by colonized nations on regaining independence) are all such rituals of social disintegration. So, too, may the execution of a criminal or a wayward spouse take ritual form. Such also may be true of massacre, which can all too readily assume the form of a purificatory sacrifice through which a troubled society is bloodily deconstructed and a novel (if truncated) society constructed in its place.

7

Revolutionary Exhumations in Spain

On the Brink of Civil War: July 1936

Like France during the Wars of Religion, Spain under the Second Republic (1931–39) was divided into two broad and mutually hostile segments that differed from one another in numerous fashions and eyed one another with mixed suspicion, hostility, and contempt. In blunt terms, one can characterize this as a cleavage between Left and Right, these distinctions being simultaneously socioeconomic (the Right drawing its primary support from the bourgeoisie and its clients; the Left from the working classes) and political (Marxists, libertarians, and most republicans on the Left; monarchists [of varying stripes], Falangists, Radicals, and members of the CEDA [*Confederación Española de Derechas Autónomas*] on the Right). Regional divisions further complicated the picture, the Left being more powerful in Catalonia, Andalusia, and the Levante; the Right in Castile, Navarre, and Galicia, with Aragon, Estremadura, and the Basque country divided. Religious considerations also figure: Whereas the Right was generally supportive of, and supported by, the Catholic Church, the Left was openly—and in varying degrees, militantly—anticlerical (Fig. 7.1).

Three times between 1931 and 1936 elections were held (June 1931, November 1933, February 1936), a procedure that can be described as the normal ritual whereby modern democratic states are periodically reconstructed. For here, not only are the formal structures and dominant ideologies of such societies legitimated, but rival parties and factions are also integrated as they cooperate in waging a rule-governed competition for (temporary) control of state power. In this case, however, little was gained either by way of political stability or of national unity. Rather, all three campaigns—the first and third of which were won by the Left, the second by the Right—were bitterly fought, and the rival segments of Spanish society emerged from each one more deeply estranged than ever before. In parliament both blocs sought to press their advantage when they had the upper hand and sought to stymie the other's programs when in opposition. More-

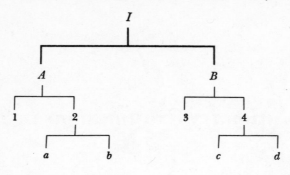

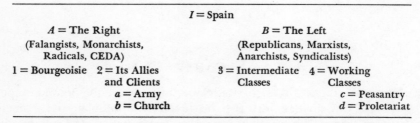

Figure 7.1. Social segmentation in the Second Spanish Republic (1931–39).

over, within this short period, both sides had increasing recourse to direct and often violent action by way of strikes, lockouts, capital flight, land occupation, insurrection, and assassination.[1]

Finally, on 17–19 July 1936, beginning in Morocco and then in the major population centers of the Spanish mainland, army officers sympathetic to the Right staged an extraordinary (but hardly unprecedented) ritual: a *pronunciamiento* (literally, a pronouncement) aimed at deconstructing the republican state and replacing it with a more authoritarian order. The gestural discourse of such rituals was well known, well rehearsed, and well understood, for there had been some forty-odd of them since 1814 (the most recent in August 1932; the most recent to succeed to 1923). In general a *pronunciamiento* involved a brief show of armed force; a public proclamation in which it was alleged that the current government had lost the ability to maintain order; an invocation of national unity through recollection of past glories and denunciation of present woes; and, sometimes, exemplary arrests and executions.[2] Always, however, the staging of a *pronunciamiento* took no more than a few days, and usually (but not always) they were successful, at least with reference to the short-term objective of effecting a change in regime.

The *pronunciamiento* of July 1936, however, failed even in this minimal goal. Taking unprecedented action, the government distributed arms to members of the two great labor federations (the socialist **UGT** [*Unión*

General de Trabajadores] and the anarcho-syndicalist CNT [*Confederación Nacional del Trabajo*]), who confronted and defeated the army in most of the major Spanish cities, making common cause with loyal members of the armed forces wherever possible.[3]

This is not to say that the republican state remained in control. On the contrary, throughout that portion of the country that came to be referred to as Loyalist Spain, effective power at this moment fell to the proletariat in arms, previously only a subordinate, if highly important, subsegment of the Left. Seizing the opportunity the workers now enacted their own extraordinary rituals—parades, rallies, and endless meetings of rapidly improvised committees; these were not only a spontaneous celebration of the victory they had won, but simultaneously (and more important) an attempt to dismantle the bourgeois social, political, and economic order and to construct a radically egalitarian, militantly solidary working-class society in its place. Toward this end, even the etiquette of greetings and partings saw sweeping revisions, as the title *Camarada* displaced all others, *"Salud!"* replaced *"Adios"* (the latter rejected for its religious connotations), and the clenched-fist salute became *de rigueur* (Figs. 7.2–7.4).

Virtually overnight the rules and habits of centuries dissolved, and a sweeping transformation in the conduct of human relations was accomplished. Suits and neckties disappeared, and overalls became the preferred dress. Women took to the streets and catcalls were forgotten. Waiters stared customers in the eye and spoke to them as equals. Bootblacks refused tips as signs of condescension and charity. But also, those identified too closely with the Right stood exposed to terror and repression, being deprived of the

Figure 7.2. July 1936: The proletariat in arms accompanied by loyal Assault Guards (in uniform), marches through the streets of Madrid. (Photo from Pemán, *Comentarios a mil imagenes*, p. 139.)

Figure 7.3. July 1936: Jubilant crowd in Barcelona. Note women in *miliciana* caps. (Photo from Péman, *Comentarios a mil imagenes*, p. 197.)

norms and institutions that had previously protected them. In particular, throughout that portion of Spain where the rising was defeated, churches were burned, priests were shot, and works of religious art were shattered.[4]

Of all the actions taken against the Church, however, perhaps the most striking was a macabre spectacle that was played out in numerous towns and cities: the exhumation and public display of the long-buried corpses of priests, nuns, and saints, some of whom had been naturally mummified by the dry Spanish heat. Such incidents were reported from Batea, Belchite, Berga, Canet de Roig, Fuenteovejuna (now Fuente Obejuna), Minorca, Orihuela, Oropesa, Peralta de la Sol, Vich, and elsewhere; photographic evidence survives of such events in some of the larger cities. Thus, in Toledo, at the Church of San Miguel, disinterred corpses were set out upon the central altar (Fig. 7.5). The altar of the Carmelite Church in Madrid was similarly adorned with skulls, as *milicianos* clowned and masqueraded about it (Fig. 7.6). Within the same church, the mummified remains of two young women were put on public display (Fig. 7.7). Perhaps the most notorious incident occurred at the convent cemetery attached to the Iglesia de la Enseñanza in Barcelona, where the bodies of nineteen Salesian nuns were exhumed and exhibited, flanking the doors of the church and spilling out into the street. Here, they remained for a full three days (23–25 July), during which time more than forty thousand people filed past them, sometimes

Figure 7.4. July 1936: *Milicianos* leave for the Aragon front: The intials UHP stand for *Unidad, Hermanos Proletarios (*Unity, Proletarian Brothers). (Photo from Thomas, *Spanish Civil War,* following p. 130.)

silent, but more often jeering (Figs. 7.8–7.10).[5] As one spectator was to recall, some forty years later:

> They dug up the nun's corpses, and displayed the skeletons and mummies. I found that quite amusing; so did all the kids. When we got bored looking at the same ones in my neighbourhood, we'd go to another *barrio* to see the ones they'd dug up there. In the Passeig de Sant Joan, they were exhibited in the street. Not for very long, but long enough for us to go and look. We kids would make comments about the different corpses—how this one was well-preserved, and that one decomposed, this one older; we got a lot of amusement out of it all.[6]

Almost immediately, such incidents were seized on by propagandists for the Nationalist cause, who cast the exhumations as conclusive proof, not only of the "anti-religious" nature of the Second Republic, but of its very "inhumanity," "barbarity," and "bestiality."[7] Throughout the war and long after, religion proved to be the sole issue with which international sympathy could consistently be rallied for the cause of Francisco Franco's Nationalists; accounts of the exhumations, often accompanied by grisly photographs, accordingly occupied a prominent position in his apologists' writings. In truth, they sought to establish a sweeping view of the Spanish struggle in

Figure 7.5. Bodies exhumed at the Church of San Miguel in Toledo and placed upon the main altar. (Photo from Péman, *Comentarios a mil imagenes*, p. 158.)

which their *movimiento* appeared as nothing less than a holy war: a righteous Crusade on behalf of Christian civilization, the guiding precedents of which were the *reconquista* and the Inquisition.[8]

Partisans of the Left were thus thrown on the defensive with regard to the religious issue, and they sought to justify the early assault on the Church in various ways, although the exhumations themselves were rarely mentioned. Since the war, liberal historians sympathetic to the Republic have been forced to take note of these events, which they depict as a regrettable excess perpetrated by uncontrollable fanatics in the heat of a crisis.[9]

Figure 7.6. *Milicianos* at the Carmelite Church in Madrid. Note man in bishop's vestments and mitre (rear, fourth from left); man pointing pistol at candlesticks (far left); clenched fist salutes (man seated at left and man kneeling behind him); a woman with her head uncovered in church (rear, fourth, from right); and four disinterred skulls, three placed upon the altar and one upon the knee of the man seated at the right. (Photo from Estelrich, *La persécution religieuse,* facing p. 80.)

Such a case, of course, could also be made on behalf of the perpetrators of the St. Bartholomew's violence or for any like episode. Moreover, this position is ironically close to that of the Nationalist propagandists, who also portrayed the exhumations as an aberration from the normal human realm. In this, the difference between the two sides lies only on whether such aberrations ought be deplored and forgiven or ferociously requited. However, serious analysts (unlike polemicists) can dismiss no human action as aberrant but must seek the sources and meanings of even the strangest and most repugnant actions that on closer analysis often prove to be more revealing than the stereotypical, automatonic behaviors that we are pleased to think comprise "normality." What follows is an attempt to remove the Spanish exhumations of July 1936 from the realm of the aberrant: to place them within a specific historical context, to locate phenomenological analogues to them, and to speculate on what may have been expressed in, and accomplished through, these dramatic and chilling acts.

Figure 7.7. One of the mummies put on display at the Carmelite Church in Madrid. (Photo from Péman, *Comentarios a mil imagenes*, p. 157.)

The Spanish Church and Anticlerical
Violence in the Nineteenth and Twentieth Centuries

July 1936 was hardly the first time that mobs had attacked the Church in Spain. Churches and convents were burned in many cities in 1833–35 during the First Carlist War and again in 1868 at the onset of the Second Carlist War. This was repeated in Catalonia during the "Tragic Week" ("*Semana trágica*") of 1909, and once more throughout the nation in 1931 during the first months of the Second Republic. On several of these occasions, religious were murdered and other atrocities committed, including

Figure 7.8. Mummies of Salesian nuns placed on display at the Iglesia de la Enseñanza in Barcelona. (Photo from Peréz de Urbel, *Los martires,* facing p. 97.)

Figure 7.9. Crowd reactions to the mummies placed on display in the streets of Barcelona. (Photo from Peréz de Urbel, *Los martires,* facing p. 49.)

Figure 7.10. Viewer's reaction to the mummies placed on display in the streets of Barcelona. (Photo from Estelrich, *La persécution religieuse,* facing p. 33.)

the exhumation and public display of the bodies of cloistered nuns in Barcelona on 27–31 July 1909.[10]

Details aside, one is struck by the frequency of these assaults, for almost without exception in recent history, whenever there was rebellion in Spain, the Church was a prime target of the masses. And although the political complexion of the Church's enemies changed—the Liberals taking the lead in the nineteenth century, the Radicals in 1909, and the Anarchists in 1931 and 1936—the fact that those seeking change felt compelled to attack the Church with physical and material violence remained a constant. Not only did they sense the Church to be antipathetic to their cause, they also felt it to be a sufficiently important (and vulnerable) target to invite direct confrontation.

The reason in all instances was fundamentally the same: From the period following the Peninsular Wars down to the present day, the Spanish Church has been a classic model of what I have elsewhere called "the religion of the status quo," that is, a religious institution that, in exchange for the material support of the dominant class within a given society, propagates an ideology that furthers the sociopolitical and material interests of that class, claiming for this ideology the status of sacred and eternal truth.[11]

From the restoration of the Bourbons in 1814, the Church allied itself with the monarchy and the wealthy, an alliance that was made indispensable to its very survival when Church land was appropriated in the late 1830s. Operating as a state church, the Spanish Catholic hierarchy made telling use of their monopoly on primary and secondary education, their dominant role in charity, and their control over the formalities of birth, marriage, and death. Through all possible channels, they sought to disseminate certain doctrines possessed of powerful political implications: obedience to authority, redemption through suffering, and trust in otherworldly rewards.

Although the Church's wealth was regularly denounced by its opponents, it was less the possessions of the Church itself that gave offense than its consistent subservience to the interests of the wealthy while paying lip service to the cause of social justice. Nowhere may one better perceive the masses' view than in the rumors that prompted church burnings. Thus, in 1834 popular belief had it that a cholera epidemic in Madrid had been caused by monks' poisoning of the well water and in February 1936 a similar story spread widely that nuns were giving children poisoned sweets. These tales as well as other persistent rumors (arms stored in convents, women cloistered and tortured aginst their will, priests firing on crowds from church towers, etc.), whether possessing any facticity or not, are best understood as metaphors in which popular opinion found graphic expression. For here, in the discourse of gossip and rumor the Church was consistently cast as a lethal masquerader: a superficially benign eminence that preyed on the young and polluted the very sources of life.

With the establishment of the Second Republic in 1931, the condition of the Church changed suddenly. One article of the new constitution—the sole one to be hotly debated—abolished Church schools, establishing secular education in their place; dissolved the Jesuit order and required all others to register with the Ministry of Justice; and forbade the Church from acquiring property or engaging in commerce. More important than any of these specific reforms, however, was the fact that the class the Church had served so well no longer held secure political control of Spain. Of necessity, the Church shifted to become a "religion of the counterrevolution," accommodating the new regime as best it could while working for the restoration of the old ruling class.

Support for the old order was clear from the stance assumed by the primates of the Spanish Church[12] and from Church involvement in the parties of the Right. With the Left's electoral victory in February 1936, however, elements of the Right prepared to retake power by other means. The July *pronunciamiento* and the Civil War that followed are best understood as their counterrevolution.

Wherever the *pronunciamiento* failed (with the notable exception of the Basque country, where attitudes toward the Church were quite different from elsewhere in Spain), the Church stood exposed as the chief remaining representative of the Right, the army having been defeated and the wealthy having earlier fled. Accordingly, it was not long after the immediate threat from the insurgents had been put down that the newly armed militants of the Left turned their attention to the Church.

Such a sketch of the longer duration may help us to understand in a general way what prompted violence against the Church in July 1936, but we are still far from fathoming the specific significance of the exhumations. In the absence of direct testimony from knowledgeable participants—and things being what they are, it is unlikely that such testimony will ever be forthcoming—one can only speculate on what their authors meant to communicate and accomplish through such acts.[13] What follows is a set of such speculations.

Millennial Antinomianism

One of the most obvious points that can be made regarding the Spanish exhumations is still one of the most important: They were an affront to decency. A fundamental norm of civilized behavior—that the dead be treated with respect—was violently and publicly, wantonly and even gleefully trampled. Yet for all that abusing the dead has been universally abhorred, one must emphasize that this is a cultural norm and not a natural law. That is to say, like all prohibitions, the rule of respect for the dead is a social construction propagated by the members of society for the good of society but still transgressible by those who define themselves as standing outside and in revolt against the established social order.

Western literature, in fact, begins with the story of just such a rebel: Achilles, who began by contesting the unjust distribution of wealth, power, and prestige within his social ambit and, as the ultimate consequence of his protest, was driven to an obscene display of rage in which he refused burial to a fallen enemy, whose corpse he, instead, dragged obsessively through the dust. Nor need one turn to literature for such examples, as the history of religions is replete with them. Among the better known are the practices of the *Aghorins* (those without dread), a class of Tantric ascetics still operative in Benares, India, whose cult centers in cemeteries, where they drink from skulls; eat faeces and all manner of flesh (human included) in defiance of normative vegetarianism; engage in incestuous intercourse and relations with prostitutes; and meditate on exhumed corpses. Far from being orgiastic revels, however, these are taken to be sacred rituals in which the Aghorins seek to enact their absolute liberation from the human condition itself, together with all its arbitrary restraints. It is significant, also, that they live lives of vagabondage and thoroughly reject the fundamental structure of Indic society: the caste system.[14]

One might also consider the *Hamatsa* (Cannibal) dance of the Canadian Northwest Coast, which forms the centerpiece of the Kwakiutl winter ceremonial. After a period in the wild, during which time he is said to commune with the deity Man Eater, the Hamatsa reenters society in spectacular fashion, smashing his way through the roof of the house in which the ceremonial is held. Raging beyond control, he assaults the others present, biting them and swallowing their flesh before he escapes to the wild once more. Lured back by magical songs and dances in which naked women carry corpses that they offer him to eat, the Hamatsa is captured and ritually tamed. In this way do the Kwakiutl acknowledge the power of absolute, unrestrained hunger as a drive that threatens—quite literally—to tear society apart, but that can and must be mastered.[15]

It is in millenarian movements, however, that the deliberate flouting of such fundamental taboos as incest, cannibalism, and abuse of the dead has been best attested and most seriously studied. Describing the antinomian excesses of Melanesian cargo cults, Peter Worsley considered them to be "the deliberate enactment of the overthrow of the cramping bonds of the past, not in order to throw overboard all morality, but in order to create a new morality."[16] More probing still is the analysis of Keneim Burridge, who also interpreted such episodes as part of a transition from the old order to the new, but who also went further, describing antinomianism as a liminal stage or dialectic moment in which "no rules" appear as the radical antithesis of "old rules" and the necessary precursor of synthetic "new rules" yet to come.[17]

That portions of Spain were in the throes of a millenarian upheaval in the weeks after the defeat of the *pronunciamiento* is clear from the testimony of those who were there. A militant, almost ecstatic egalitarianism was evident, in which all signs of social hierarchy in dress and demeanor were obliterated. The state for all intents and purposes ceased to function, power falling to spontaneous workers' committees and the proletariat in arms. Factories, farms, and utilities were collectivized, wages equalized, and money abolished in places. A militia sprang into existence in which there were no ranks, commands, or formal discipline. Women were released from the domestic sphere and entered the streets, factories, committees, cafés, and armed forces. Peasants refused to wait for the attention of bureaucrats and demanded their right to be seen and heard.[18] In their daily activities, ordinary people experienced themselves as agents of social change, energetically and enthusiastically constructing a new society possessed of radically new rules. As part of the process, they were also systematically deconstructing the old rules that had previously ordered their existence. But between new rules and old, there was a violent and profoundly disquieting phase of no rules in the summer of 1936, during which time political and class enemies were murdered, churches were burned, and disinterred corpses were placed on public display. In part these acts may have been practical steps aimed at demolishing what remained of the ancien régime, but they were also the spontaneous dramatization of *absolute* liberation from all constraints of the past, including those of "common decency."

Rituals of Collective Obscenity

Revolutionary or millenarian outbursts of antinomianism generally appear to be quite spontaneous and unpremeditated. Speaking of participants in the incestuous orgies of several cargo cults, Burridge recalled:

> The fact of the matter is that whenever millenarian movements assert themselves you get a period of no laws, no time. This is the period of excesses, when all social boundaries are symbolically transgressed, in order to start again. . . . The generally human myth—that order first came out of chaos—is, as it were, inside them. This is enacted, not wholly self-consciously. *The people to whom I've spoken cannot really explain, afterwards, why they've done that in particular. They're in a daze.*[19]

Yet in other instances, it is clear that participants in such violations do have a clear consciousness of purpose and through their unprecedented acts intend to transform themselves, others, and society in general.

The famous Mau Mau oaths provide an important case in point. As designed by the rebellion's leaders, these drew on traditional Kikuyu symbolism in new and creative fashion in order to stress two themes. The first of these was initiation, a ritual form that had atrophied badly under British rule but was supplanted by the oaths, which conferred upon those who took them a level of adult status and responsibility unattainable under colonialism. The statement of Karari Njama, one of the foremost Mau Mau leaders, regarding the effects of his own oath-taking is most significant. He observed: "I had been born again in a new society with a new faith."[20] As Njama recognized, the results of this initiation were not just individual, but social as well. For not only had he personally experienced a ritual rebirth, but through the administration of the same ritual to other individuals, a new society was being constructed. Moreover, this new society was placed in direct and conscious opposition to the existing social order, as seen in the ritual sequences revolving around the second main theme, that of purity and defilement. For through such forbidden deeds as the drinking of blood, eating of excrement, intercourse with animals, and so on, oath-takers entered a state of *thahu* (spiritual stain). By freely assuming this state, they effectively estranged themselves from society as it is officially constructed, and they renounced its demands for normative ("proper") behavior. Moreover, they assumed this status collectively, being bound together by the stain and the ritual they shared.

Nor is it only exotic peoples under colonial rule who have had recourse to such "rituals of collective obscenity."[21] It is told that the rebels who joined in the conspiracy of Catiline against the Roman Republic (63 B.C.E.) performed a human sacrifice and feasted on the victim's flesh as a means to bind themselves together (Plutarch, *Life of Cicero* 10.3, Dio Cassius 37.30.3, and Sallust, *Bellum Catilinae* 22). Again, the most radical phase of the Nizārī Ismāʿīlī (Assassin) movement was inaugurated by the Festival of the Resurrection *(Qiyāma)*, a feast staged 8 August 1164 in such a way as to produce "a solemn and ritual violation of the law," for not only were all participants obliged to break the fast of Ramadān, but the pulpit was erected so that all attending turned their backs on Mecca.[22] Hardly an oversight, this coincided with the explicit message of the Qiyāma: the end of traditional law and authority and the entry of all present into a new and paradisal state of being. At a more practical level, this festival also announced and effected the Nizārīs' estrangement from other more orthodox Muslims, who could scarce be expected to embrace them after such desecrations.

Even the Terror of the French Revolution may be considered—in part at least—as a ritual of collective obscenity, although one might hesitate to offer such a characterization had not one of its chief authors done so first. For it is reported that Danton told the future Louis XVIII, "It was my will that the whole youth of Paris should arrive at the front covered with blood *which would guarantee their fidelity. I wished to put a river of blood between them and the enemy.*"[23] In similar fashion the exhumations and other atrocities both manifested and established the radical estrangement of the Spanish Left from their adversaries, with whom there could subsequently be no hope of reconciliation.

Iconoclasm

In considering the exhumations as an instance of millennial antinomianism and as a ritual of collective obscenity, I have tended to focus on what they accomplished *for* those who performed them: enactment of their radical freedom, in the first instance, and forging of their militant solidarity, in the second. But we must also consider what exhumation did to those *against* whom it was performed, for there can be no mistaking the aggression implicit in the act. That aggression, of course, was not directed principally against the individuals actually exhumed,[24] but against the religious institution they represented and, beyond that, against the social order that institution served. Like the widespread burning of churches (Figs. 7.11, 7.12), decapitation and disfigurement of religious statues (Figs. 7.13, 7.14), parodic appropriation of religious images and ecclesiastic paraphernalia (Figs. 7.15, 7.16), and acts of symbolic violence against the same (Figs. 7.17, 7.18), the exhumation of religious may be considered—in a broad sense, at least—as an act of iconoclasm.

Although we still lack a general theoretical understanding of iconoclasm, there are certain observations that may be ventured.[25] To begin, if it is true, as I have repeatedly argued, that in some measure society is constructed (and continually reconstructed) through the exercise of symbolic discourse, then the destruction of widely recognized and even revered symbols may be seen as an attempt to undo their effects, that is, to deconstruct the social forms that others have constructed and maintain through them. The iconoclastic act is thus less a matter of the icons themselves than it is an attack

Figure 7.11. Crowds view the burning of the Jesuits' residence in Madrid. (Photo from Peréz de Urbel, *Los martires,* facing p. 289.)

launched by members of one segment of society against those of another, designed to isolate the latter and to deprive them of an important instrument with which they have in the past maintained social forms in which they hold privileged positions.

In and of itself, iconoclasm has no specific political content, although it has always a political dimension, being an assault on those who hold, recently held, or conceivably might hold power. Often it is employed as an instrument of conquest or colonial domination, for instance, in St. Boniface's destruction of the Germans' sacred oak at Geismar or in later missionaries'

Figure 7.12. Interior of a gutted church, Madrid. (Photo from Thomas, *Spanish Civil War,* following p. 130.)

campaigns against the sacred art of the missionized. Conversely, revolutionary movements also make frequent use of iconoclasm as a weapon against the regimes they seek to overthrow. Thus, during the massive de-Christianization campaign of 1793–94, Hébertists and other radicals staged spectacular demonstrations, such as that in Lyons where asses decked out in cope and mitre dragged copies of the Gospels through the streets. Similarly, the English Civil War abounds with instances of radical soldiers tearing down altar

Figure 7.13. Statue of Christ, defaced and dis-
armed. (Photo from Péman, *Comentarios a mil
imagenes,* p. 159.)

rails, crosses, and images, and the Taiping Rebellion saw like assaults on
Confucian religious trappings.[26]

It should be stressed that no act of iconoclasm is ever carried out with
the intent of destroying an icon's sacred power, for iconoclasts—who are regularly estranged from their adversaries on lines of class, politics, or national
origin as well as those of religion—act with the assurance either that the specific image under attack has no such power or the more radical conviction
that there is no such thing as sacred power. It is their intent to demonstrate
dramatically and in public the *powerlessness* of the image and thereby to inflict a double disgrace on its champions, first by exposing the bankruptcy of
their vaunted symbols and, second, their impotence in the face of attack.

Figure 7.14. Crucifix from the Church at Cabra, with Christ decapitated, Magdalene and the Virgin defaced. (Photo from Estelrich, *La persécution religieuse*, before p. 121.)

Any number of examples could be cited to show that such dynamics were at work in the anticlerical violence of 1936. To take but one, it is related that during the famous siege of the Alcázar, a group of *milicianos* brandished a famous religious statue in front of this fortress, taunting the Nationalist soldiers within, "Here we have the Cristo de la Vega! We're going to burn it. If you are Catholics, come down and stop us. We'd stop you if you did the same with a figure of Lenin!" As is evident, the goal of the *milicianos*—if there is any truth to the story—was not just to burn a statue. Rather, they meant to create a situation in which two images and two correlated social groupings were set in contrast to one another: the image of Lenin, which the Left regarded as authoritative, and that of Christ, which was similarly regarded by the Right. Moreover, they hoped to show that whereas the figure of Lenin (and the vision that figure encoded) provided an effective charter and rallying slogan for the Left, Christ had lost such sta-

Figure 7.15. Statue of the Baby Jesus from an unspecified part of Catalonia, dressed in *miliciano*
uniform and holding a republican flag. (Photo
from Estelrich, *La persécution religieuse*, facing
p. 64.)

tus, for *as of that very moment* the Right was sufficiently cowed that it
would not and could not venture forth to defend its image.[27]

In the early days of the Civil War, devotional objects, including great
works of art, were destroyed in vast numbers, provoking an anguished response from the Right. Ordinarily, Nationalist denunciations of anticlerical
actions treated iconoclasm and the exhumations separately, for the bodies of
religious are not normally considered to be icons nor is exhumation, strictly
speaking, an act of iconoclasm. However, it is also true that religious are
consecrated persons, their very bodies made holy according to Church dogma,
not only by their moral lives, but also by the sacraments they receive. As
one Jesuit apologist put it, those who suffered exhumation had been nothing
less than "living temples of God."[28] To tear these from their hallowed rest-
ing places and subject them to public derision may surely be considered an

Figure 7.16. *Milicianos* clown with ecclesiastical regalia (I). Note woman with reliquary, seated at center of the group, and man with bishop's mitre and vestments holding rifle. (Photo from Peréz de Urbel, *Los martires,* facing p. 145.)

Figure 7.17. *Milicianos* clown with church regalia (II). Note figure at left threatening a crucifix with his revolver. (Photo from Peréz de Urbel, *Los martires,* facing p. 336.)

Figure 7.18. *Milicianos* shoot at statue of the Sacred Heart, Cerro de los Angeles, Madrid. (Photo from Estelrich, *La persécution religieuse*, facing p. 81.)

act of iconoclasm even in a conventionally religious sense. More important, it was very much an act of iconoclasm in the sense described earlier, being a potent attack upon a highly charged symbol, the precise nature and significance of which we have only begun to fathom.

Sanctity, Corruption, Profanophany

For all that the preceding analyses may help shed light on the exhumations, we have not yet considered the act of exhumation itself as an instance of symbolic discourse. The question remains: Why would anyone rip the ancient bodies of religious from their tombs and set these up on public display? What was signified in such a gesture?

In many instances, including some of the most publicized, no motives for the acts were ever offered or elicited, a fact that left Nationalist propagandists free to invoke necrophilia, sadism, and satanic possession as the only possible explanations. But in other cases the exhumers did not remain mute, but spoke directly, claiming that the specific corpses they displayed gave concrete evidence either of sexual depravity or the practice of torture. Thus, fetal remains and those of young children who had been buried within convents were prominently exhibited, as were those of monks and nuns in penitential orders who had been interred with their scourges and implements of penance.[29] Moreover, the trials that followed events of Barcelona's "Tragic Week" of 1909 developed a significant record concerning the motives of those who exhumed and displayed corpses of religious at that time, individuals who claimed, apparently with full sincerity, that they did so in an attempt to produce graphic evidence of the Church's corruption.[30]

The category of corruption is of considerable interest in the present context because like its near-synonyms rottenness and decadence, corruption is most concretely and emphatically manifest in the state of bodily decomposition. The most disquieting of all natural processes, bodily corruption comes inevitably with the passage of time as dead flesh putrefies and decays. From a theological perspective, however, bodily corruption is less a natural process than a moral one, for decay is the final physical result of a sinful (i.e., a "corrupt") life. And, what is more, the bodies of those who are purified of sin through the sacraments of the Church and the practice of a saintly life *do not decay,* but partake of eternity, freedom from decomposition being one of the foremost proofs of sanctity.

If the absence of corruption correlates with and, by implication, signifies the presence of sainthood, conversely the presence of corruption bears witness to sainthood's absence. Such an analysis stands at the heart of the celebrated section of *The Brothers Karamozov* entitled "The Breath of Corruption," where it is related how during the funeral of the widely revered Father Zossima, his corpse began to stink. This turn of events, moreover, catalyzed a latent cleavage in the monastic community to which Zossima belonged, between those who had accepted the doctrines he propounded and those who had been skeptical or had actively opposed him. And the latter group rejoiced, taking the stench which emanated from Zossima's body to be a sign of divine judgment, whereas his supporters stood unable to defend him or his doctrines, particularly given that the corpse had decomposed even more rapidly than is normal.

Ordinarily, putrefaction arouses only revulsion, this being the reaction of those who would deny their mortality when confronted with the palpable evidence of human finitude. Father Zossima's enemies, however, perceived something quite different in his reeking corpse: something that caused them to exult rather than recoil, for the fumes revealed to them that one for whom great claims had been made was, in fact, no different from other men, but equally subject to death, time, and decay. The episode was nothing less than what I will call a *profanophany:* a revelation of the profanity, temporality, and corruption inherent to someone or something.

Like the funeral of Father Zossima, the Spanish exhumations may be understood as profanophanies, in which inherent corruption was revealed through profoundly distressing bodily means. Indeed, it is difficult even now to look at the pictures of those pathetic remains without some terror or disgust. Yet we are told that the crowds laughed and jeered at them in July of 1936, a response that is only comprehensible, I submit, if we consider that the derision was directed not at the corpses of these unfortunate individuals, but at the pretensions of the Church, a church that found graphic representation in their tortured bodies. For just as the thin layer of preserved skin spread across the mummified corpses served only to accentuate the death and decay beneath, so also the veil of sanctity in which the Church cloaked itself served only to accentuate *its* underlying corruption. And its claim to eternity notwithstanding, the Church in this moment stood revealed in its full temporal reality: a human institution, not one divine. Moreover, it was clear that the Church, like all things temporal, was itself subject to death and decay. At this, some spectators laughed, experiencing joy and liberation at the degradation of the mighty, whereas others—now more radically estranged than ever from the laughers—could only mourn and brood on revenge.

In this moment society itself was reorganized. In the presence of such iconoclastic acts, the whole of Loyalist Spain was divided into two radically separate groups, in which all prior and potential sentiments of affinity one for the other were eradicated: those of the Left, who gloried in their new-won victories and those of the Right, who found themselves constrained to an unaccustomed (and temporary) silence, waiting for the day when the tables would be turned once more (Fig. 7.19).

Figure 7.19. Shortly after having taken Barcelona (January 1939), Nationalist troops under the command of Colonel Yague (center left foreground, wearing spectacles) celebrate a monumental outdoor Mass. (Photo from Jackson, *Spanish Republic*, following p. 210.)

Although the exhumations have consistently been presented as an aberrant and impious act of violence, such a simplistic analysis is untenable. Like all anticlerical violence throughout Spanish history, they were not an assault on religion per se, but rather on one specific religious institution: an institution closely aligned with, and subservient to, the traditionally dominant segment of society. At the same time that the exhumations were a ferocious assault on and mockery of that institution, they were also an assault on the segment of society with which it was symbiotically entangled, and—what is more—they were a ritual in which the traditionally subordinate segment of Spanish society sought by means of a highly charged discourse of gestures and deeds to deconstruct the old social order and construct a new, radically different order in its place.

Part III

CLASSIFICATION

8

The Tyranny of Taxonomy

The Classificatory Logic of a Domestic Arrangement

A significant portion of my childhood, including some of its most pleasant moments, was spent around the dining room table where my parents, my sister, and I gathered each day for the ritual of our evening meal. The seating arrangement was absolutely invariant, nor (so far as I can recall) did the possibility of variation ever occur to any of us. Always my father and mother sat facing one another at that end of the table which we all understood to be its head, with myself to my father's right, across from my sister, who sat at the left of my mother (Fig. 8.1, where F = Father, M = Mother, S = Son, and D = Daughter). The pattern was a comfortable one, although the nature of that comfort seems more problematic in retrospect than it did at the time. Although such a question never arose, had we been asked to explain or justify this pattern, I am reasonably certain we would have pointed to its practical advantages, such as the fact that my mother was placed closest to the kitchen, and the left-handed family members (my father and sister) were distributed in such a way that they were not constantly bumping elbows with their right-handed neighbors.

Beyond such utilitarian concerns, we all were aware, and at times remarked openly, that our dining arrangement provided a convenient map of the major family subsystems, for were the table bisected vertically, adults were divided from children; horizontally, males from females (Fig. 8.2). The potentially incestuous diagonal groupings also happened to divide right-handed family members from lefties and were jokingly recognized in this latter form as a means to round out the system. When and how this pattern originated, I have no idea, nor do my parents or sister. What is clear, however, is that through it we gave tangible expression to a classificatory system quite common among American families of the 1950s and early 1960s.

This system—that of the patriarchal nuclear family—is logically constructed on two binary oppositions, the first based on distinctions of age, the second on those of gender. Moreover, such distinctions are hardly neu-

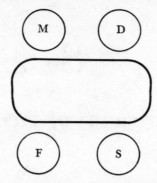

Figure 8.1. Seating arrangement at the Lincoln family table.

tral or value free: they never are. Rather, adults (i.e., those who possess the preferential age, that of majority) outranked children (those who lack it), and males (those who possess the preferential gender) outranked females. The result is a four-part hierarchic set, which in those days was commonly accepted as natural and right: (1) Father (Adult Male = +Age/+Gender); (2) Mother (+Age/−Gender); (3) Son (−Age/+Gender); (4) Daughter (−Age/−Gender).[1] In daily practice this same hierarchy found expression in countless other fashions (rights in conversation, bedtime order, portions at meals, etc.), and it may also be schematized in two analytically convenient forms that hardly occurred to any of us who lived within the confines of this system. These forms, however—a taxonomic tree and a serial ranking—are only somewhat more abstract ways of encoding or representing the same information that was daily enacted within our seating pattern (Fig. 8.3).

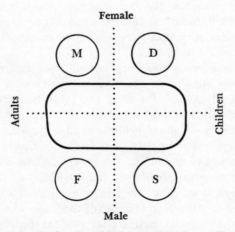

Figure 8.2. The Lincoln family table bisected horizontally and vertically.

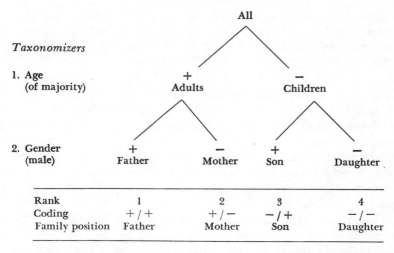

Figure 8.3. Taxonomy and hierarchy in the patriarchal nuclear family.

Taxonomic Structure and Hierarchic Rank

Within this system, age and gender function as taxonomizers, that is, each one establishes the basis for an act of discrimination through which all members of a given class are assigned to one of two subclasses: those who possess the trait or property in question, and those who do not. Although common enough in this role, age and gender are hardly universals, but they reflect the values and preoccupations of those cultures that employ them in this fashion. Other taxonomizers can be (and regularly are) so used in other parts of the globe and periods in history. What seems to remain constant, however, is the logical structure whereby social hierarchies are recoded in taxonomic form. As an example, consider a classic of anthropological literature: the Trobriand Islands' myth of emergence, which is, in effect, the narrative re-presentation of a taxonomy.[2]

> The problem of rank which plays a great role in their sociology was settled by the emergence from one special hole, called Obukula, near the village of Laba'i. This event was notable in that, contrary to the usual course (which is: one original "hole," one lineage), from this hole of Laba'i there emerged representatives of the four main clans one after the other. Their arrival, moreover, was followed by an apparently trivial but, in mythical reality, a most important event. First there came the Iguana, the animal of the Lukulabuta clan, which scratched its way through the earth as iguanas do, then climbed a tree, and remained there as a mere onlooker, following subsequent events. Soon there came out the Dog, totem of the Lukuba clan, who originally had the highest rank. As a third came the Pig, representative of the Malasi clan, which now holds the highest rank. Last came the Lukwasisiga totem, represented in some versions by the Crocodile, in others by the Snake,

in others by the Opossum, and sometimes completely ignored. The Dog and Pig ran round, and the Dog, seeing the fruit of the *noku* plant, nosed it, then ate it. Said the Pig: "Thou eatest *noku*, thou eatest dirt; thou art a low-bred, a commoner; the chief shall be I." And ever since, the highest subclan of the Malasi clan have been the real chiefs.[3]

As Malinowski observed, this story legitimates or "charters" (to use his terminology) a social hierarchy: a hierarchy that differs from the serial order in which the totemic animals of Trobriand clans are said to have emerged from the primordial "hole" at Laba'i. Thus, while the emergence sequence was (1) Iguana, (2) Dog, (3) Pig, and (4) Crocodile (or other representatives of the Lukwasisiga clan in variant traditions), the normative hierarchy has Pig in first position and Dog second, with Iguana and Crocodile together bringing up the rear.

To begin, we ought note a certain inconsistency regarding the Lukwasisiga clan, which is "represented in some versions by the Crocodile, in others by the Snake, in others by the Opossum, and sometimes completely ignored." Consideration of this inconsistency is helpful, however, in sorting out the taxonomic system that lies behind and is explained through the mythic narrative, for in two of the four cases, Lukwasisiga is represented by a reptile (crocodile and snake), in another by a marsupial (opossum), and in the final case lacks totemic representation altogether. In no case, however, is either Lukwasisiga or Lukulabuta, the other low-ranking clan, ever represented by a mammal, for the totem of Lukulabuta is another reptile, the iguana. Together Lukwasisiga and Lukulabuta thus stand in contrast to the high-ranking clans, Lukuba and Malasi, as nonmammals to mammals since the latter are represented by the dog and the pig, respectively.

As recorded by Malinowski, the myth shows no interest in differentiating members of the two low-ranking clans from one another and is content to group them together at the bottom of the Trobriand sociopolitical hierarchy. One can well imagine other variants, however, in which Lukwasisiga is contrasted to Lukulabuta as reptile to marsupial (iguana–opossum), quadruped to aped (iguana–snake) or land to river (iguana–crocodile). The variant at hand is more concerned, however, with differentiating members of the upper-ranking clans through a narrative episode in which dietary purity is at issue and figures, in effect, as a second-order taxonomizer. This is the incident of the *noku* plant, a plant that in normal Trobriand usage is considered an abomination.[4] Dog thus violates normative standards of propriety by nosing this plant and eating it, and Pig rightly denounces the transgression. As a consequence of these events—so the myth would persuade us—Dog ceded his position of primacy to Pig, and the Malasi clan came to outrank Lukuba, a position that it continues to enjoy down to the present day. The myth thus serves to legitimate and perpetuate a socially and historically contingent state of affairs by providing an authoritative discourse in which four social groups are organized in hierarchic fashion. Within that discourse two taxonomizers are deployed: mammalian identity and dietary purity, and the classificatory structure is much the same as that

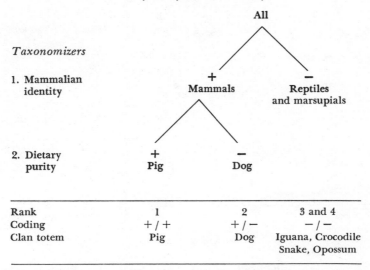

Figure 8.4. Taxonomy and hierarchy in the Trobriand Islands' myth of emergence.

which found expression in my family's dinner table (compare Figs. 8.3 and 8.4).

Examples of other taxonomic systems that operate on these same logical principles while deploying different taxonomizers could easily be multiplied,[5] for instance, the theory of the soul expounded in Plato's *Republic* and *Timaios,* where three different types of soul are identified, each having a different bodily locus and associated with a different social class of the ideal Platonic state. Thus, the "rational" soul, located in the head, is associated to the vaunted philosopher-kings; the "spirited" soul, located between the diaphragm and the throat, is related to the military class; and the "appetitive" soul, found in the torso below the diaphragm, is linked to the "commercial" class, that is, the bulk of the freeborn population. Further, at *Timaios* 69D–70A, Plato makes explicit the taxonomizers on which these distinctions are founded when he observes that divinity, which is characteristic of the rational soul, is lacking in the other forms that together are identified as mortal, whereas masculinity, found in the rational and the spirited soul, is absent in the appetitive. The resultant system can be graphed in a fashion by now familiar (Fig. 8.5).

Although similar in form to the other taxonomies we have considered, this system differs from them in one important fashion. Whereas the others organized only one order of phenomena (i.e., social statuses) in a single taxonomic module or classificatory set, Plato constructs a multimodular taxonomy by simultaneously categorizing three different entities that are brought into correlation with one another: varieties of the soul, parts of the body, and social classes.

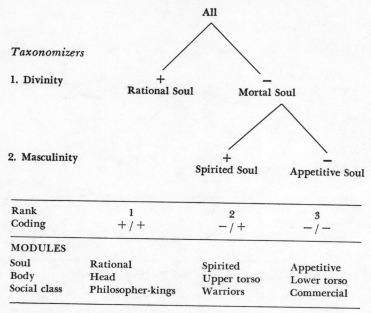

Figure 8.5. Taxonomy and hierarchy in Plato's theory of the soul.

Multimodular Classification

Such multiplication of taxonomic modules has several significant effects. First, and most obviously, it makes for a more complex system, encompassing a far broader range of phenomena. More important, the system's persuasive power is also increased, for insofar as any individual module carries conviction, it supports the others, all modules being mutually implicative and mutually reinforcing. Thus, in the case at hand, the bodily module is the strongest of the three, in that it finds apparent confirmation in the natural world, being so constructed as to reflect the vertical pattern of the human body: (1) head, (2) upper torso, and (3) lower torso.[6] By correlating modules for the soul and society to that for the body, Plato thus implicitly advances the claim that they reflect the same natural and hierarchic order. For just as the head is (quite literally) superior to the torso, he would have us conclude that reason, being seated in the head, is superior to other gifts, and thus philosophers, being most possessed of reason, are superior to other men.

Among students of taxonomy, it was Durkheim and Mauss who first insisted on the social foundations of classificatory logic;[7] more recently Pierre Bourdieu has contributed to our understanding of the ways in which taxonomic systems provide ideological mystification for sociopolitical realities.[8] Yet there remain those who, taking their lead from Kant, maintain that taxonomy is primarily an epistemological instrument, that is, a means of gathering, sorting, and processing knowledge about the external (especially the natural) world: a "science of the concrete" in which the infinite atomized data of experience are organized and given a form in which they become knowable and manipulable.[9] For all that the epistemological functions of taxonomy are undeniable,[10] placing primary emphasis on them obscures the fact that all knowers are themselves *objects* of knowledge as well as subjects insofar as they cannot and do not stand apart from the world that they seek to know. One consequence of this (and far from the least important) is that categorizers come to be categorized according to their own categories. Taxonomy is thus not only a means for organizing information, but also—as it comes to organize the organizers—an instrument for the classification and manipulation of society, something that is particularly facilitated by the fashion in which taxonomic trees and binary oppositions can conveniently recode social hierarchies, as we have begun to see.

The extent to which concern with the social world predominates over concern with the natural can be seen in a taxonomic system found in a famous work of ancient Indian philosophy: the *Chandogya Upanishad* 6.1–6, a text that is of particular interest precisely because society and social categories are never once mentioned in it. Briefly, this theory holds that the entire universe and everything in it are compounds of three quasi-substantial entities. These entities—the primordial Forms (Sanskrit, *rūpās*)—are: (1) Brilliance, or radiant energy (Sanskrit, *tejas*); (2) Water (Sanskrit, *āpas*); and (3) Food (Sanskrit, *annam*), and they are distinguished one from another in several different ways. Thus, on a scale of relative density, Brilliance is the most rarefied and least corporeal of the three, Food the densest and most gross, and Water in between. In color, Brilliance is red, Water white, and Food dark.[11]

A ranking of the Three Forms is evident in their order of creation: Brilliance first, Water second, and Food third. This sequential order further corresponds to a vertical ranking encoded in a module given over to classification of the cosmos that posits heaven as the realm of Brilliance (associated with the sun); atmosphere, that of Water (associated with clouds); and earth, that of Food (associated with plants and the soil).

Numerous modules are set forth, it being claimed that all things can be analyzed according to the Forms. To cite but a few examples, fire is said to consist of Brilliance in the form of flame (which is red, highest vertically, most rarefied, most heavenly, and most like the sun), Water in the form of smoke (white, intermediate in density and vertical locus, most atmospheric, and most like the clouds), and Food in the form of fuel (dark, most gross and substantial, lowest vertically, most earthy and most like plants). The course of a day is classified such that sunrise is that portion most marked by Brilliance (i.e., first and most red), daytime by Water (second and most white), and night by Food (last and most dark). Storms are subdivided into lightning (= Brilliance), rain (= Water), and clouds (= Food). A similar analysis is suggested for milk products, with ghee (clarified butter) being associated to Brilliance, milk to Water, and curds to Food. In like pattern living organisms are categorized as (1) those born from eggs, that is, birds

	Brilliance	Water	Food
Brilliance	Speech	Breath	Mind
Water	Marrow	Blood	Flesh
Food	Bone	Urine	Feces

Figure 8.6. Classification of the body according to the system of the Three Forms.

(= Brilliance); (2) those born live, that is, mammals (= Water, probably by association to amniotic fluid); and (3) those born from the earth, that is, plants (= Food).

Obviously, the logic of the system is more persuasive in some modules than in others that have a rather procrustean ring to them. Among the most elaborate of its applications is the megamodule for the body, which incorporates a full nine items by squaring the Three Forms, as shown in Figure 8.6.

This is not the place to give full treatment to the ideas summarized in this diagram; it may suffice to consider just a few of its constituent modules. For instance, the second vertical column presents a classification of bodily fluids, in which breath is established as the highest and most rarefied, its incorporeal nature resulting from the intermixture of Brilliance with Water. Conversely, urine is the lowliest and most gross owing to the intermixture of Food and blood is the quintessential bodily fluid, intermediate to breath and urine, being Water compounded upon itself without intermixture.[12] Grouped with Water on the diagonal descending from left to right are the two other bodily essences: speech (Brilliance compounded upon Brilliance, highest of the high and rarest of the rare), and feces (densest of the dense and lowest of the low, being nothing save Food compounded upon itself).

One could pursue details almost infinitely and with almost infinite fascination (as does this text and others like it), but for our purposes, it is more important to identify the taxonomizers from which the system is generated, something that must be done by induction because the text remains mute on this point. Nevertheless, it is reasonably clear that the first-order taxonomizer is elevation, whereby anything that is either literally or figuratively above zero grade on a relevant vertical plane is set apart from that which is at the bottom, the former being accorded high status and the latter low status on the strength of this distinction. Thus, to cite but a few examples, heaven and atmosphere possess elevation, whereas earth does not; likewise flame and smoke, in contrast to fuel; breath and blood, in contrast to urine; and—more broadly—Brilliance and Water in contrast to Food. The second-order taxonomizer, then, would seem to be purity, more specifically a purity that finds expression in such characteristics as radiance, luminosity, rarefication, and incorporeality, that is to say, the kind of purity possessed

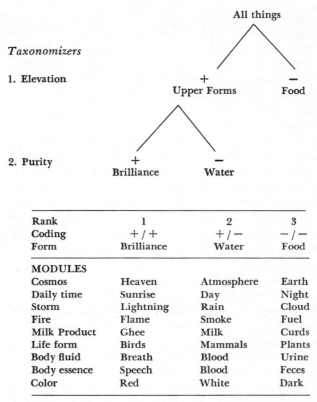

Figure 8.7. Taxonomy and hierarchy in the system of the three Forms (*Chandogya Upanishad* 6.1–6).

by heaven, flame, and breath in contrast to atmosphere, smoke, and blood. This system may be diagramed in the same form we have previously employed, as in Figure 8.7.

For all that this system may encompass many more modules than the other taxonomies we have considered, it is identical to them in its formal structure: It deploys successive binary oppositions as the means to encode a ranked hierarchic series.[13] Yet whereas the hierarchy established in those other systems was explicitly social in all cases, for all of its multimodular complexity, the system of the Three Forms as presented in the *Chandogya Upanishad* is silent on the question of social classification. Or so it might seem.

Surely, such silence is curious as one could well employ the system's taxonomizers to generate a social module; what is more the resultant module would replicate perfectly the givens of the Indic caste system.[14] Thus, the first-order taxonomizer, elevation, distinguishes the two noble classes—Priests (who are associated with the heavens and with speech) and Warriors (associated with the storm and with blood)—from the Commoners, who are associated with the earth and the production of food. The second-level taxonomizer, purity, then differentiates Priests from Warriors, with the resultant hierarchy: (1) Priests (+Elevation/+Purity), (2) Warriors (+Elevation/−Purity), and Commoners (−Elevation/−Purity). Moreover, when ancient Indian legal and ethical texts present taxonomies on the pattern of the Three Forms, a social module is regularly included, one that conforms precisely to the lines we have indicated.[15]

Obviously, one can distinguish the text of the *Chandogya Upanishad* from the system of the Three Forms, the former being but a partial expression of the latter, and one might argue that the author of this specific text was simply uninterested in such social applications as the system might have. Such a bland line of argument, however, beyond being both superficial and casuistic, leaves unresolved the central question of whether taxonomic systems are more concerned with nature than with culture: That is, are they primarily epistemological or sociopolitical in their orientation and instrumentality?

In order to assess properly the valuable evidence of the *Chandogya*, one must begin with the recognition that all modules of a multimodular taxonomy, being constructed on the same formal principles, contain not only specific information, but also the logical basis of the entire system, this being the precise sequence of binary oppositions (which organizes the system's form) and the identity of the taxonomizers deployed (which gives it its specific content). As a result each module contains the mechanism for generating—and thus implies—all others, not only those that chance to find expression in a given text or on a given occasion, but *all* those modules that can potentially be produced.

Although the *Chandogya* never advances a social module, one may *not* conclude that the text has no interest in things social. Rather, it leads its audience to infer a social module, a module for which it never takes responsibility, speaking only of such matters as the classificatory superiority of heaven to earth, ghee to curds, and speech to feces while tacitly suggesting the parallel superiority of Priests (who address the heavens with speech in the form of prayer and offerings in the form of ghee) to Commoners (who work the earth to produce food, but are dismissed as shitty fellows). Moreover, by remaining implicit, which is to say masked, this hierarchic classification of social strata is placed beyond question, challenge, or debate. The *Chandogya* need never make mention of caste, for the social hierarchy may equally well—perhaps even better—be justified and maintained through discussions of abstract Forms or parts of the natural world, given that all these modules simply recode the givens of the caste system.

The vast majority of modules within complex taxonomic structures are likely to derive from the natural world and, insofar as taxonomies are in part epistemological instruments, the claim is advanced that they make possible knowledge of the underlying patterns of the natural order. But insofar as taxonomies are also instruments for the organization of society, those patterns are extended to—better yet, imposed upon—social groupings, as the social module (whether explicit or not) is associated to the modules of the natural world, being treated as if it were but one more instance of a general cosmic law. More than legitimate, arbitrary social hierarchies are thus represented as if given by nature, and agitation against their inequities—which tends to come from those who have been subordinated and marginalized by these systems—is made to seem but the raving of lunatics. Still, there remain other instruments that can be used to challenge an entrenched sociotaxonomic order, instruments such as inversion and anomaly, the nature and utility of which we shall examine in the succeeding chapters.

9

The Dialectics of Symbolic Inversion

Toward the end of the last chapter, I suggested that among the instruments through which sociotaxonomic structures can be attacked or undermined, anomaly and inversion figure prominently, and of these, it is inversion that has been most discussed in recent years.[1] At times, the threat posed by acts of inversion to entrenched sociopolitical orders (and the symbolico-ideological orders on which they depend) has been taken quite seriously: Headstands are said to have been forbidden at the imperial Chinese court as images of social and cosmic chaos.[2] In other instances, however, dominant classes have themselves employed processes of inversion to defend the status quo. In this chapter, I hope to explore two questions: First, how it is possible for an inversion to challenge a given order successfully, forcing significant modifications in it; second, why it is that inversions frequently contribute more to enhanced sociopolitical stability than to dynamic change.

A Provocative Inversion and the Disruption of Society: Duchamp's *Fountain*

Let us begin with a famous example from the history of modern art in which a symbolic inversion was successfully employed to subvert the habitual assumptions of a given society, and precipitated a crisis that led to that society's reorganization. The example I have in mind is the set of events surrounding the exhibition of Marcel Duchamp's *Fountain,* a work he submitted under the name of R. Mutt[3] to the first exhibition organized by the New York based Society of Independent Artists (February 1917), a group of which he was a prominent member. Although the show was announcedly open to all exhibitors who paid a $6.00 entry fee, *Fountain* gave the organizers pause, for it was nothing other than a urinal, with its pseudonymous signature so placed as to force it to be hung upside down (Fig. 9.1).

Figure 9.1. Marcel Duchamp, *Fountain*. 1917. (Courtesy Sidney Janis Gallery, New York.)

Believing *Fountain* to be the work of an unknown, the steering committee of the society pondered how to deal with an object they considered profoundly embarassing. Ultimately, they decided to exhibit the piece only in the back of the hall, where it would be screened off by a partition, and Duchamp—who had been present, but remained silent throughout the deliberations—tendered his resignation. Shortly thereafter, the work disappeared from view entirely, until Walter Arensberg (Duchamp's patron) arrived in the exhibit hall, asked to see Mutt's *Fountain,* and was told that such a work did not exist. Only when he announced that he wished to purchase it was the piece located, whereupon he, too, resigned from the society, as did several others of the Duchamp–Arensberg circle.[4]

Historians of art have generally treated this incident as a turning point in the formation of the New York avant-garde, and such a view undoubtedly has its merit. Yet it is also possible to consider these actions as a social drama, following the methods of processual analysis developed by Victor Turner.[5] Thus, one may trace the same dramatic sequence within the Society of Independent Artists as was evident to Turner in the socioritual processes of the Ndembu people of central Africa and others elsewhere: (1) there occurred a violation of an accepted norm; (2) this violation provoked a crisis,

Figure 9.2. Marcel Duchamp, *Bicycle Wheel*. New York, 1951
(Third version, after lost original of 1913). Assemblage: metal
wheel, mounted on painted wood stool. (Collection, The Mu-
seum of Modern Art, New York. The Sidney and Harriet
Janis Collection.)

in which a previously latent cleavage within the group was called into focus; (3) attempts were made to resolve the crisis; but (4) these proving unsuccessful, schism followed along the lines of the preexisting cleavage. Further, what is of paramount interest to us in the present instance is that the
initial violation was nothing other than an act of symbolic inversion.

Even at the most literal level, *Fountain* was an act of inversion, in which
a familiar object was turned upside down, this being a technique that Duchamp commonly employed. Thus, for instance, in *Bicycle Wheel* (1913), he
inverted a wheel and mounted it upon a stool, thus transforming an instrument of motion into an image of stability, simultaneously changing a common
object into privileged (i.e., art) goods (Fig. 9.2).

Such pieces were deliberate provocations, challenging numerous categories fundamental to modern Euro-American society and shared by the Society of Independent Artists, its pretensions of nonconformity notwithstanding. Among the most important of these is the distinction commonly drawn between that which can be termed the High and the Low, by which is meant not only the physical top and bottom, but also the associated categories of the elevated and the base or degraded. Implied within this distinction are also such opposed categories as the public and the private, the hidden and the manifest, the spiritual and the corporeal, the ridiculous and the sublime, and the privileged sphere of Art, which stands in contrast to all utilitarian goods.

It is these neat, simple, and commonly accepted categories that *Fountain* rendered impossible to sustain. The initial reaction of the Independent Artists' Steering Committee—that is, the suggestion that *Fountain* be displayed in a back corner, screened from public view by a partition—is an interesting one, for it represents an attempt to find a solution by way of synthesis and compromise. They hoped to create a space that was neither public nor private, neither open nor closed, to house an object simultaneously art and nonart, an object related to both the corporeal and the spiritual, certainly ridiculous, but possibly also sublime, in which the top had become the bottom and the lowly had been raised up: a toilet in the salon, a urinal meant for viewing. Ultimately, however, such an artificial solution proved unworkable, satisfying neither the champions of the work nor those who defended the normal order against its challenge. In the final reckoning, members of the society's steering committee chose to preserve the normative structures of their world, with the result that: (1) the group that challenged those structures withdrew from the society of which they had previously been a part and (2) the previously encompassing society was thereby weakened, not only by the loss of these members, but also by its demonstrated inability to defend itself and its principles adequately in a moment of crisis.

Inversion, Counterinversion, and Political Reform: Menenius Agrippa and the Plebeian Secession

Let us consider another classic example of inversion, a case more complex, if less amusing than that of Duchamp's *Fountain:* the first secession of the Roman plebes and the so-called "Apologue of Menenius Agrippa," as recounted by Titus Livy 2.32. According to Livy, already in the first decades of the Roman Republic, there existed powerful tensions between the upper (i.e., patrician) order and the lower (i.e., the plebes), with debt and the treatment of debtors as particular areas of contention. Unable to win concessions from the patricians—who controlled governmental institutions, the army, and the bulk of the national wealth—the plebes are said to have physically withdrawn from the city and established themselves as an independent community on the Aventine Mount, leaving the patricians to tend their own needs without the support of plebeian labor (c. 494 B.C.E.).[6] Obviously, this could be—and has been—considered as an early instance of aggravated class conflict. Moreover (and this in no way contradicts the Marxist interpretation), it may also be understood as a social drama of the same type as that involving Duchamp and the Society of Independent Artists, in which a latent social cleavage was activated by specific violations and a situation of crisis followed, during which time schism loomed as a real possibility.

Given the numerical imbalance between patricians and plebes, the ability of the former to subdue the latter by force seems doubtful. Moreover, we are told that the patricians were fearful of attack both by those plebeians who had not retired to the Aventine (and who thus formed a potential fifth column within the city) and by foreign enemies who might try to exploit the crisis. Direct coercion of the plebes being thus impossible, the patricians chose the other classic instrument of ruling elites for preserving the social order intact: a discourse that mystifies exploitative social relations while stimulating strong sentiments of affinity among those who might otherwise find themselves enemies. Toward this end they sent an emissary to the plebeian camp, one Menenius Agrippa, a man who had himself been born into the plebeian order and who was well liked and well respected among the plebes, being thus a *mediator* in the most literal sense: a man in-between. Moreover, he had a reputation for eloquence, which he showed to be much deserved,[7] for on his hospitable reception, he told the plebes the following story (Livy, 2.32.9–11):

> There was a time when the parts of the human body did not all agree, as they do now, but individual limbs had their own opinions and their own powers of speech. At that time, the other parts were outraged at having to work for the belly, while the belly rested idly, savoring their delicious gifts. Therefore, they conspired that the hands would not bear food to the mouth, the mouth would not swallow, and the teeth would not chew. As a result, they starved the belly, but all of them wasted away together. From this it became apparent that the belly is no idler, but just as others feed it, so it feeds the rest of the body.

Such eloquence was hardly exercised in vain. Livy concludes (2.32.12), "And by comparing how similar the rebellion of the body's organs was to the rage of the plebes against the patricians, he swayed the minds of those men." Shortly thereafter, plebeian and patrician segments were reconciled within the encompassing Roman society, patrician domination of which was modified by a significant reform. *Tribuni plebis* (tribunes of the plebes) were introduced: the first officials chosen by and from the lower social orders, whose charge it was to protect plebeian interests and who were given considerable powers toward this end.

Within this celebrated text, Livy presents a story within a story, that is, he recounts as a frame story the events of the First Secession of the Plebes, and this narrative culminates in another: the narrative that is said to have been told by Menenius Agrippa that purportedly brought the plebeians' secession to an end. Although it remains subject to debate, most experts now tend to doubt the facticity of the frame story, being more inclined to judge this legend and not history, although fully acknowledging the reality and seriousness of antagonisms between the patricians and the plebes, even at this early period. Among the Romans, in contrast, this story—which was told by others as well as Livy (cf. Dionysius of Halicarnassus 6.86)—consistently held the status of myth, providing as it did not only a credible account of events long past, but also (1) an authoritative charter for the institution of the *tribuni plebis,* and the hierarchic supremacy of the patrician class, and, what is more (2) an authoritative slogan through which could be evoked the unity of the Roman people.

To appreciate the efficacy of Menenius Agrippa's discourse, it is helpful to note that although it was a commonplace of Roman sociopolitical discourse to describe the patricians as the head of the body social, he identified the patricians not with the head, but with the belly, an organ rather more lowly in absolute spatial terms and for the way in which it is initially characterized as both insatiable in its appetites and parasitic on the other bodily members. The traditional metaphor of the social body was thus turned upside down in line with plebeian perceptions, as the ideology and practice of patrician domination was itself called into serious question.

Granting the plebes' identification of the patricians as the belly and not the head of society, Menenius Agrippa then proceeded, in a discursive *tour de force,* to invert things once more, arguing that the belly is no parasite, but a central, invaluable, and indispensable organ that appropriates food produced by other bodily members only in order to redistribute it to all (Fig. 9.3). Having abandoned claims to primacy based on a vertically encoded bodily image, he thus reasserted patrician primacy on novel grounds, arguing now that nurturance of the belly must of necessity precede that of any other organ.

Persuaded by this reformulation, the plebes (so we are told) renounced their secession and returned to the city. Through their show of force and their (temporary) reversal of the old ideological and sociopolitical order, they won a significant concession: the establishment of the *tribuni plebis.* But with the second reversal wrought in the discourse attributed to Menen-

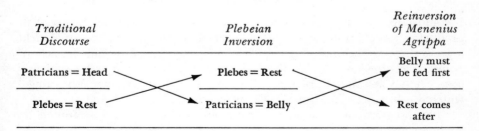

Figure 9.3. Operations of inversion and counterinversion within the Apologue of Menenius Agrippa.

	Symbolic Representations (in the discourse of Menenius Agrippa)	Sociopolitical Processes (in the frame story told by Livy)
Thesis	Patricians = Head	Patrician power
Antithesis	Patricians = Belly	Plebeian secession
Synthesis	Belly = indispensable, first to be fed	Unity restored, introduction of *Tribuni plebis*

Figure 9.4. Dialectic processes in Livy, 2.32.9–11.

ius Agrippa, the patricians reconstituted Roman society and, at the cost of this concession, regained their position as the dominant party within the social aggregate. This struggle of imagery and counterimagery, as well as that of social classes, may be described as the working of a dialectic in which symbolic formulations both reflect and help to shape sociopolitical processes, as is shown in Figure 9.4.

The persuasive power of Menenius Agrippa's discourse thus depends on a skillful operation of counterinversion. If there exists any facticity to Livy's account, one must admire, albeit grudgingly, the ability of its hero to manipulate language, logic, and imagery—and more important, to manipulate people through these other manipulations. In a critical moment he discovered an elegant dialectic solution that (at least temporarily) resolved the crisis. And if these events never did transpire (and scholars rightly judge it a legend), one ought reserve admiration for the manipulative genius of the tradition itself, on which Livy drew and that remains operative each time the tale is retold. In this regard it is perhaps worth noting that this discourse was still being employed as late as 1594, when the lieutenant general of the Cahors court, in condemning the Croquant rebels, posed as a rhetorical question: What would happen if the members of the body should rebel against the stomach and refuse to feed it?[8]

Dialectic Manipulations and Preservation of the Status Quo: "All-Star Wrestling"

I would now like to consider a case in which ritual inversions, rather than producing upheaval or significant modification within a given social field help to preserve sociopolitical and economic structures intact in the face of potential challenges. Specifically, I propose to examine an individual episode, chosen at random, of the syndicated TV show "All-Star Wrestling," which was broadcast in Minneapolis on Saturday, 28 October 1984.[9]

The program in question was composed of six bouts, interrupted by commercials, interviews, and the like. All bouts were formulaic in the extreme, quite lacking in surprise, drama, or tension. Several interlocking codes helped the audience identify—with no possibility of error—(1) who

	Entry Marked	Costume Marked	Size Marked	Heroism Marked	Victory
Entry Marked		100%	83%	33%	100%
Costume Marked	100%		83%	33%	100%
Size Marked	83%	83%		17%	83%
Heroism Marked	33%	33%	17%		33%
Victory	100%	100%	83%	33%	

Figure 9.5. Correlations in "All-Star Wrestling" (28 October 1984).

'as the hero (or babyface in the parlance of the trade) and who the villain)r heel) in each bout and (2) who would be the victor. Thus, before the :art of each bout, an announcer introduced the contestants, one of whom 'as already in the ring, whereas the other—who in all cases would win— marched through the crowd to cheers or jeers. All of the victors were also marked by costumes that were considerably more extreme than those of their opponents, either by virtue of special elegance (silk robes, capes, se- quins), special insignia (military uniforms and emblems), or a particularly ragged look (torn blue jeans, rope belts, etc.).[10] These factors also correlated strongly with superiority in size, for in five of the six bouts (83 percent), the larger man was ultimately victorious. Things were not so simple, however, with regard to the correlation between victory and heroism, that is, moral rectitude as measured by fair play, obedience to the referee, modest de- meanor, and so on, for in only two of the six matches did the heroes triumph. A graphing of these correlations is presented as Figure 9.5.

If the individual matches were relatively predictable, this is not to say that the program was devoid of suspense or interest. On the contrary, the six bouts fit together in such a fashion as to form an overarching dramatic structure that was not only utterly compelling, but elegant in the extreme, as becomes clear when one considers the matches in their proper sequence.

Thus, the first match saw the relatively easy and straightforward victory of the hero, one "Fabulous Freebird" Michael Hayes, over an unremarkable villain named "Gentleman Jerry" Valiant. Hayes was a young, heavily muscled, chestily hirsute, and deeply tanned individual with long blond hair and a short beard, who wore a sequined cape emblazoned with the Confederate flag. His entrance was accompanied by booming rock music, to which he danced in openly sexual fashion (Fig. 9.6). At the outset of the match, Valiant attempted to strangle the hero, shielding this illegal maneu- ver from the gaze of an obligingly inept referee. Hayes, however, recovered quickly and took immediate vengeance, overpowering his opponent with a

Figure 9.6. Fabulous Freebird Michael Hayes, photograph by Mike Gratchner. (Courtesy of Wrestling World.)

series of flying kicks and other athletic maneuvers. On announcement of his victory, Hayes resumed his dance to the delight of the audience. Although it was not clear at the time—this became evident only on completion of the full card—the opening match was anomalous in two respects: first, it was the sole time that a smaller man would defeat a larger (Hayes's announced weight was 250 pounds to Valiant's 285), and more important, it was the only time that the victor was not marked as more fully "American" than the vanquished, for as we shall see, in every other encounter a code of racial, ethnic, or political identity was operative such that the superior "Americanism" of the eventual victor was firmly established.

The second bout was a tag-team affair, in which the heels were identified only as "The Moondogs, Rex and Spot" (cumulative weight 601 pounds). Although said to come from "parts unknown," their unkempt hair and

Figure 9.7. The Moondogs, photograph by George Napolitano. (Courtesy of Wrestling World.)

matted beards announced a rural locale, as did their costumes, which consisted of ripped blue jeans held up by a rope. As they marched toward the ring, they carried large animal bones, from which they apparently gnawed raw meat (Fig. 9.7). Throughout their time on stage, they never spoke, but only emitted a series of canine wails and ululations as they battered their opponents: the thoroughly outclassed team of Billy Travis (225 pounds) and Mario Mancini (245 pounds), who put up only token resistance.

The next match saw George "The Animal" Steele (288 pounds) compete against "The Black Panther" (245 pounds), the only black wrestler on the program. For his part, Steele displayed a hirsute body set off by a shaven head, and like "The Moondogs," he never spoke. Rather, his manager, "The Mysterious Mr. Fuji," spoke on his behalf and called instructions to him from time to time. Such instructions were not particularly necessary. As was evident to the audience—but not, of course, to the referee—Steel had a heavy piece of metal hidden in his trunks, which he periodically extracted and used to bludgeon the hapless "Black Panther." Having quickly rendered the latter nearly defenseless, Steele threw him outside the ring into the crowd, then followed him, hit him with a chair, and dragged him back into the ring for the pin. When it was all over and Steele's hand had been raised in victory, he went back to bite the Panther who still lay insensate on the mat.

The fourth match involved that villain who was scheduled to compete for the World's Championship in a few days' time: "Big John" Studd, the largest of all the contestants, being some 7 feet in height and weighing 400 pounds, according to the announcer. Studd was accompanied by his manager, Bobby "The Brain" Heenan, who seized the announcer's microphone and insisted on extolling both Studd and himself ("He is the world's strongest man and I am the world's smartest") to the outrage of the easily aroused crowd. Both men were resplendent in sequined suits. Studd confronted a man little more than half his size at 265 pounds and many years older, one Salvatore Bellono, with whom Studd toyed briefly before hoisting him high and slamming him to the mat.

This was followed by a match in which another heel with a sexually provocative nom de guerre, Brutus Beefcake (273 pounds), was paired against an outclassed babyface, the young and attractive, but inexperienced Brian Madden (225 pounds). Beefcake, evidently confident in his own abilities and good looks, strutted and preened, wearing gold silk tights and a set of forearms guards that—in the opinion of the TV announcers—should have been declared illegal (Figure 9.8). These he used repeatedly to choke Madden, whose Irish combativeness was praised by the announcers, but whose physical abilities were palpably inadequate to the task. Having knocked Madden down, Beefcake would shout at him to get up, which Madden would gamely do, only to be knocked down again. When it was all over, Beefcake threw kisses to an unappreciative crowd.

In the four matches that followed the opener, the villains consistently triumphed, and triumphed easily, using illegal and sadistic means in every case. They strangled their victims and bit them, hit them with chairs and concealed weapons. They gouged eyes and kicked in the groin, threw their hapless opponents from the ring and smashed them to the mat. They sneered at referees, abused fallen heroes, taunted the crowd, and made mockery of the rules. Truly, these four matches constituted a chamber of horrors: an abandonment of all normative morality, without a hint of retribution.

Such, however, was not long in coming. At the start of the sixth and final match, a heel of decidedly secondary status—the bearded and surly, but diminutive 226-pound Dave Rice—occupied the ring, and expectations were clearly high as to who his opponent would be. At the announcement of the

Figure 9.8. Brutus Beefcake. (Photo courtesy of Pumpkin Press, Inc.)

hero, the crowd leapt to its feet and roared its approval, for it was none other than the formidable and much-beloved Sergeant Slaughter (296 pounds) who entered the hall, as is his fashion, to the hymn of the U.S. Marine Corps, wearing the cap of a marine drill instructor. Slowly, he made his way through the crowd, pausing to shake hands with numerous individuals (Fig. 9.9). When finally he entered the ring, he placed his right hand over his heart and led the rapturous audience in the U.S. Pledge of Allegiance. Only when this solemn rite—a regular feature of the sergeant's appearances—was complete, could the bout commence.

The first exchange was perfectly choreographed and immensely revealing. Initially, Sergeant Slaughter forced Rice into a corner, where the suddenly vigilant referee ordered him to release his opponent and "break clean." This Slaughter did with an elaborate show of sportsmanly compliance. Directly thereafter, positions were reversed, and the referee gave the same instructions to Rice, who began by ostentatiously imitating the sergeant's gesture of fair play, only to change this without warning into an illegal blow. Caught unaware, the sergeant showed surprise—and perhaps disappointment—but not pain, responding immediately with a punch of his own that sent Rice reeling across the ring. Several further exchanges followed, in which Rice's violations consistently brought overpowering retaliation. Finally, with a maneuver in which he launched himself horizontally from the top rope ("just like a B-52 bomber," in the words of the announcer) Ser-

Figure 9.9. Sergeant Slaughter, photograph by George Napolitano. (Courtesy of Wrestling World.)

geant Slaughter brought Rice to the canvas and counted him out. Rising in victory, he stood at attention and gave a last military salute to the jubilant crowd. Figure 9.10 summarizes the results of these six matches.

It is easy to describe professional wrestling as if it were a joke or a parody. Such descriptions, however, are not only condescending, but also superficial. To be sure, it is not a subtle sport, nor a mode of discourse suited to refined bourgeois tastes. Its gestures are spectacular, its contents exaggerated, and its characters larger than life. This notwithstanding, the ritual and dramatic structure of professional wrestling is anything but simple, and its efficacy is anything but negligible: These need to be studied in further detail.

At its most fundamental level—that recognized by Roland Barthes in his classic essay on the sport—wrestling offers an extravagantly staged combat

	Babyface Victor	Heel Victor
1. "Gentleman" Jerry Valiant "FABULOUS FREEBIRD" MICHAEL HAYES	X	
2. Mario Mancini and Billy Travis "THE MOONDOGS, REX AND SPOT"		X
3. "The Black Panther" GEORGE "THE ANIMAL" STEELE		X
4. Salvatore Bellono "BIG JOHN" STUDD		X
5. Brian Madden BRUTUS BEEFCAKE		X
6. Dave Rice SERGEANT SLAUGHTER	X	

Figure 9.10. Summary of bouts, "All-Star Wrestling" (28 October 1984); contestants are listed in order of appearance. (Capital letters denote the ultimate victors.)

between good and evil.[11] Considered with reference to this binary coding of morality, it is evident that our episode of "All-Star Wrestling" consisted of a drama in three acts: (1) the preliminary triumph of virtue (first match), (2) the repeated triumphs of evil (matches two through five), and (3) the definitive triumph of virtue (the grand finale).

Beyond this, however, there is another operative code that is both more subtle and more vicious: an ethnocentric and racist coding for "Americanism" and lack thereof. In order to recognize this second code, which remained always subtextual to the primary moral code, it is helpful to consider the four central matches in the program: the repeated triumphs of evil.

First let us observe that the four villains who triumphed in these matches—The Moondogs, Steele, Studd, and Beefcake—were differentiated from one another in subtle and not-so-subtle ways by their appearance, demeanor, ring tactics, and the like. Among the more significant features that set them apart are managers, articulate speech, and elegant clothes, each of which was possessed by two of the victorious villains and lacked by two. These factors may be charted as in Figure 9.11.

With regard to these variables, Beefcake appears as the opposite of Steele, and Studd as the opposite of The Moondogs. Other points are also worth making, for instance, the covariance of speech and elegance (i.e., none of the victorious heels possessed one without the other), which together distinguish those villains who are too cultured (the fops) from those too close to nature (the beasts). Further, as we have now come to expect, a hierarchy is embedded within this classificatory system, a hierarchy that was borne out

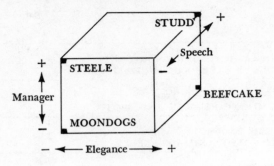

Figure 9.11. Identifying characteristics of the victorious villains, "All-Star Wrestling" (28 October 1984).

	Elegance	*Speech*	*Manager*
Moondogs	−	−	−
Steele	−	−	+
Studd	+	+	+
Beefcake	+	+	−

Figure 9.11. Identifying characteristics of the victorious villains, "All-Star Wrestling" (28 October 1984).

in the matches that unfolded in the two years after broadcast of this program. Thus, Studd (+/+/+) was ranked as the top contender for the world heavyweight championship and given a title bout (he lost); Beefcake (+/−/+) gained a manager and a tag team partner (thus → +/+/+), whereupon he gained the tag-team championship; Steele (−/+/−) lost his manager (thus → −/−/−) and disappeared for a spell (it was reported that he had gone mad and was under psychiatric treatment); and The Moondogs (−/−/−) sank to the level of those heels who invariably suffer defeat at the hands of superior heroes.

If there were thus numerous ways in which these characters differed, they were, nonetheless, united in their villainy and also in another feature, which emerges when they are considered alongside the heroes they conquered. Without exception the victorious heels lacked explicit ethnic or racial identity, unlike the vanquished heroes, who included among their number two Italo-Americans (Mario Mancini, Salvatore Bellono), an Irish-American (Brian Madden), and a Black ("The Black Panther").[12] In these matches it was those individuals most palpably "American," not those most virtuous, who emerged triumphant.

This stands in contrast to the first bout, in which "Fabulous Freebird" Michael Hayes overcame "Gentleman Jerry" Valiant. By his nickname; his youth, suntan, and long hair; his music and dance; and his Confederate flag, Hayes systematically associated himself with several groups at the margins of American society: the counterculture of the late 1960s, California surfers, and Southern good old boys.[13] In contrast, for all that he was somewhat nondescript, Valiant appeared as the more "American" of the com-

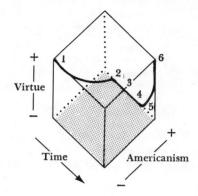

	Victor Marked for Virtue	Victor Marked for Americanism
Match No. 1	+	−
Matches Nos. 2–5	−	+
Match No. 6	+	+

Figure 9.12. Coding for virtue and "Americanism" in "All-Star Wrestling" (28 October 1984). Numerals stand for the six matches of the card.

batants—an American villain, to be sure, and ultimately a vanquished American villain but American nonetheless, it being not Americanism, but virtue in the form of fair play, hard work, and native ability that led to victory in this match.

The second act was thus an inversion of the first, a systematic reversal of its contents with regard to the moral and ethnic/racial codes, codes that were also powerfully operative in the third and final act, as is seen in Figure 9.12.

The victory of Sergeant Slaughter is thus the end toward which the entire program was structured, he being that hero who was not only most virtuous, but also most totally—indeed hyperbolically—"American," given his open patriotism, his obedience to the rules (except when provoked), his blend of strength and modesty (reminiscent of such American icons as Gary Cooper, Humphrey Bogart, and John Wayne), and his abundant violence: a violence that differed from that of all other contestants in its legitimation through military trappings.

It is not sufficient however, to treat professional wrestling as a collection of interlocking symbolic codes, without grounding those codes in their proper social context, along lines explored by Jim Freedman, who argued persuasively that what is most fundamentally at issue in wrestling as it is staged throughout North America is the nature of modern capitalism and the fabled "American Dream" of success through individual talent, effort,

	Symbolic Representations	Sociopolitical Processes
Thesis (Match #1)	Virtue triumphs (even if not American)	Hegemonic status of the "American Dream"
Antithesis (Matches #2–5)	Evil triumphs (over those not fully American)	Severe doubts raised by experience
Synthesis (Match #6)	Virtue together with "Americanism" is invincible	Hegemony of "American Dream" firmly reestablished

Figure 9.13. Dialectic processes in "All-Star Wrestling" (28 October 1984).

and virtue.[14] Freedman began his analysis by noting two important facts about professional wrestling: First, that heels triumph considerably more often than do babyfaces and, second, that they triumph by different means, relying on secret holds, sly managers, hidden weapons, and illegal maneuvers, whereas babyfaces trust to their physical abilities and athletic training alone. Given this, Freedman argued that the fascination wrestling exerts on its predominantly lower-class audience[15] derives from its ability to present a convincing picture of the contradictions between the Horatio Alger ideology of upward mobility within a free market economy and lived experience, where hard work and ability are seldom adequately rewarded, whereas other methods—unscrupulous dealings, family connections, obsequiousness, flattery, and the like—are regularly keys to success.

The second act of "All-Star Wrestling" thus sets forth a pointed challenge to the "American Dream," dramatically and effectively portraying a world in which bastards triumph and the virtuous suffer: a world all too familiar to the audience. Yet the task that wrestling undertakes—and it is hardly alone in this—is to rescue the "American Dream" from such a challenge: that is to say, to repersuade the audience of the dominant ideology's enduring validity, their own contradictory experiences notwithstanding. Toward this end it proceeds, as did Menenius Agrippa, by making use of inversion and counterinversion to rescue an embattled ideology and sociopolitical order. Further, like the elements in Livy's account, those that figure in "All Star Wrestling" can be presented as a form of dialectic, as in Figure 9.13.

If this is a dialectic, its structure differs significantly from the familiar Hegelian model. To be sure, the symbolic representations of "All-Star Wrestling" are formally constructed in proper Hegelian fashion, so that the confrontation of polar opposites gives rise to a novel configuration partaking of thesis and antithesis alike, while also differing from them both. This play of symbolic constructs, however, serves to produce decidedly nondialectic (at least, non-Hegelian, and emphatically non-Marxian) developments at the level of sociopolitical process: developments that these symbolic representations not only help shape, but also help mask. At this level the last phase of the dialectic offers no synthesis at all in the traditional sense, merely an emphatic restatement of the thesis. In such a dialectic the antithetical position is reduced to the status of an aberration that surfaces when the once-and-future thesis temporarily flags, and is effectively contained between the initial and the final presentation of the thesis, where it is rendered harmless, deprived of whatever persuasive power it might otherwise have had.[16]

Such a result does not derive from any inherent weakness of the antithesis: Even the most powerful positions are vulnerable to the skillful and subtle manipulation of symbols. Inversion and counterinversion, when perfectly performed, lead back to the initial starting point. And for all that inversion can be an effective instrument of agitation, skillful use of which can prompt significant reform (as in the story of Menenius Agrippa) or radical upheaval (as with Duchamp's *Fountain*), dominant orders are capable of employing their own symbolic inversions to defend against just such threats. To be sure it is a powerful act to turn the world upside down, but a simple 180-degree rotation is not difficult to undo. An order twice inverted is an order restored, perhaps even strengthened as a result of the exercise.

10

The Uses of Anomaly

Places Outside Space and Moments Outside Time

A well-known myth of ancient India relates that after having engaged in an inconclusive combat, the god Indra and the demon Namuci concluded a pact of friendship. Namuci, however, took advantage of this pact and stole from Indra the miraculous and highly prized ritual intoxicant known as soma. Thereupon Indra sought help from several other deities, recounting to them the nature of his pact with the demon,[1] "I have sworn to Namuci thus: 'I will not kill you by day, nor by night; not with a staff, nor with a bow; not with an open hand, nor with a clenched fist; not with anything dry, nor anything wet.' Yet he has stolen my soma. Please help steal it back!" And after exacting a goodly price—a share in the soma-offerings that form the core of Vedic ritual—the others extended their assistance, "They poured out the froth of the waters as a weapon, saying, 'Neither dry, nor wet.' With that froth, Indra cut off Namuci's head when the night was giving way to dawn, saying, 'Neither day, nor night.' "[2] Thus ends the encounter and the story, a seemingly simple point having been established: There is no contract without its loophole.

Quite similar in theme and content is a medieval Welsh tale, *Math, Son of Mathonwy*, in which the hero, one Lleu Llaw Gyffes, possesses what is known as a *cyneddr* (literally, a peculiarity—but more accurately described as a supernatural set of rules by which the hero is bound). Specifically, Lleu's *cyneddr* establishes the conditions under which he can be killed.[3]

Math is a long and complicated tale, but the episode that concerns us begins with the seduction of Lleu's wife, Blodeuedd, by one Gronw Pebyr at a time when the latter is a guest in Lleu's house. Shortly thereafter, the lovers decide to kill Lleu, but first they need learn the precise nature of his "peculiarity." This Blodeuedd wheedles from him as they lie in bed. First, only a spear that has been forged over the course of an entire year can harm him. Second, work on this spear must be done only on Sundays, that is, it must be a weapon constructed wholly within moments of sacred time or—

to put it conversely—wholly outside of normal time. And finally, the unsuspecting Lleu explains to his wife:

> "I may not be killed inside a house. I may not be killed outside. I may not be killed while on horseback. I may not be killed when on foot."
> And she said: "How can you be killed, then?"
> And he said: "I'll tell you. Make a bath upon the river shore. Make a well-thatched, vaulted roof over the top of the tub. Bring a he-goat, and place it close by the tub, and I'll put one foot on the goat's back and the other on the rim of the tub. Whoever could strike me a wound then would surely cause my death."
> And she said: "I say thanks to God for those things. One is able to escape them easily." And no sooner had she gotten that information than she sent it to Gronw Pebyr.

Blodeuedd's last words fairly drip with irony, "I say thanks to God for those things. One is able to escape them easily." But escape what—the perilous situation or the protective conditions? In this skillfully constructed speech-act, Blodeuedd encompasses two seemingly exclusive alternatives, "Thank God you can't be killed" and "Thank God you can be killed." Embracing neither one nor the other fully and openly, she reveals and exploits the inadequacy of such oversimplified binary distinctions.

The action that follows is not terribly difficult to predict. Every Sunday for the next year Gronw works on a spear and when it is ready, Blodeuedd lures Lleu to his mortal position, neither inside nor out (but halfway under a straw roof), neither on horse nor on foot (but straddling a tub and a goat), neither wet nor dry (but dripping from his bath), neither clothed nor naked (but wrapped in a towel). In such a condition, betwixt and between, Lleu is slain, whereupon the lovers take straight to their bed. On the following day, Gronw assumes control of Lleu's realm and possessions. Scandalized by this turn of events, other characters manage a miraculous resurrection of Lleu, who returns to kill Gronw on the very same spot and in the very same fashion that earlier he had himself been killed.

One could cite many other examples of this same mythic topos, with varying details but the same general story line.[4] These two variants, however, are sufficient for several important observations. In both, struggle derives from competition over scarce and valued resources, a competition that is waged covertly at first, and then with open force. In the one case it is a miraculously beautiful woman who is contested; in the other, a potent ritual beverage, which is the very source of the gods' strength and power.[5] So great is their desire for these goods that the actors in these stories are led to betray whatever oaths, bonds, and expectations join them to others—others who are their comrades, their rivals, and ultimately their victims.

Social Bonds and Interstitial Categories

Such an observation leads us to consider the nature of social relations as depicted therein. At the heart of the Indic myth we find a solemn pact of friendship and alliance (Sanskrit, *samdhā*) that binds the protagonists together, whereas in the Welsh tale, two other forms of social bond are at issue, both equally solemn: marriage, which unites Lleu and Blodeuedd, and hospitality, which joins them to Gronw. Yet none of these bonds proves durable or sure, and one can understand both stories—in part at least—as explorations of the great theme of the fragility of social bonds and thus of society itself.

Alliance, marriage, and hospitality, as is well known, are all important mechanisms for bringing individuals into close and abiding relation with one another. Through mechanisms such as these (and one could add filiation, friendship, patronage, and many others), persons who initially stand separate from one another come to share sentiments of affinity in such forms as loyalty, affection, mutual attachment, or common purpose, these being the sentiments out of which society is constructed. Moreover, when such sentiments prevail over those of estrangement, some measure of peace and harmony is won thereby, however temporary or partial it may be.

Always there persists, however, a certain risk or insecurity in even the closest and most enduring of social relations. For if one can draw near to others and thus diminish the extent of their otherness, one can never close completely—mystics and romantics of various stripes notwithstanding—the existential gap that separates self from other. In a sense those with whom one shares social bonds are themselves interstitial creatures: neither self nor alien, but somewhere in between. And, like all interstitial entities, such persons can be dangerous.

There is, for example, the possibility of exploitation, as in the Indic story we have considered. There, Namuci proves appreciably more dangerous to Indra as an ally than he had as an enemy, as he is able to employ the terms of the very bond that joins them in order to take material advantage of his new-found ally and friend. Another danger is that of betrayal, as in the story of Lleu, Blodeuedd, and Gronw, where a guest (i.e., an outsider sufficiently trusted to enter inside one's home) turns seducer, and a spouse, who is, after all, another variety of outsider-come-in, turns unfaithful.

The question of marital fidelity and infidelity is a highly charged one in those kinship systems where sexual relations are restricted by rule to marital partners. By definition, such structures fuse two logically separable considerations—marriage (a jural relation) and sex (a physical relation)—into one complex taxonomizer. The result is a system of sexual morality that is, in effect, a classificatory system having but two categories: spouses and others, sexual relations being licit with the former and forbidden with the latter. Now, within such a system, nonmarried lovers hardly disappear,[6] but rather are marginalized, relegated to the position of anomalies (i.e.,

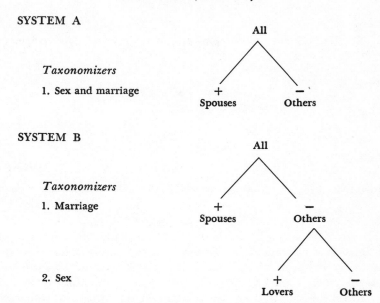

Figure 10.1. The relations of lovers, anomalous under the rules of System A (marital exclusivity), can potentially dissolve that system and force its reorganization as System B.

entities that escape the categories of an operative taxonomic structure). Yet the existence of nonmarried lovers exerts a certain pressure for separation of the system's two fused taxonomizers, with the consequent emergence of a different sociotaxonomic order, as is shown in Figure 10.1.[7]

Like Gronw's spear or Indra's foam, the lovers' relation is an anomalous entity, and one that can present serious challenges to an established sociotaxonomic order. In its narrative line, *Math, Son of Mathonwy* entertains this anomalous relation, and acknowledges its corrosive power. In its final episode, however—Lleu's return and vengeance—it conclusively rejects that relation, and restores the preexistent classification and norms of marriage and sexuality.

In truth, the two stories are equally explorations of the tensions that exist between taxonomic order and countertaxonomic anomaly, for both the pact that guards Namuci and Lleu's "peculiarity" are nothing other than taxonomic stuctures, built upon serial binary oppositions of the type "Neither *A* nor not-*A*."[8] Given the logical principle of the excluded middle, any proposition of this form ought to cover all possibilities, yet stories of this type tend to multiply such propositions, sometimes in more and sometimes in less systematic fashion, thereby constructing ever-more difficult conditions for their heroes to overcome. Thus, for example, in its specification "not with a staff, nor with a bow; not with an open hand, nor with a clenched fist;" the pact of Indra and Namuci attempts to classify and pre-

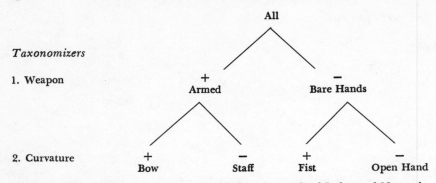

Figure 10.2. Types of assault, as classified in the myth of Indra and Namuci.

clude all possible types of assault through the deployment of two taxono-mizers. The first of these is fairly obvious, the presence or absence of a weapon in the hands of the assailant. The second is rather less obvious and depends on a perceived analogy between the bow and the fist, on the one hand, vis-à-vis the staff and the open hand on the other. In both cases the more dangerous form of assault (bow, which can kill at a distance, in con-trast to staff; fist as opposed to a slap with the open hand) employs the same material items as do the safer forms, with the difference that the bow and fist are bent, whereas the staff and open hand remain straight. Accord-ingly, the presence or absence of curvature seems to be the second-order taxonomizer (Fig. 10.2).

Against such a system of defense, victory becomes possible only with the discovery and aggressive use of some entity that escapes the restrictions of the classificatory system. Thus in the present instance, an attack with foam can properly be considered neither assault with a weapon nor one that is empty-handed, in addition to its avoiding the further stipulation, "neither dry nor wet." It is thus not the strength of Indra or Gronw (although both characters possess these in abundance) that leads to their success, but their cunning, their genius for locating the seams in the logical (and ideological) armor of their adversaries.[9] Moreover, one should stress that those adver-saries not only appear invincible at first, but also retain their privileges, possessions, and positions as long as would-be opponents remain persuaded of their invincibility.

Anomaly and Danger

That interstitial, liminal, or anomalous entities are frequently charged with danger in complex and mysterious ways has been a commonplace of scholarly literature at least since Arnold van Gennep's work on the rites of passage was published in 1908.[10] Recently, however, this idea has been called into question, as by Rodney Needham, who writes:

Just as there are no necessary anomalies so there are no necessary responses to anomalies. Certainly it cannot be alleged that an anomaly automatically gives rise to wariness or unease or a fear of danger. One proof of this is that everywhere people make up classificatory oddities: they are attracted by them, and it might even be said that they seem to need them.[11]

Although not without a measure of justice (especially if one stresses the modifiers "necessary" and "automatically"), this corrective does not get us as far as one might like. Moreover, there are ways, particularly in the lack of specificity regarding the "people" to whom he refers, in which Needham further obscures the very problem he, to his merit, isolates: Why (and how) is it that an anomaly can be a source of amusement or fascination under one set of circumstances and a source of danger under another, yet be totally ignored under still a third?

Resolution of this question begins, I believe, with Needham's observation that there is nothing that is intrinsically, inherently, and automatically anomalous. Rather, there are only things that appear anomalous within the framework of a given taxonomic system: specifically, a system that is incompetent—given the nature of the taxonomizers it deploys—to classify those specific things in a satisfactory manner. One can, in fact, define anomaly in rather neutral terms as any entity, the existence of which goes unrecognized under the terms of a given taxonomy. That definition can be modified, however, in two rather opposite but equally pointed formulations, and this takes us to the heart of the matter. Thus, (1) an anomaly is any entity that defies the rules of an operative taxonomy or (2) an anomaly is any entity, the existence of which an operative taxonomy is incapable of acknowledging. In the first case the taxonomy is taken to be normative and the anomaly deviant. In the second the anomaly is judged legitimate; the taxonomy, inadequate, distorting, and exclusionary. Under the terms of both definitions, however, it is possible to see how an anomaly may both pose danger to and be exposed to danger from the taxonomic order in which it is anomalous, just as deviants are considered outlaws when the legitimacy of legal systems is affirmed, but rebels when such systems are judged illegitimate.[12]

The responses of taxonomic systems—or more properly, of those who construct, maintain, and deploy such systems—to those things they cannot classify and thereby constrain are many and varied. Anomalies can be ignored, ridiculed, distorted, or suppressed, these all being means whereby they are relegated to the margins and interstices of both a given classificatory system and of lived experience. Alternately, the system under which they are judged anomalous can be modified or abandoned. This is what happens (or so we are told) in scientific revolutions as these have been described by Thomas Kuhn.[13] Where Kuhn's analysis falls short, however, is his inadequate attention to the sociopolitical dimensions of such revolutions. Thus, for instance, one must stress that defenders of a given paradigm struggle to maintain not only an intellectual construct, but also the privileges, positions, and prestige they enjoy while that construct (which may itself encode social hierarchy, as in the case of Ptolemaic cosmology) remains dominant. Treatment of anomalous data thus have obvious and powerful implications for the society of scientists (and others) as well as for the discourse of science.

Anomalies remain always a potential threat to the taxonomic structures under which they are marginalized, for in the very fact of their existence they reveal the shortcomings, inadequacies, contradictions, and arbitrary nature of such structures. A paradoxical relation and a dialectic tension thus exist between taxonomy and anomaly: The latter, called into existence by the former, can also prove its genitor's undoing. What is more—and this is the central point—it is not simply a matter of logical structures because just as taxonomy can encode and legitimate, indeed, help construct sociopolitical and economic orders, so conversely can anomaly be used to delegitimate and deconstruct those same sociotaxonomic orders.

Androgynes, Toadstools, and Others

In recent decades we have seen sociotaxonomic orders based on age, class, ethnicity, and gender called into question by numerous anomalies, including a "white man who sounds black" (Colonel Tom Parker's description of the singer he sought and ultimately found in Elvis Presley), a fifteen-year-old "perfectly enlightened master" (the Guru Maharaj Ji),[14] and the phenomenon of couturier-designed blue jeans. Feminists and others have been particularly active in undermining established gender classification and hierarchy, using the theme of androgyny as an instrument of countertaxonomic agitation, as in the vogue for unisex fashions, "whole-brain learning," and the recovery and publication of hermaphrodites' diaries. In this they follow in an extremely ancient tradition, although it was not always feminists who so employed the image of the androgyne.[15]

An interesting case in point is the speech attributed to Aristophanes in Plato's *Symposium* 189E–192E, where it is told that before the emergence of humanity proper, there were three primordial beings, each having two faces, four arms, four legs, and two sets of genital organs. Of these, one was doubly male, the second doubly female, and the third an androgyne. These beings ran afoul of Zeus, however, who used his thunderbolt to cut them in half, thereby creating human beings in their present form. Further, although surface appearances might lead one to believe that there are only two types of humans—male and female—there are, in fact, three. For from the doubly male being there emerged male homosexuals, from the doubly female, lesbians, and from the androgyne, heterosexuals of both genders. And in their sexual relations these three types of humanity all seek the same thing: reunion with their lost half.

For all that the story is a work of fanciful delight, it is also a serious work of agitation, for by introducing the anomalous figure of the androgyne, it reveals the inadequacy of a bipartite classification of humanity on straightforwardly gender-based categories. In place of such a system (the hierarchic dimensions of which are obvious), it advances a taxonomy based on sexual preference: that is, a system in which the gender of one's sexual partners is taken into account as well as one's own. Moreover, such a change in taxonomy carries with it a change in hierarchy, to the benefit of certain men and certain women (i.e., those who prefer sex with males) and to the detriment of others (those whose taste runs to females). For the text asserts that male homosexuals are "most excellent" and "most manly" (Greek, *beltistoi . . . andreiotatoi,* 192A), whereas heterosexuals tend to be adulterers and adulteresses (*hoi polloi tōn moikhōn . . . moikheutriai,* 191D). Lesbians, for their part, are dismissed as "whores" (*hetairistriai,* 191E). Further, this ranking is reinforced by means of the vertical structure of an associated cosmic module (190B), for the sun is said to have been the father of the doubly male being (and thus of homosexuals), the moon of the androgyne (and thus of heterosexuals), and the earth of the doubly female (and thus of lesbians). Having struggled to deconstruct one sociotaxonomic order (System A in Fig. 10.3) through the anomaly of an androgyne, Plato's Aristophanes labors, with partial success,[16] to replace it with another (System B in Fig. 10.3).

The view I am advancing is that anomaly can serve as a (potentially potent) instrument with which opponents of an entrenched sociotaxonomic order may attempt to undermine the latter. Such an analysis is quite different from that of Clifford Geertz, who argued that experience of the anomalous prompts a general, if not universal, response of a cognitive, intellectual, and ultimately religious nature. He states:

> It does appear to be a fact that at least some men—in all probability, most men—are unable to leave unclarified problems of analysis merely unclarified, just to look at the stranger features of the world's landscape in dumb astonishment or bland apathy without trying to develop, however fantastic, inconsistent, or simple-minded, some notions as to how such features might be reconciled with the more ordinary deliverances of experience.[17]

In support of this view, he recounted an incident from his fieldwork in Java, where "a peculiarly shaped, rather large toadstool" suddenly sprouted in the house of a carpenter. The toadstool received considerable attention, as Geertz explained:

> Toadstools play about the same role in Javanese life as they do in ours, and in the ordinary course of things Javanese have about as much interest in them as we do. It was just that this one was "odd," "strange," "uncanny"—*aneh.* And the odd, strange, and uncanny simply must be accounted for—or, again, the conviction that it *could be accounted for* sustained. One does not shrug off a toadstool which grows five times as fast as a toadstool has any right to grow. In the broadest sense the "strange" toadstool did have implications, and critical ones, for those who heard about it. It threatened their most general ability to understand the world, raised the uncomfortable question of whether the beliefs which they held about nature were workable, the standards of truth they used valid.[18]

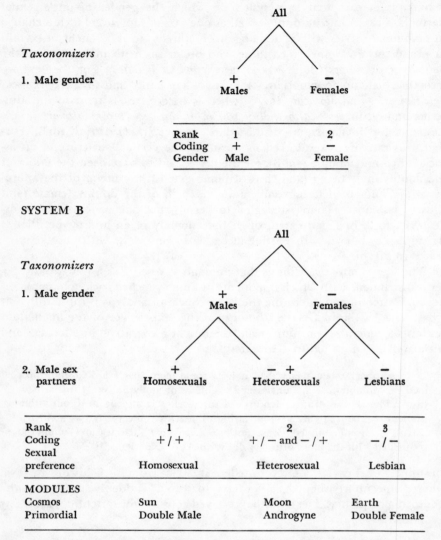

Figure 10.3. Taxonomy by gender (System A) is rendered unworkable by the anomaly of the androgyne and replaced by a taxonomy based on sexual preference (System B) following the analysis of Plato's *Symposium* 189E–192E.

The broadly humanistic nature of Geertz's analysis and rhetoric is initially attractive, not to say seductive. To be sure, it is worth noting that a strange mushroom can call into question an entire system of thought and belief, although this is hardly something which any toadstool does either necessarily or in and of itself. *Pace* Geertz's assertion that "the odd, strange, and uncanny simply must be accounted for," there is nothing simple here and nothing categorically imperative. Rather, like any anomaly, a fast-growing toadstool *may be employed by human actors* who seek to discredit a given system of belief and thereby challenge a social order that is in some measure sustained by that belief system. What one longs to know—and what Geertz does not tell us—is the position within the local sociopolitical hierarchy of (1) those people who first recognized the toadstool and posed questions about it, (2) those who spread word of it, (3) those who argued that it rendered established beliefs unworkable, and (4) those who argued it did not. Given such information as this, one might be able to draw reasonable conclusions about what was at issue in this celebrated incident; such information lacking, one can only hypothesize.

In other instances, we are better informed and may observe how members of subordinate classes have, on occasion, made telling use of anomaly as an instrument of revolutionary agitation. Among such anomalies ought to be numbered lascivious monks, cake-eating peasants, and mad tea parties in which Indians who are not Indians consume vast amounts of tea without drinking any. Also noteworthy is the attribution of treason to Louis XVI, treason being in 1793 formally defined as a crime against the king. The moral, legal, and logical conundrum of trying and executing a man for a crime committed against himself was hardly lost on those who participated in the trial, yet far from recoiling at the seemingly self-contradictory nature of the charge, several of the chief actors—Saint-Just and Robespierre above all—ably exploited it, their aim being not merely to convict one king, but to deconstruct kingship and its correlated sociopolitical order.[19]

Having mentioned the trial of Louis XVI, it is worth considering certain aspects of the discourse implicit in his execution. For if—as divine right monarchs and their ideological apologists regularly claimed—a king stands in relation to the rest of society as does the head to the body, then regicidal decapitation is an act in which the very body of a king is transformed into a model of the nonmonarchic (i.e., acephalous) society, which is through that very action and in that very moment being constructed. This same point was raised to explicitude in the famous aside Cromwell is said to have made to Algernon Sydney during the trial of Charles I: "I tell you, we will cut off his head with the crown on it." And when the house of Stuart was restored in 1660, this same system of symbolic discourse was put to opposite use, for at that time the regicides of 1649 were hung and not beheaded, a mode of execution that accentuates the very distinction between head and torso that decapitation annihilates. Moreover, as the ultimate act of deconstructing nonmonarchic society, the second Charles had those regicides who had died during the interregnum—most prominently Cromwell and Ireton—exhumed and hanged, reasserting through the anomalous image of hanged dead men, not only the absolute, even capricious, power of monarchic rule, but also the shape of monarchic society, wherein heads remain always atop the body (see Fig. 10.4).

In all of this, there is nothing "automatic" or "necessary," to return to

	Body	Society
Norm	Head atop body	King as head of society
Revolutionary anomaly	Decapitated king	Kingship overthrown
Counterrevolutionary counteranomaly	Regicides hung, even when dead	Kingship restored

Figure 10.4. Symbolic dimensions of regicide and restoration in seventeenth-century England.

Needham's terms. Actors in any given situation may or may not recognize and employ anomalies in such fashion, depending on strategic considerations and other contingencies. Headless monarchs, exhumed regicides, wayward holymen, and cake-eating peasants are no more inherently dangerous than are toadstools, androgynes, foam, dawn, or spears forged on Sundays. In the right hands, however, and under the right circumstances, such anomalous entities can become potent weapons, for like all others, the social contract has also its loopholes—if only one knows where to find them.

Unconcluding Postscripts

The final chapters of scholarly books—regularly and almost obligatorily entitled "Conclusion"—are the sites in which authors pretend there is something conclusive to be said, and provide satisfying closures for the stories they have told. In some cases "Summation" or "Synopsis" would be a more honest, if less inviting title: Such chapters can provide a useful rehash for those readers who have bothered with the preceding pages and an even more useful précis for those who have not. Were the contents of this book even minimally summarizable, I would be sorely tempted to adopt such a strategy.

Authors who need to draw nonlinear and open-ended stories to a graceful finish, however, are afforded no such easy solution and must find other ways to accomplish their aims. Often they choose to take leave of their data altogether and raise the discussion to an entirely different level, producing thereby finales that might well be entitled "Transcendental Aroma of the Preceding Work" or "Abstractions of a Theoretical (and De-natured) Nature." Such a strategy gives me pause, less for its pomposity (although there is that) than for the hierarchical structure implicit in the vertical imagery of the verb *to raise* and the notion of *levels,* through which it is insinuated that theory and those who advance it stand somehow above practice and its practitioners, just as concluding chapters stand as the head to their preceding textual bodies.

In recent years the dichotomization of theory and practice, with corollary privileging of the former has become such a commonplace of intellectual and academic life that it generally passes unquestioned. On closer scrutiny, however, one finds that this taxonomic system, like others, encodes and helps to construct an associated social hierarchy. Specifically, it reflects and reproduces in its essentials the division of labor into mental and manual components, with primacy of place reserved for the former. Thus, if one grants the initial premise that working with words and ideas is better than working with hands and matter, it consequently follows that theory (i.e., thinking and speaking about thought and speech, or that activity we can designate as Mental Labor[2] must exceed in the same measure thinking and speaking about matters more concrete. Still better must be that mode of discourse that some term *metatheory* (= Mental Labor[3]), that is, thinking and speaking about the thought and speech lesser theoreticians employ in their thinking and speaking about the thought and speech of others yet, who themselves stand closer to concretion. In principle this privileging of theory could be extended more or less infinitely (Mental Labor$^{[n + 1]}$ always being greater than Mental Labor^n), such that thought and speech might move to planes as rarefied as they are sterile.

Preferable, I believe, is to leave theory embedded in practice whenever possible, so that generalizations may gradually emerge from the detailed analysis of specific materials. When such generalizations are finally presented, however, they might well be announced with more trepidation than bombast as the precipitate, not the essence or transcendence, of specific, concrete studies.

In the researches that constitute this book, I have tried to explore how the complementary instruments of force and discourse have been and can be used in the construction and reconstruction of social groups and hierarchies. In order to engage that vast topic, I have mixed studies of different historic eras, geographic locales, discursive forms, political situations, and cultural contexts, which seems to me the only possible way one can work toward generalizations that are truly general and not merely representative of some select subsection of human experience. Nor does the charge of comparatism bother me, for—to put it bluntly—the only alternative to comparison is one brand of parochialism or another: That is, the stance of those who privilege the data with which they happen to be familiar while ignoring, and thus remaining ignorant of, the rest.[1] Among the more prevalent brands are ethnocentrism, androcentrism, Eurocentrism, and the other centrisms as yet unnamed (e.g., those of class, temporality, and genre), all of which yield generalizations of a highly prejudicial nature—and not accidentally so.[2]

In this work I must also acknowledge that I have drawn upon the work of other scholars without paying particular attention to their disciplinary identities and have profited much from the researches of those who call themselves historians, anthropologists, sociologists, historians of religions, classicists, indologists, semioticians, and area specialists of various sorts. Those who champion such profligate pilferage tend to call it interdisciplinary research, whereas others may view it as simply undisciplined. I prefer to think of it as actively and aggressively antidisciplinary, for I understand and intend my practice to be a form of resistance to and an act of sabotage against, a tendentious taxonomy of knowledge and its legitimating discourses.[3] Inquiry into the relation between discourse and society inevitably reflects back on the society and discourse of academics, and among its other virtues cuts across the divide that is thought to separate the humanities from the social sciences, thereby calling into question the classificatory logic through which such a division is authorized and commonly accepted.

With regard to the issue of discourse and society, I cannot pretend to have reached any conclusive answers. Indeed, for reasons I have tried to spell out, I would distrust any answers for which such a claim were advanced, because the inquiry is not so much inconclusive as it is unconcluded and unconcludable. Accordingly, the following generalizations, which have been artificially abstracted from the preceding chapters, are meant to be neither exhaustive nor definitive, but to provide a simplified and schematic summary of the views to which these studies have led me:

1. Society in its essence consists not of impersonal structures, but of human beings who feel or come to feel more affinity for, than estrangement from, one another. This being so, society is reconstructed in some measure whenever sentiments emerge that draw together those who previously felt separated or separate those who previously felt commonality.

2. The useful metaphor of social borders describes that situation in which persons who, feeling more estrangement from, than affinity toward, one another, regard each other as members of different societies.[4]

3. Within any society there exist (in actuality and even more in potential) a large number of varied subgroups, the members of which feel ambivalent mixes of affinity for, and estrangement from, one another. This situation may be described through the metaphors of segmentation and cleavage.

4. The integration of any society depends on the peaceful management of cleavages such that sentiments of affinity predominate over those of estrangement, whereas social disintegration (through schism, civil war, etc.) follows from situations in which sentiments of estrangement come to prevail.

5. The constituent subgroups of any society are encompassed within hierarchic orders and enjoy differential rank and privileges, including (most importantly) differential access to, and control over, scarce resources of a material and nonmaterial nature.

6. Such hierarchies and the inequities they engender are always subject to contestation. They are defended, above all, through those discourses that legitimate or mystify their structures, premises, and workings. Insofar as such discourses remain broadly persuasive, hierarchic orders are able to sustain most challenges.

7. Those discourses that disrupt previously persuasive discourses of legitimation and those that mobilize novel social formations by evoking previously latent sentiments of affinity or estrangement are among the most powerful instruments of social change.

8. When previously persuasive discourses no longer persuade and previously prevalent sentiments no longer prevail, society enters a situation of fluidity and crisis. In such moments competing groups continue to deploy strategic discourses and may also make use of coercive force as they struggle, not just to seize or retain power, but to reshape the borders and hierarchic order of society itself.

Minneapolis, Minnesota
21 June 1988

Notes

Introduction

1. Roland Barthes, *Mythologies* (London: Jonathan Cape, 1972), p. 142.
2. Several other studies have advanced analyses that are formally (if not materially) similar to that of Barthes, in that they characterize myth (or some subset of myth) as inherently reactionary and attempt to locate another category of discourse that is its dialectic (and political) opposite. Thus, for example, Antonio Buttitta, *Semiotica e antropologia* (Palermo, It.: Sellerio, 1979), pp. 126–33 contrasted myth to utopia; Roger Bastide, "Mythes et utopies," *Cahiers internationaux de sociologie* 28 (1960): 3–12, contrasted myth-as-defined-by-Barthes to myth-as-defined-by-Georges Sorel; and in "Der politische Gehalt des Mythos," in Hans-Peter Duerr, ed., *Alcheringa, oder die beginnende Zeit: Studien zu Mythologie, Schamanismus, und Religion* (Frankfurt am Main: Qumran Verlag, 1983), pp. 9–25, an article that I would now reject as too simplistic, I contrasted cosmogonic to eschatological myth.
3. Barthes, p. 146.
4. Maurice Bloch, "The Past and the Present in the Present," *Man* 18 (1977): 284–85; cf. idem, "Symbols, Song, Dance and Features of Articulation: Or Is Religion an Extreme Form of Traditional Authority?" *Archives européennes de sociologie* 15 (1974): 55–81. Influenced by, and supportive of, Bloch are, inter alia, Diane J. Austin, "History and Symbols in Ideology: A Jamaican Example," *Man* 14 (1979): 497–514; Arjun Appadurai, "The Past as a Scarce Resource," *Man* 16 (1981): 201–19; and J.D.Y. Peel, "Making History: The Past in the Ijesha Present," *Man* 19 (1984): 111–32. Critical have been M.F.C. Bourdillon, "Knowing the World or Hiding It? A Response to Maurice Bloch," *Man* 13 (1978): 591–99; and Leopold E.A. Howe, "The Social Determination of Knowledge: Maurice Bloch and Balinese Time," *Man* 16 (1981): 220–34.
5. Bloch, "Past and Present in the Present," p. 281.
6. Ibid., p. 278.
7. Myth and ritual apparently held little interest for Marx per se, insofar as he would have viewed them as component parts of religion. It should be stressed, however, that it was Marx's early analyses of religion, in which he pursued lines

opened up by Ludwig Feuerbach and other of the Young Hegelians, that culmi-nated in his broader and infinitely more far-reaching theory of ideology. For the development of his thought along these lines, see in particular *Contributions to a Critique of Hegel's Philosophy of Right* (1844), *Theses on Feuerbach* (1845), and (with Engels) *The German Ideology* (1845–46).

8. Émile Durkheim and Marcel Mauss, *Primitive Classification* (Chicago: Uni-versity of Chicago Press, 1963), see esp. p. 8; cf. Pierre Bourdieu, *Outline of a Theory of Practice* (Cambridge: Cambridge University Press, 1977), pp. 97, 163–65.

9. This is hardly a new idea. Already in the fifth century B.C.E., the pre-Socratic philosopher Empedocles described all social (and all cosmic!) processes as the con-sequence of two opposed forces: that which draws things together and that which divides them, which he rather poetically termed *Love* (Greek, *philotēs*) and *Strife* (Greek, *eris*), respectively. More recently, see Bourdieu, *A Theory of Practice*, pp. 124–30. I am aware, of course, that use of the term *sentiment* is likely to cause some problems, given the almost insuperable difficulty of speaking with precision about the affective dimension of social life; at times I have considered coining a neologism to avoid talk of sentiment, for example, speaking of the sociogravitational forces of attraction and repulsion that can be stimulated by discourse. Always, however, the cure has seemed worse than the disease.

Chapter 1

1. A.S.P. Woodhouse (ed.), *Puritanism and Liberty: Being the Army Debates, 1647–1649, from the Clarke Manuscripts,* 2d ed. (London: J.M. Kemp, 1974), p. 52 (emphasis added). That Ireton foresaw the likelihood of such an objection being raised is indicated by his initial specification that "no memory of *record*" could go beyond the constitution then current. Interjections such as Cowling's were quite rare in the debates, which were characterized by a remarkable decorum throughout, at least to judge from the transcripts. Also atypical is the brevity of Ireton's inter-rupted speech. Most fully on these debates, see Austin Woolrych, *Soldiers and Statesmen: The General Council of the Army and its Debates 1647–1648* (London: Oxford University Press, 1987).

2. Ibid., p. 53. On this theme, see Christopher Hill, "The Norman Yoke," in John Saville, ed., *Democracy and the Labour Movement: Essays in Honour of Dona Torr* (London: Lawrence and Wishart, 1954), pp. 11–66.

3. Woodhouse, *Puritanism and Liberty,* p. 52.

4. Ibid., p. 54.

5. John Wildman sought to turn this state of affairs to the Levellers' advantage, by rendering problematic the question of who produced written texts and why, arguing as follows: "Our case is to be considered thus: that we have been under slavery, that's acknowledged by all. Our very laws were made by our conquerors; and whereas it's spoken much of chronicles, I conceive there is no credit to be given to any of them; and the reason is because those what were our lords, and made us their vassals, would suffer nothing else to be chronicled." (Woodhouse, *Puritanism and Liberty,* pp. 65–66).

6. Christopher Hill, *The Century of Revolution: 1603–1714* (Edinburgh: Thomas Nelson, 1961), p. 179.

7. Leon Trotsky, *The Spanish Revolution (1931–1939)* (New York: Pathfinder Press, 1973).

8. Ibid., p. 139.

9. Ibid., 385.

10. On the nature of such systems, see, for example, Meyer Fortes and E.E. Evans-Pritchard, eds., *African Political Systems*. (Oxford: Oxford University Press, 1940); Laura Bohannon, "A Genealogical Charter," *Africa* 22 (1952): 301–15; M.G. Smith, "Segmentary Lineage Systems," *Journal of the Royal Anthropological Institute* 86 (1956): 39–80; Marshall Sahlins, "The Segmentary Lineage: An Organization of Predatory Expansion," *American Anthropologist* 63 (1961): 322–45; P.C. Salzman, "Does Complementary Opposition Exist?" *American Anthropologist* 80 (1978): 53–70; and John Galaty, "Models and Metaphors: On the Semiotic Explanation of Segmentary Systems," in L. Holy and M. Stuchlik, eds., *The Structure of Folk Models* (New York: Academic Press, 1981), pp. 63–92.

11. See, inter alia, Émile Durkheim, *The Elementary Forms of the Religious Life*, J.M. Swain, trans. (London: Allen & Unwin, 1915), pp. 240–42, 431–32; Durkheim and Mauss, *Primitive Classification*, pp. 85–88; Marcel Mauss, *The Gift* (New York: Norton, 1967), pp. 76–81; idem, *Oeuvres*. Vol. 3: *Cohésion sociale et divisions de la sociologie* (Paris: Éditions de Minuit, 1969), pp. 17, 314–15. Cf. Clifford Geertz, *The Interpretation of Cultures* (New York: Basic Books, 1973), p. 449.

12. As might be expected, such tampering is quite common. See, for instance, the classic discussions of Bronislaw Malinowski, *Magic, Science and Religion and Other Essays* (Garden City, N.Y.: Doubleday, Anchor Books, 1954), pp. 125–26, 146; Gregory Bateson, *Naven* (Stanford, Calif.: Stanford University Press, 1958), pp. 125–28; Edmund Leach, *Political Systems of Highland Burma* (London: Athlone Press, 1954), pp. 264–78. Also relevant in a broader fashion are E.J. Hobsbawm, "The Social Function of the Past: Some Questions," *Past and Present* 55 (1972): 3–17; and Eric Hobsbawm and Terence Ranger, eds., *The Invention of Tradition* (Cambridge: Cambridge University Press, 1983).

13. E.E. Evans-Pritchard, *The Nuer* (Oxford: Oxford University Press, 1940). This is the standard source on the Nuer and remains a classic of anthropological writing. In recent years, however, some of the limitations of this work have been brought to light and a number of authors have attempted to reassess the nature of Nuer society and of Nuer–Dinka relations. For a variety of views, see Peter J. Newcomer, "The Nuer Are Dinka," *Man* 7 (1972): 5–11; Maurice Glickman, "The Nuer and the Dinka: A Further Note," *Man* 7 (1972): 586–94; Aidan Southall, "Nuer and Dinka Are People: Ecology, Ethnicity and Logical Possibility," *Man* 11 (1976): 463–91; Idem, "The Illusion of Nath Agnation," *Ethnology* 25 (1986): 1–20; John W. Burton, "Ethnicity on the Hoof: On the Economics of Nuer Identity," *Ethnology* 20 (1981): 157–62; Bruce Lincoln, *Priests, Warriors, and Cattle* (Berkeley: University of California Press, 1981), pp. 13–48; Douglas H. Johnson, "The Fighting Nuer: Primary Sources and the Origins of a Stereotype," *Africa* 51 (1981): 508–27; idem, "Tribal Boundaries and Border Wars: Nuer–Dinka Relations in the Sobat and Zaraf Valleys, c. 1860–1976," *Journal of African History* 23 (1982): 183–203; Ivan Karp and Kent Maynard, "Reading *The Nuer*," *Current Anthropology* 24 (1983): 481–503; and Raymond C. Kelly, *The Nuer Conquest: The Structure and Development of an Expansionist System* (Ann Arbor: University of Michigan Press, 1985). Details on cattle raiding are found in the last-named source, pp. 36–44; some related mythic materials are discussed in R. Godfrey Lienhardt, "Getting Your Own Back: Themes in Nilotic Myth," in J.H.M. Beattie and R.G. Lienhardt, eds., *Studies in Social Anthropology: Essays in Memory of E. E. Evans-Pritchard* (Oxford: Clarendon Press, 1975), pp. 213–37.

14. Evans-Pritchard, *The Nuer,* p. 125.

15. Ibid., pp. 126–27.

16. E.E. Evans-Pritchard, "The Nuer, Tribe and Clan," *Sudan Notes and Records* 17 (1934): 2. Emphasis added.

17. As always, the presence of an observer distorts the phenomenon observed. It is clear to me that stories of Montaperti were told in part for my benefit and that my obvious interest produced elaborated versions. This notwithstanding, many Sienese were competent to produce highly wrought versions of the story and did so with little prompting and evident pleasure.

18. The use of select moments from the past as an instrument through which hostilities are maintained between contending groups that are superficially integrated within a weak state is an important feature in some of the most bitter conflicts of the contemporary world, as for instance in Northern Ireland and Sri Lanka, on which see S. Saugestad Larsen, "The Glorious Twelfth: The Politics of Legitimation in Kilbroney," in A.P. Cohen, ed., *Belonging: Identity and Social Organisation in British Rural Cultures* (Manchester: Manchester University Press, 1982), pp. 278–91, and Bruce Kapferer, *Legends of People, Myths of State: Violence, Intolerance, and Political Culture in Sri Lanka and Australia* (Washington: Smithsonian Institution Press, 1988), respectively. Also of interest regarding the microdiscursive politics of social formation, with reference to Sri Lanka is Michael Roberts, "Ethnicity in Riposte at a Cricket Match: The Past for the Present," *Comparative Studies in Society and History* 27 (1985): 401–429.

19. One runs the risk of unduly stressing this point. Perhaps it is most accurate to say that a story like that of Montaperti is an instrument *capable* of arousing such sentiments. Whether it actually does so on any given occasion depends on many factors: the precise composition of the audience, the skill of the teller, external circumstances at the time of the telling, and so forth.

20. It is worth stressing that the Nuer make truth-claims for their narrative no less fully warranted by their own criteria of verifiability than are the parallel claims of Sienese and Swedes. By relegating the Nuer story to the category of myth and regarding the others as history, we merely ratify shared Euro-American criteria, and reject other criteria that are foreign to us. For a discussion of norms invoked in different cultures to adjudicate narratives' truth-claims, see Appadurai, "The Past as a Scarce Resource."

21. Although one may speak of credibility as if it were inherent within a narrative, such, of course, is not the case. Rather, this is a measure of the audience's response to the narrative's contents, and as the composition of an audience will inevitably change over time, as will the circumstances in which a given narrative is told and heard, so it may gain or lose credibility, thereby moving from the class of Legend to that of History, or vice versa. In a deservedly celebrated article "The Truth of Myth" (in *Essays on the History of Religions* [Leiden, Neth.: E.J. Brill, 1967], pp. 11–23), Raffaele Pettazzoni showed a sense of the categoric mobility possessed by mythic narratives, but he undercut the value of his own analysis by speaking of myth as "true stories" instead of "stories the truth-claims of which are generally accepted."

22. Malinowski, *Magic, Science and Religion,* pp. 93–148; Geertz, *Interpretation of Cultures,* pp. 93–94.

Chapter 2

1. Hilda Kuper, *The Uniform of Colour: A Study of White–Black Relationships in Swaziland* (Johannesburg, S. Afr.: Witwatersrand University Press, 1947), pp. 103–4.

2. Another version collected by J.P. Crazzolara (*Zur Gesellschaft und Religion der Nueer* [Vienna: Missionsdruckerei St. Gabriel, 1953], pp. 68–69) is essentially identical to that of Evans-Pritchard; still another version shows considerable and significant variation in its details (V.H. Fergusson, "The Nuong Nuer," *Sudan Notes and Records* 4 [1921]: 148–50).

3. H.C. Jackson, "The Nuer of the Upper Nile Province," *Sudan Notes and Records* 6 (1923): 70–73.

4. P.P. Howell, *A Manual of Nuer Law* (London: Oxford University Press, 1954), pp. 190–94.

5. Burton, "Ethnicity on the Hoof," p. 159.

6. H.C. Jackson, "Nuer of the Upper Nile Province," p. 59. Emphasis added.

7. Evans-Pritchard, *The Nuer,* p. 221; cf. Howell, *Manual of Nuer Law,* pp. 56, 83.

8. The most recent literature (see chap. 1, n. 11) has emphasized that any attempt to draw a hard and fast distinction between two groups called, respectively, Nuer and Dinka is simplistic and misleading in the extreme. See, for example, Southall, "Nuer and Dinka Are People," p. 487; Johnson, "The Fighting Nuer"; idem, "Tribal Boundaries and Border Wars"; and Burton, "Ethnicity on the Hoof." The last states bluntly, "The static ethnic designations which anthropologists have come to regard as empirically verifiable in this region of Africa serve to mystify rather than clarify extant realities of economic and ecological adaptation" (p. 157).

9. Within a large and growing literature, I have found the following particularly useful: Michael M.J. Fischer, *Iran: From Religious Dispute to Revolution* (Cambridge: Harvard University Press, 1980); Nikki Keddie, *Roots of Revolution* (New Haven, Conn.: Yale University Press, 1981); Hans Kippenburg, "Jeder Tag 'Ashura, Jedes Grab Kerbala," in Kurt Greussing, ed., *Religion und Politik im Iran: Mardom Nameh—Jahrbuch zur Geschichte und Gesellschaft des mittleren Orients* (Frankfurt am Main: Syndikat, 1981), pp. 217–56; Jerrold D. Green, *Revolution in Iran: The Politics of Countermobilization* (New York: Praeger, 1982); Theda Skocpol, "Rentier State and Shi'a Islam in the Iranian Revolution," *Theory and Society* 11 (1982): 265–84; Shahrough Akhavi, "The Ideology and Praxis of Shi'ism in the Iranian Revolution," *Comparative Studies in Society and History* 25 (1983): 195–221; Gudmar Aneer, *Imam Ruhullah Khumaini, Shah Muhammad Riza Pahlavi and the Religious Traditions of Iran* (Uppsala, Swed.: Almquist & Wiksell, 1985); Asaf Hussain, *Islamic Iran: Revolution and Counter-revolution* (New York: St. Martin's Press, 1985); Mary Hegland, "Two Images of Husain: Accommodation and Revolution in an Iranian Village," in Nikki R. Keddie, ed., *Religion and Politics in Iran* (New Haven, Conn.: Yale University Press, 1983), pp. 218–35; Christian Bromberger, "La seduzione del potere: Procedure simboliche di legittimazione nel Islam rivoluzionario," in Carla Pasquinelli, ed., *Potere senza stato* (Rome: Riuniti, 1986), pp. 115–34; and Ali Reza Sheikholeslami, "From Religious Accommodation to Religious Revolution: The Transformation of Shi'ism in Iran," in A. Banuazizi and M. Weiner, eds., *The State, Religion, and Ethnic Politics* (Syracuse, N,Y.: Syracuse University Press, 1986), pp. 227–55.

10. In the course of the revolution, this calendric reform was reversed, but the concession had little effect. Significantly, new holidays were introduced after the revolution and served as part of the attempt to construct an Islamic republic. Among these was celebration of the Battle of Qādisīyyah, in which the Arab Muslims effected the conquest of Zoroastrian Iran in 642 C.E. Almost simultaneously, the same holiday was established in Iraq by Saddam Husayn, for whom it was the Arab–Iranian dimension of the conquest that was of focal importance, not the triumph of Islam over Zoroastrians and, in the shah's case, suspected crypto-Zoroastrians.

11. William O. Beeman, "Images of the Great Satan: Representations of the United States in the Iranian Revolution," in N. Keddie, ed., *Religion and Politics in Iran* (New Haven, Conn.: Yale University Press, 1983), p. 210. It was even rumored that when informed that Zoroastrians do not accept converts, the shah replied this was no problem, for Iranians had always, in effect, been Zoroastrians, their apparent conversion to Islam having been only superficial.

12. Marshall G.S. Hodgson, *The Venture of Islam*, Vol. 1. *The Classical Age of Islam* (Chicago: University of Chicago Press, 1974), p. 217.

13. Although consideration of events since 1979 falls beyond the scope of the present discussion, one may observe that insofar as the 'ulama supplied the chief instrument through which the revolutionary coalition was constructed, they maintained considerable control over revolutionary discourse and praxis. In the months after the shah's departure, those elements within this coalition who had thought that they could use the clergy and the Karbala myth in an opportunistic fashion—for example, the predominantly secular politicians such as Abolhassan Bani-Sadr, Mehdi Bazargan, members of the Tudeh, the Mujahedeen i Khalq, and others—found themselves rapidly estranged from the new Iranian society in one way or another: exile, execution, or simple marginalization.

Chapter 3

1. Earlier discussions of this text are to be found in James Hope Moulton, *Early Zoroastrianism* (London: Williams & Norgate, 1913), pp. 399–402; Émile Benveniste, *The Persian Religion According to the Chief Greek Texts* (Paris: Paul Geuthner, 1929), pp. 69–117; Joseph Bidez and Franz Cumont *Les mages hellénisés*, Vol. 2. (Paris: Société les belles lettres, 1938), pp. 70–79; and J. Gwyn Griffiths, ed., *Apuleius of Madauros, The Isis-Book (Metamorphoses, Book XI)* (Leiden, Neth.: E.J. Brill, 1970), pp. 470–92.

2. See Bruce Lincoln, *Myth, Cosmos, and History: Indo-European Themes of Creation and Destruction* (Cambridge: Harvard University Press, 1986), pp. 141–71, esp. p. 146.

3. On this text, see H. Windisch, *Die Orakel des Hystaspes. Verhandelingen der koninklijke Akademie van Wetenschappen te Amsterdam*, Afdeeling Letterkunde, Nieuwe Reeks 28/3 (1929); and John R. Hinnells, "The Zoroastrian Doctrine of Salvation in the Roman World: A Study of the Oracle of Hystaspes," in J.R. Hinnells and E.J. Sharpe, eds., *Man and His Salvation: Studies in Memory of S.G.F. Brandon* (Manchester, Eng.: Manchester University Press, 1973), pp. 125–48. A bibliography of earlier literature is found in the latter, p. 126.

4. Hinnells, "Zoroastrian Doctrine of Salvation," pp. 138–39.

5. In citing these comparative data, I do not mean to imply that there exists

any historic connection among them (although such is possible in some instances) nor any sort of archetypal symbolism that informs them. Nor does it seem that the image in every instance bears the same generalized sociopolitical content. As always, only a thorough examination of a given text along with its full social and historic context will permit reasonable interpretation. Among other occurences within the ancient world, note: *Isaiah* 2.14 and 40.4, *Ezekiel* 38.20, *Habbakuk* 3.6, *Job* 9.5, *Psalms* 46.2–3, the *Assumption of Moses* 10.4, *Baruch* 5.7, *Ethiopic Enoch* 1.6, and the *Sibylline Oracles* 3.777–79 among Jewish sources; *1 Corinthians* 13.2, *Revelation* 16.20, the *Sibylline Oracles* 8.236, and Lactantius's *De Ave Phoenice* 5–6 among Christian sources; Euripides, *Trojan Women* 612ff., Asclepius 25, Eustatius, *Ad Iliadem* 16, and Seneca, *Consolatio Marcus* 26.6 among classical authors; Qu'rān, Sūra 18.47, 20.105–8, 56.5–6, 69.14, 73.14, 78.20, and 81.3 as well as *Haft Bāb-i Bābā Sayyid-nā*, chapter 3 (quoted by Marshall G.S. Hodgson, *The Order of Assassins* [The Hague, Neth.: Mouton, 1955], pp. 295–96) among Islamic sources; and among Buddhist texts, *Sukhāvatīyūha* 17–18. More recently, see *Macbeth* IV i, ll. 55–60 or the prophecies of John Frum, one of the earliest and most important leaders of cargo cult activity in Melanesia, in Peter Worsley, *The Trumpet Shall Sound: A Study of Cargo Cults in Melanesia* (New York: Schocken, 1968), pp. 99, 154. Also relevant and of considerable interest are the Paiela materials discussed by Aletta Biersack, "Prisoners of Time: Millenarian Praxis in a Melanesian Valley," in *Clio in Oceania*, A. Biersack, ed. (Washington, D.C.: Smithsonian Institution Press, forthcoming). Among these inhabitants of the New Guinea highlands, the practice of exogamy is conceptualized and strategically pursued as having for its ultimate goal the eradication of all the tribal and kinship distinctions that separate human beings one from another. Moreover, when this audacious project is ultimately accomplished, it is expected that the distinctions between sky and earth, night and day, good and evil, living and dead, and so forth will all disappear in a sweeping transformation of natural and social existence that is referred to as the time "when the ground ends."

6. Trans. Hok-lam Chan, "The White Lotus-Maitreya Doctrine and Popular Uprisings in Ming and Chi'ing China," *Sinologica* 10 (1969): 212–13.

7. Trans. A.C. Graham, *The Book of Lieh-tzü* (London: John Murray, 1960), p. 102.

8. Irwin Scheiner, "The Mindful Peasant: Sketches for a Study of Rebellion," *Journal of Asian Studies* 32 (1973): 587.

9. Quoted in Norman Cohn, *The Pursuit of the Millennium* (New York: Oxford University Press, 1970), p. 321. Typography as in the original. Regarding Coppe, the Ranters, and radical movements more generally during the English Civil War, the discussion of Christopher Hill, *The World Turned Upside Down* (New York: Viking, 1972) remains fundamental, notwithstanding the revisionist views of J.C. Davis, *Fear, Myth, and History: The Ranters and the Historians* (Cambridge: Cambridge University Press, 1986). See further A.L. Morton, *The World of the Ranters* (London: Lawrence and Wishart, 1970), J.F. McGregor and B. Reay, eds., *Radical Religion in the English Revolution* (London: Oxford University Press, 1984), and Jerome Friedman, *Blasphemy, Immorality, and Anarchy: The Ranters and the English Revolution* (Athens: Ohio University Press, 1987).

10. Quoted in Christopher Hill and Edmund Dell, eds., *The Good Old Cause: The English Revolution of 1640–1660* (London: Frank Cass, 1969), p. 331.

11. The efficacy—that is, the persuasive power—of a discourse such as "The Levellers' Rant" depends, of course, on the class identity and consciousness of its

audience. As a defense of the established order, it temporarily entertains a suggested inversion of that order only to disqualify the inversion, thereby restoring the status quo ante. See further discussion in chapter 9.

Chapter 4

1.   It should be obvious from the discussions that follow that I do not regard ritual as something necessarily, or even primarily, religious in nature. Rather, some rituals (like some myths) have a religious dimension, whereas others do not. Diagnostic in this regard is whether or not the claim is advanced that the origin or import of the ritual in question transcends the human sphere. Note in this regard the studies collected in Sally F. Moore and Barbara Myerhoff, eds., *Secular Ritual* (Amsterdam, Neth.: Van Gorcum, 1977).

2.   Reprinted in Max Gluckman, *Order and Rebellion in Tribal Africa* (New York: Free Press of Glencoe, 1963), pp. 110–36.

3.   Hilda Kuper, *An African Aristocracy: Rank Among the Swazi* (London: Oxford University Press, 1947/1961), pp. 197–225. Among Kuper's other works on the Swazi, note in particular *Uniform of Colour:* "A Royal Ritual in a Changing Political Context," *Cahiers d'études africaines* 12 (1972): 593–615; "Costume and Cosmology: The Animal Symbolism of the Ncwala," *Man* 8 (1973): 613–30; "Costume and Identity," *Comparative Studies in Society and History* 15 (1973): 348–67; *Sobhuza II: Ngwenyama and King of Swaziland* (New York: Africana Publishing Co., 1978); and "The Monarchy and the Military in Swaziland," in J. Argyle and E.P. White, eds., *Social System and Tradition in Southern Africa: Essays in Honour of Eileen Krige* (Cape Town, S. Afr.: Oxford University Press, 1978), pp. 222–39. Other important literature on the Swazi and the Ncwala ceremony includes T.O. Beidelman, "Swazi Royal Ritual." *Africa* 36 (1966): 373–405; Laura Makarius, "Une interprétation de l'Incwala Swazi: Étude du symbolisme dans la pensée et les rites d'un peuple africain," *Annales économies société civilisation* 28 (1973): 1403–22; John J. Grotpeter, *Historical Dictionary of Swaziland* (Metuchen, N.J.: Scarecrow Press, 1975); J.S.M. Matsebula, *A History of Swaziland,* 2d ed. (Cape Town, S. Afr.: Longman/Penguin Southern Africa, 1976); Christian P. Potholm, "The Ngwenyama of Swaziland: The Dynamics of Political Adaptation," in R. Lemarchand, ed., *African Kingships in Perspective: Political Change and Modernization in Monarchical Settings* (London: Frank Cass, 1977), pp. 129–59; Pierre Smith, "Aspects of the Organization of Rites," in M. Izard and P. Smith, eds., *Between Belief and Transgression: Structuralist Essays in Religion, History, and Myth* (Chicago: University of Chicago Press, 1982), pp. 103–26; Philip Bonner, "Classes, the Mode of Production and the State in Pre-colonial Swaziland," in Shula Marks and Anthony Atmore, eds., *Economy and Society in Pre-industrial South Africa* (London: Longman, 1980), pp. 80–101; *Kings, Commoners and Concessionaires: The Evolution and Dissolution of the Nineteenth-Century Swazi State* (Cambridge: Cambridge University Press, 1983); Andrew Apter, "In Dispraise of the King: Rituals 'Against' Rebellion in South-east Africa," *Man* 18 (1983): 521–34; Alan R. Booth, *Swaziland: Tradition and Change in a Southern African Kingdom.* Boulder, Colo.: Westview Press, 1983).

4.   My colleague, Richard Leppert, a musicologist by training, has pointed out to me regarding the songs:

It would be most interesting to investigate the nature of the sonorities, rhythms, etc., themselves, especially as the rituals proceed/change. Given the extraordinary importance of music to such cultures, the specific musical characters undoubtedly mediate powerfully the social and political issues. I'm reminded here of John Blacking's comments in *How Musical Is Man?* about the specific ways in which some South African music (carefully "preserved," with acute understanding of the cultural-political implications) served as a site of resistance to the inroads of European culture, via Christian evangelism's homogenized Western hymnody imposed on its "converts." It seems clear that the traditional music's changed function—no longer "simply" cultural replication, but now a political and cultural *resistance*—bears relation to the ritual as you've analyzed it (Personal communication 16 September 1987).

5. Kuper, *African Aristocracy*, p. 204. Translations of all other songs are taken from the same source.

6. The use of the third-person pronoun "they" in this song is ambiguous, and some authors have argued that it signifies the king's foreign enemies only. This line of argument is contradicted, however, by the use of such third-person locutions within ritual contexts as a means to express anger felt by the speaker but shared with numerous others, thus "the legalized, ritual and non-personal expressions of hatred" (Axel-Iver Berglund, *Zulu Thought Patterns and Symbolism* [Uppsala: Swedish Institute of Missionary Research, 1976], p. 326). Note also the statement of Selby Msimang in his unpublished study of the Ncwala, who says of this song that it is "an indirect allusion to the king's enemies, not necessarily from outside, but may be from members of the royal family, or among the tribesmen" (cited in Kuper, *African Aristocracy*, p. 207).

7. This song anticipates the success of both Ncwala and king insofar as one aim of the ritual is to produce rains at the end of the dry season, and it is the monarch who holds a monopoly on rain magic, thus on the production of thunder.

8. Reprinted in Gluckman's *Order and Rebellion in Tribal Africa*, pp. 110–36; on the Ncwala in particular, see esp. pp. 119–30. Gluckman's views were adopted and expanded on by Pierre L. van den Berghe, "Institutionalized Licence and Normative Stability," *Cahiers d'études africaines* 3 (1963): 413–23.

9. The latter half of the nineteenth century saw the rebellions of Fokoti, Somcuba, and Malambule against Mswati (r. 1839?–65); the rebellion of Mbilini against Ludvonga (heir to Mswati 1868–72, but never installed as king) and Ludvonga's murder, probably by Ndwandwe, his uncle and regent; as well as the rebellion of Mabedla against Mbandzeni (r. 1872–89). In addition there were countless plots with varying degrees of seriousness in which Dlamini princes conspired against different kings.

10. Beidelman, "Swazi Royal Ritual," esp. pp. 374–75, 401–4. For other critiques, see, inter alia, Edward Norbeck, "African Rituals of Conflict," *American Anthropologist* 65 (1963): 1254–79; and O.F. Raum, "The Interpretation of the Nguni First Fruit Ceremony," *Paideuma* 13 (1967): 148–63.

11. Beidelman, "Swazi Royal Ritual," p. 394.

12. For examples of what can be gained when rituals are studied with attention to *both* their social and their historic context, see Jean Comaroff, *Body of Power, Spirit of Resistance: The Culture and History of a South African People* (Chicago: University of Chicago Press, 1985); and Maurice Bloch, *From Blessing to Violence: History and Ideology in the Circumcision Ritual of the Merina of Madagascar* (Cambridge: Cambridge University Press, 1986).

13. Bonner, *Kings, Commoners and Concessionaires*, pp. 48–49.

14. Kuper, "A Royal Ritual in a Changing Political Context" and "Costume and Identity."

15. Kuper's attitudes toward the issue of change and continuity within the Ncwala are quite complex. She states that even though her initial observations were made at a time "when British colonialism appeared to be firmly entrenched," she was still "able to observe and describe a distinctive Swazi culture and the persistence of a social structure centered on Swazi Kingship" ("A Royal Ritual in a Changing Political Context," p. 593). Her interest in the Ncwala thus seems to have stemmed in large measure from her appreciation of the ways in which Swazi traditions were preserved therein, notwithstanding the ways in which other aspects of Swazi life were being transformed under colonialism. Tradition, however, is a more problematic category than is usually recognized, as Hobsbawm and Ranger, *Invention of Tradition*, have shown. For my part, I would argue that tradition was celebrated within the Ncwala precisely because of the encroachments of colonialism; it served as an instrument strategically employed to rally Swazi solidarity against such encroachments. Regarding the Ncwala of 1966, Kuper stressed the formal conservatism of the ceremony ("A Royal Ritual, in a Changing Political Context," 605–7), at the same time recognizing its profoundly different political implications during the precolonial, colonial, and postcolonial periods (ibid., pp. 595, 613–14).

16. On the *tinsila*, see Kuper, *African Aristocracy*, pp. 58, 78–79, 81–83. The only relationship paralleling that of the king and his *tinsila* is that which exists between the king and his two ritual wives, the only other persons with whom he exchanges his blood. Like the *tinsila*, these women also come from non-Dlamini clans, and the ritual of blood exchange appears an attempt to construct a category of person with whom the king can have ties as close as those of kinship, but lacking the potential for rivalry that kinship entails.

17. Ibid., pp. 82, 198. On codes of right and left among the Swazi, see Beidelman, "Swazi Royal Ritual," pp. 378–79, 381–83; more broadly, Rodney Needham, ed., *Right and Left: Essays on Dual Symbolic Classification* (Chicago: University of Chicago Press, 1973); and Serge Tcherkézoff, *Le roi Nyamwezi, la droit, et la gauche: Révision comparative des classifications dualistes* (Cambridge: Cambridge University Press, 1983).

18. Kuper, *African Aristocracy*, pp. 81–82.

19. Ibid., p. 82.

20. Cited in Kuper, *African Aristocracy*, p. 24. Emphasis added.

21. Ibid. More fully on this incident, see Bonner, *Kings, Commoners and Concessionaires*, pp. 192–94.

22. Cited in Kuper, *African Aristocracy*, p. 26.

23. Ibid., p. 28.

24. Ibid., pp. 28–29.

25. In this regard it is instructive to consider the struggle over rank and terminology that was evident in Sobhuza's dealings with Prince Arthur of Connaught, high commissioner for Basutoland, Bechuanaland, and Swaziland in the early 1920s. When the two first met (6 June 1921), they were introduced (by Prince Arthur's predecessor) as "The Paramount Chief, Sobhuza" and "His Royal Highness," respectively (Kuper, *Sobhuza II*, p. 76). Then, on Prince Arthur's first visit to Swaziland (6 September 1921), Queen Regent Gwamile Mdluli publically introduced him as "the grandson of the Most Gracious Sovereign, Queen Victoria, of

Blessed Memory," while stressing Sobhuza's more immediate connection to royalty, calling him "the son of Ngwane [= Bhunu], the son of Mbandzeni, the son of Mswati, the son of Sobhuza, the son of Ndungunye, the son of Ngwane, the son of Dlamini, all Kings of Swaziland" (ibid., p. 79). Also revealing is Prince Arthur's response to the first petition he received from Sobhuza, in which the latter called himself king. To this, Prince Arthur stated, in a letter of 19 December 1921:

> There is one matter which I wish to mention. I notice that the Petition contains numerous references to the Paramount Chief as "the King of Swaziland." The word "King" is not a correct translation of the word "Nkosi" by which the Paramount Chief is addressed in the Swazi language, and the style "King of Swaziland" is not one which I should be prepared to recognize. I do not think there could be a more dignified or a more appropriate title for the Chief of the Swazi than "Paramount Chief." . . . A Native Chief, like an official of the Government gains more dignity by using a title which is appropriate to his position than by using one which people might regard as high-sounding and pretentious. I hope in the future the title "Paramount Chief" will be used instead of the title "King" (cited in Matsebula, *History of Swaziland*, p. 167).

26. Kuper, "Monarchy and the Military," pp. 73–74.

27. I prefer this formulation to that advanced by A.W. Hoernlé (in her introduction to Kuper, *Uniform of Colour*, p. viii) which posited "one society with two cultures struggling to adjust themselves to one another." Beyond the understandable liberal delusions that informed such a statement (hardly were the British "struggling to adjust themselves"), it is the very question of whether there was *one* society present (this being the British view, which directly served their political and economic interests) or two rival societies (as the Swazi saw it) which lies at the heart of the issue. This same conflict over the proper placement of social borders might also be expressed in the politically volatile question of whether the British were aliens in Swaziland or not.

28. Kuper, *African Aristocracy*, p. 216; cf. idem, "A Royal Ritual in a Changing Political Context," p. 610.

29. Kuper states, "When I wrote that the presence of the Resident Commissioner 'in no way interfered with the proceedings,' I was aware of the extent of the subtle interplay between ruled and the rulers, but really meant that the performance was seen by the former as if the latter had not come; it was, of course, seen by the Resident Commissioner as an act of patronage, etc. (Private communication 9 April 1986).

30. On flight as a mode of resistance, see Cristiano Grottanelli, "Archaic Forms of Rebellion and their Religious Background," in Bruce Lincoln, ed., *Religion, Rebellion, Revolution* (London: Macmillan, 1985), pp. 17–22.

31. Kuper, *African Aristocracy*, p. 217.

32. Gluckman, *Order and Rebellion*, p. 124.

33. Kuper, *Sobhuza* II, p. 70n.

34. The *Mfukwane* are not used for plowing or other normal forms of labor; they are believed to possess great stores of magico-religious power. Their relation to normal cattle is thus analogous to that of royalty to commoners. Although the king, queen mother, and chief ritual queen anoint themselves with fat of the *Mfukwane*, should other individuals do so, they would go mad as a result.

35. Kuper, *African Aristocracy*, pp. 217–18.

36. Victor Turner, *The Forest of Symbols: Aspects of Ndembu Ritual* (Ithaca, N.Y.: Cornell University Press, 1967), p. 106.

37. Kuper, *African Aristocracy*, p. 219; cf. Beidelman, "Swazi Royal Ritual," p. 399; and Harriet Ngubane, *Body and Mind in Zulu Medicine* (London: Academic Press, 1977), pp. 151–53.

38. On 6 September 1968 the Kingdom of Swaziland (as it is officially known) celebrated its independence of British rule. Although this date fell outside the normal Ncwala period, it is noteworthy that Sobhuza, the queen mother, the other queens, the princesses, and the Swazi regiments all wore full Ncwala costumes to the formal ceremonies (Kuper, "Costume and Identity," p. 362). In all of sub-Saharan Africa, Swaziland is the only nation in which traditional kingship survived colonialism and emerged as the central political institution of the postcolonial era. Although hardly the full explanation for such a state of affairs, the ability of King Sobhuza II to use the Ncwala as an effective instrument for resisting the British and for solidifying his paramount position within the Swazi Nation, contributed in no small measure. Consideration of Swazi kingship and the Ncwala in the post-colonial period falls outside the scope of this study.

39. Partial exceptions are Gluckman's 1940 article "Analysis of a Social Situation in Modern Zululand," *Bantu Studies* 14: 1–30, 147–74; and Isaac Schapera, "Contact Between European and Native in South Africa: Bechuanaland," in Lucy Mair, ed., *Methods of Study of Culture Contact in Africa* (London: Oxford University Press, 1938), pp. 25–37.

40. Alternatively, and with certain advantages, one may treat such situations under the model of "plural societies" developed in Leo Kuper and M.G. Smith, eds., *Pluralism in Africa* (Berkeley: University of California Press, 1969).

41. See, for instance, Stuart Hall and Tony Jefferson, *Resistance Through Rituals: Youth Subcultures in Post-war Britain* (New York: Holmes & Meier, 1976); James C. Scott, *Weapons of the Weak: Everyday Forms of Peasant Resistance* (New Haven, Conn.: Yale University Press, 1985); Comaroff, *Body of Power; Spirit of Resistance;* and Bruce Lincoln, "Notes Toward a Theory of Religion and Revolution," in B. Lincoln, ed., *Religion, Rebellion, Revolution: An Interdisciplinary and Cross-cultural Collection of Essays* (London: Macmillan, 1985), pp. 272–76.

42. Kuper, *African Aristocracy*, p. 224.

Chapter 5

1. For the older tendency, see for example, Edmund Leach, "Ritual," in *International Encyclopedia of the Social Sciences* (New York: Macmillan, 1968), 13: 523–27; idem, *Culture and Communication* (Cambridge: Cambridge University Press, 1976). The more recent trend includes the work of such varied authors as Mikhail Bakhtin, Maurice Bloch, Pierre Bourdieu, Natalie Zemon Davis, Louis Dumont, Norbert Elias, Michel Foucault, Clifford Geertz, Stuart Hall, Sherry Ortner, Marshall Sahlins, Michael Taussig, E.P. Thompson, and Jean-Pierre Vernant, to name but a few.

2. Most recently on Tara, see Francis J. Byrne, *Irish Kings and High-Kings* (New York: St. Martin's Press, 1973). George Petrie, "On the History and Antiquities of Tara Hill," *Proceedings of the Royal Irish Academy*, sec. C, 18 (1839): 25–232 retains value, particularly for its collection of textual and archaeological evidence. It remains controversial whether the Feast of Tara was held annually, every three years, or only at each king's inauguration. On banquets and feasting

in general, see: Norbert Elias, *The History of Manners,* 2 vols. (New York: Pantheon Books, 1982); Cristiano Grottanelli, "L'ideologia del banchetto e l'ospite ambiguo," *Dialoghi di Archeologia* 3 (1981): 122–154; Jack Goody, *Cooking, Cuisine and Class: A Study in Comparative Sociology* (Cambridge: Cambridge University Press, 1982); and Sergio Bertelli and Giuliano Crifo, eds., *Rituale, Cerimoniale, Etichetta* (Milan: Bompiano, 1985), esp. the article of Cristiano Grottanelli, "Cibo, Istinti, Divieti," pp. 31–52.

3. A discussion of the Feast of Tara, with reproductions of the two diagrams can be found in Petrie, "Tara Hill," pp. 204–11. Two other Old Irish sources describe arrangements for the banquet and aid in the interpretation of these diagrams: The description of the hall that accompanies the diagram in both manuscripts (see Petrie, "Tara Hill," pp. 196–202) and a section of the *Metrical Dindsenchas* (1.3.149–80). A detailed discussion of how the reconstruction presented in Figure 5.1 was arrived at would be too technical for a work of this type. My attention was first called to the materials treated herein by the excellent discussion of Diego Poli, "La distribuzione nel banchetto celtico," *L'Uomo* 9 (1985): 75–97.

4. See Eoin MacNeill, "Ancient Irish Law. The Law of Status or Franchise," *Proceedings of the Royal Irish Academy,* (N.S.) sec. C, 16 (1923): 265–316, where the most important legal texts are presented in translation. Also, more recently, see Neil McLeod, "Interpreting Early Irish Law: Status and Currency," *Zeitschrift für celtische Philologie* 41 (1986): 46–65, and 42 (1987): 41–115.

5. See Wolfgang Meid, *Dichter und Dichtkunst im alten Irland* (Innsbruck, Aus.: Innsbrucker Beiträge zur Sprachwissenschaft, 1971); idem, "Dichtkunst, Rechtspflege und Medizin im alten Irland: Zur Struktur der altirischen Gesellschaft," in W. Meid et al., eds., *Antiquitates Indogermanicae: Gedenkschrift für Hermann Güntert* (Innsbruck, Aus.: Innsbrucker Beiträge zur Sprachwissenschaft, 1974), pp. 21–34.

6. Some of those without independent honorprice were also located in the serving area or toward the bottom of both tables on the inner sides: charioteers (D/1), pilots (C/6), jugglers (B/8), buffoons (C/8), and clowns (C/9).

7. The term *maél* recurs at positions B/1 and C/1, and is quite difficult to interpret. An ambiguous word, in different contexts it can mean any of the following: (1) the dishorned head of an animal; (2) some part of the shoulder, either the blade or scapula; (3) the lower end of the thighbone or femur. In the interpretations proposed here, I have been guided by the structure of the diagram. Thus, in its occurrence at the top (positions B/1 and C/1), the *maél* stands in contrast to the coccyx at the bottom (B/12): head as opposed to rectum. In its other occurrences (B/5 and C/5), it stands in contrast to the *loarc,* or haunch, at positions A/5a and D/5a: uppermost portion of the forelegs as opposed to uppermost portion of the hind.

8. The best discussion of the Irish data is Poli, "Distribuzione nel banchetto celtico." In English, see Philip O'Leary, "Contention at Feasts in Early Irish Literature," *Eigse* 20 (1984): 115–27. More broadly on this theme, see Marcel Detienne and Jean-Pierre Vernant, eds., *La cuisine du sacrifice en pays grec* (Paris: Gallimard, 1979); Gregory Nagy, *Best of the Achaeans* (Baltimore, Md.: The Johns Hopkins University Press, 1979), pp. 123–37; Gerhard J. Baudy, "Hierarchie oder: Die Verteilung des Fleisches," in B. Gladigow and H.G. Kippenberg, eds., *Neue Ansätze in der Religionswissenschaft* (Munich: Kösel Verlag, 1983), pp. 131–74; Cristiano Grottanelli, Nicola Parise, and Pier Giorgio Solinas, eds., "Sacrificio, organizzazione del cosmo, dinamica sociale," *Studi storici* 25 (1984): 829–956; idem,

"Divisione delle carni: Dinamica sociale e organizzazione del cosmo," *L'Uomo* 9 (1985): 3–298, and Grottanelli and Parise, eds., *Sacrificio e società nel mondo antico* (Rome: Laterza, 1988).

9. Two notes are in order regarding the translation. First, Greek *kôlēn* cannot simply mean thighs or legs here because it must be differentiated from *mērion*, which occurs later in the passage. It thus must mean hams or hind legs (cf. the byform *kôlē* ["thighbone with the flesh on it, ham"]). Second, it is a mark of the precision with which Posidonius observed these customs that he specifies the Celtic champion took only *one* thigh (presumably the right one) as his portion because the word for thigh (*to mērion*) appears in the singular here, but elsewhere in Greek literature always in the plural (*ta mēria*).

10. J.J. Tierney, "The Celtic Ethnography of Posidonius," *Proceedings of the Royal Irish Academy*, sec. C, 60 (1960): 201–2.

11. It is remarkable that this feast, the very point of which is to award hierarchically graded portions, should be called an "equal feast" (*daitos eisēs*). Several explanations are possible: (1) the adjective *eisos, eisē* here means just, not equal, signifying that appropriate, if disproportionate shares are awarded each person; (2) the phrase is formulaic (it recurs at *Iliad* 1.468, 1.602, 2.431, 9.225; *Odyssey* 11.185, 16.479, etc.) and was inserted within the present passage almost automatically, without cognizance of the contradictions it entails; or (3) the assertion that this feast is "equal" serves to mystify its otherwise all-too-transparent inequality. I favor the third option, but cannot entirely preclude the other two: In any event the three are not mutually exclusive. See Nagy, *Best of the Achaeans*, p. 128n; Detienne and Vernant, *Cuisine du sacrifice*, pp. 23–24; Anna Lydia Motto and John R. Clark, "Isē Dais: The Honor of Achilles," *Arethusa* 2 (1969): 109–125.

12. One clear distinction that emerges between Greek and Celtic practices is that whereas Ajax received the undivided tenderloin, the highest and most prestigious cut of all, Celtic champions received lesser pieces: thighs according to Athenaeus, shoulders according to the Feast of Tara diagram (D/2). What is more, in the latter text, the higher-ranking tenderloin was reserved for kings, judges, literati, and foremost nobles, all of whom remained superordinate to champions, however distinguished in battle the latter might be.

13. Stella Georgoudi, "L'égorgement sanctifié en Grèce moderne: Les Kourbánia des saints," in Detienne and Vernant, *Cuisine du sacrifice*, pp. 271–307; idem, "Viande sacrificielle et structures sociales dans la pratique du kourbani néogrec," *L'Uomo* 9 (1985): 201–14.

14. Wendy Doniger has alerted me to a story told by her mother, in which the same point is made, "Bismarck finds himself in the countryside as night falls and must take refuge at a humble inn. The innkeeper, being flustered at the presence of the great man, scurries about and finally apologizes: "Herr Bismarck, I am terribly sorry, I know you always sit at the head of the table, but here all we have is a round table. What shall we do?" "That's all right," says Bismarck, *"Wo ich setze ist oben"* (Personal communication, 5 June 1988). Also relevant is the earliest evidence on circular seating patterns among the Celts, Athenaeus's testimony that "when many dine together, they sit in a circle, and the most powerful man—he who surpasses the others either in his fortitude in battle, the eminence of his family, or his wealth—is in the middle, like the leader of a dramatic chorus. And the host is next to him, then on either side are the others, in order of their preeminence" (*Deipnosophistae* 4.152b).

15. The best source for this society is Walter Arnold, *The Life and Death of*

the Sublime Society of Steaks (London: Bradbury, Evans & Co., 1871). Other accounts (largely but not entirely dependent on Arnold) may be found in Louis C. Jones, *The Clubs of the Georgian Rakes* (New York: Columbia University Press, 1942), pp. 142–55; and Charles Cooper, *The English Table in History and Literature* (London: Sampson, Low, Marston, n.d.), pp. 81–96. The earl of Sandwich was, in fact, expelled from the club, apparently as the result of a political struggle that pitted its Whig against its Tory members. On this, see further, Jones, *Clubs of the Georgian Rakes,* pp. 135–139.

16.   Cited in Arnold, *Life and Death,* p. xiv.
17.   Ibid., p. 5.
18.   A list of the original members as well as one of all succeeding members is contained in Arnold, *Life and Death,* pp. xi–xii, and pp. xvii–xxiv, respectively.
19.   Quoted in Arnold, *Life and Death,* p. 22.
20.   See, inter alia, Victor Turner, *The Ritual Process: Structure and Anti-structure* (Chicago: Aldine, 1969), pp. 93–130.
21.   Arnold, *Life and Death,* p. 16.
22.   In an account of the club that was published in 1833 and quoted in Arnold, *Life and Death,* pp. 20–23, the author, having stated that he could never hope to join the society, "as they are a' far aboon my sphere" (p. 20), reports its chief attraction was that members dined "solely on Beef-steaks—and what glorious Beef-steaks!" (p. 21). That members understood themselves as an elite is evident from remarks such as Arnold's observation (p. 24f.) that election to the society was a distinction "coveted by many, but of necessity conferred on few."
23.   Arnold, *Life and Death,* p. 9. (Emphasis added.)
24.   See, for instance, the songs that appear in Arnold, *Life and Death,* pp. 81–84, 96–99, 143–47.
25.   Ibid., p. 24.
26.   It is of some theoretic interest to note that it was not the inherent contradictions of this group that brought about its demise. On the contrary, so long as those contradictions were intact, the Beefsteak Society thrived, and it was, in fact, when the contradictions dissolved that its existence became threatened.

Chapter 6

1.   Émile Durkheim, *The Elementary Forms of the Religious Life,* J. M. Swain, trans. (London: Allen and Unwin, 1915).
2.   See, in particular, Moore and Myerhoff, *Secular Ritual* and such cases as those in which revolutionary and postrevolutionary states attempt to construct secular rituals that will advance social integration, solidarity, and common purpose as studied by Mona Ozouf, *La fête révolutionnaire 1789–1799* (Paris: Gallimard, 1976); and Christel Lane, *The Rites of Rulers: Ritual in Industrial Society—the Soviet Case* (Cambridge: Cambridge University Press, 1981).
3.   Max Gluckman, "Les rites de Passage," in Max Gluckman, ed., *Essays on the Ritual of Social Relations* (Manchester, Eng.: Manchester University Press, 1962), p. 40.
4.   Emmanuel Le Roy Ladurie, *Carnival in Romans* (New York: George Braziller, 1979).
5.   From the large and rapidly growing literature on Carnival, see in particular: Yves-Marie Bercé, *Fête et révolte: Des mentalités populaires du XVIe au*

XVIIe siècle (Paris: Hachette, 1976); Bob Scribner, "Reformation, Carnival, and the World Turned Upside-Down," *Social History* 3 (1978): 303–29; Julio Caro Baroja, *Le Carnaval* (Paris: Gallimard, 1979); Laura Barletta, *Il carnevale del 1764 a Napoli: Protesta e integrazione in uno spazio urbano* (Naples: Società Editrice Napoletana, 1981); Pietro Clemente et al., "Il linguaggio, il corpo, la festa: Per un ripensamento della tematica di Michail Bachtin," *Metamorfosi* 7 (1983); particularly see ibid., Antonio Mélis, "Figure del rovesciamento e figure dell' alterità," pp. 153–68; Mikhail Bakhtin, *Rabelais and His World* (Bloomington: Indiana University Press, 1984); and Robert Dirks, *Black Saturnalia: Conflict and Its Ritual Expression on British West Indian Slave Plantations* (Gainesville: University of Florida Press, 1987).

6. The most important work on the St. Bartholomew's Massacre remains Janine Estèbe, *Tocsin pour un massacre: La saison des Saint-Barthélemy* (Paris: Éditions du Centurion, 1968), which I have followed for the most part.

7. Although I have focused on the broadest and most significant line of cleavage in French society of the late sixteenth century, there existed—as always—other lines of cleavage and subdivision. Among these, one of the most important is that which separated relative moderates within the Catholic party from their more militant coreligionists. In the period leading up to the massacre (i.e., August 1570–August 1572), the former group included most prominently the king and the queen mother; the latter, the heir apparent (Anjou), his younger brother the duc d'Alençon, the duc de Guise, and the cardinal of Lorraine (Guise's uncle). One can show the relations of these groups in a diagram.

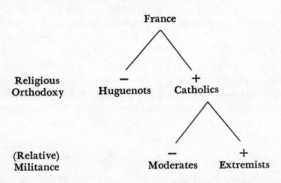

The position of the moderate Catholics was an ambiguous and mediating one, and their policies tilted alternately toward the Huguenots and toward the militant Catholics. A shift in their position was always significant and often had dramatic consequences, for instance, in the royal council on the night of 23 August 1572 when the St. Bartholomew's Massacre was authorized and planned. Protestant discourses that took the massacre as their starting point have also been studied by Robert M. Kingdon, *Myths About the St. Bartholomew's Day Massacres: 1572–1576* (Cambridge: Harvard University Press, 1988).

8. The extent to which one can interpret the French Wars of Religion as exhibiting features of class struggle remains controversial. For differing views, see the dispute between Janine Estèbe, "The Rites of Violence: Religious Riot in 16th Century France: A Comment," *Past and Present* 67 (1975): 127–30; and Natalie Zemon Davis, "A Rejoinder," *Past and Present* 67 (1975): 131–35.

9. See the discussion of Denis Richet, "Sociocultural Aspects of Religious Con-

flicts in Paris During the Second Half of the Sixteenth Century," in Robert Forster and Orest Ranum, eds., *Ritual, Religion, and the Sacred: Selections from the Annales*, Vol. 7 (Baltimore, Md.: The Johns Hopkins University Press, 1982), pp. 182–212.

10. Michael Walzer, *The Revolution of the Saints: A Study in the Origins of Radical Politics* (Cambridge: Harvard University Press, 1965), pp. 68–92.

11. Estèbe, *Tocsin pour un massacre*, p. 192.

12. Estèbe, "Rites of Violence," p. 130.

13. Barbara Diefendorf has stressed to me the extent to which sentiments of affinity based on ties of kinship, propinquity, and so on, continued to exist between Catholics and Huguenots in spite of their growing estrangement, even up to the time of the massacre. She states that "the process of disintegration was a very complex one whose progress was slowed by the persistence of many traditional social bonds, such that the ultimate rupture was all the more wrenching. [The view that] the Huguenots were by their religious affiliation alone immediately and directly cast out of traditional French society . . . results in oversimplification and obscures the true dynamic of the situation" (Personal communication, 19 July 1986).

14. See in particular Natalie Zemon Davis, *Society and Culture in Early Modern France* (Stanford, Calif.: Stanford University Press, 1975), pp. 152–87; Barbara Diefendorf, "Prologue to a Massacre: Popular Unrest in Paris, 1557–1572," *American Historical Review* 90 (1985), 1067–91.

15. Claude Lévi-Strauss, *The Elementary Structures of Kinship* (Boston: Beacon Press, 1969); cf. Pier Giorgio Solinas, "Guerra e matrimonio," in Pasquinelli, *Potere senza stato*, pp. 21–47.

16. On the reactions of Navarre's mother to the marriage, see Nancy Lyman Roelker, *Queen of Navarre: Jeanne d'Albret, 1528–1572* (Cambridge: Harvard University Press, 1968), pp. 354–83. On the general norms of marriage during this period and specifically on the emphasis accorded the freely given consent of bride and groom, see André Burguière, "The Marriage Ritual in France: Ecclesiastical Practices and Popular Practices (Sixteenth to Eighteenth Centuries)," in Forster and Ranum, *Ritual, Religion, and the Sacred*, pp. 8–23.

17. Estèbe, *Tocsin pour un massacre*, p. 103.

18. Ibid., p. 196.

19. The account of these masques is found in Estèbe, *Tocsin pour un massacre*, p. 105. Further details are in Roy Strong, *Art and Power: Renaissance Festivals 1450–1650* (Berkeley: University of California Press, 1984), pp. 111–13, although the interpretation of the latter is rather superficial.

20. For a critical discussion of the various sources, see N.M. Sutherland, *The Massacre of St. Bartholomew and the European Conflict 1559–1572* (London: Macmillan, 1973), pp. 312–37. Regarding the question of responsibility as ultimately unresolvable (both here and in "The Massacre of St. Bartholomew and the Problem of Spain," in Alfred Soman, ed., *The Massacre of St. Bartholomew: Reappraisals and Documents* [The Hague, Neth.: Martinus Nijhoff, 1974], pp. 15–24), Sutherland has argued forcefully that the motives for the assassination of Coligny were more related to international politics—specifically, the need to keep him from precipitating war with Spain—than to any domestic considerations. This ignores, however the relative dependence of foreign policy at this time on domestic considerations and explains only Coliguy's assassination, not the general massacre that followed.

21. The processes involved in the reshaping of society are nowhere more evi-

dent and more dramatic than in the deliberations that lead up to a purge. In this specific case disagreements centered on the fate of the Huguenot princes Navarre and Condé, who were ultimately spared by virtue of their royal blood. Alternatively, one might observe that in this moment the sentiments of affinity deriving from their membership in the royal family outweighed the sentiments of estrangement provoked by their religious affiliation. In the months following St. Bartholomew's, they were made virtual prisoners at court and were pressed to renounce their Protestantism, which they did in a formal abjuration and letter of confession that they sent to the pope on 29 September 1572 (see Estèbe, *Tocsin pour un massacre,* pp. 157–59).

22. Estèbe, *Tocsin pour un massacre,* p. 121.

23. For the fullest discussion, see Victor W. Turner, *Schism and Continuity in an African Society* (Manchester, Eng.: Manchester University Press, 1957).

24. Both the *Kristallnacht* (9–10 November 1938) and the Sicilian Vespers (30 March 1282), like the Carnival in Romans and the Massacre of St. Bartholomew's Day, were festivals that culminated in widespread and lethal attacks on a segment of society that—having long been imperfectly integrated—came to be regarded as fully alien. The *Kristallnacht* pogrom was staged on the Nazi party's celebration of the anniversary of the Beer Hall Putsch; the Sicilians' massacre of their Angevin overlords came on Easter Monday.

25. Davis, *Society and Culture,* p. 181; more broadly, see G. Wylie Sypher, "Faisant ce qu'il leur vient à plaisir: The Image of Protestantism in French Catholic Polemic on the Eve of the Religious Wars," *Sixteenth Century Journal* 11 (1980): 59–84. One is inevitably reminded of the notorious delousing showers at Auschwitz.

26. Estèbe, *Tocsin pour un massacre,* p. 22.

27. This line of interpretation has been adopted by Estèbe, *Tocsin pour un massacre,* pp. 132–33, 143–55, 197–98; Davis, *Society and Culture,* pp. 178–79; Richet, "Sociocultural Aspects of Religious Conflicts," p. 194; and Diefendorf, "Prologue to a Massacre," p. 1067 n.2. Davis gathered numerous examples from the years leading up to the massacre in which celebration of holy days led to sectarian confrontations and assaults, and observed, "The violence seems often a curious continuation of the rite" (Davis, *Society and Culture,* p. 170; and more broadly, pp. 152–87). Many examples resembled St. Bartholomew's Day in all but scale, for instance, a case in Lyon where participants in the Corpus Christi procession of 1561 ran amok, assaulting Protestants to the cry, *"For the flesh of God,* we must kill all Huguenots" (Ibid., p. 171). Emphasis added.

28. Although most historians' attention has been focused on sorting out the motives and deeds of the massacre's chief authors, an important study of the Huguenot consciousness in this period, with special emphasis on their attitudes toward martyrdom, is Donald R. Kelley, "Martyrs, Myths, and the Massacre: The Background of St. Bartholomew," in Soman, *Massacre of St. Bartholomew,* pp. 171–202.

29. See, for example, Mary Douglas, "The Lele of Kasai," in Daryll Forde, ed., *African Worlds: Studies in the Cosmological Ideas and Social Values of African Peoples* (London: Oxford University Press, 1954), pp. 17–22; or Alvin P. Cohen, "Coercing the Rain Deities in Ancient China," *History of Religions* 17 (1978): 224–65.

30. Cohen, "Coercing the Rain Deities," p. 247 n.11.

31. In truth, those normal rituals that foster social integration are never fully adequate to their weighty task. Inevitably, competition over such chronically scarce

resources as wealth, power, and prestige creates sentiments of estrangement and animosity that can be offset only partially and temporarily by ritually stimulated sentiments of affinity. Particularly in situations of rapid social, economic, and political change, with their attendant stress and dislocations, the normal rituals are increasingly incompetent to forge a harmonious and stable society.

Chapter 7

1. There is a large and uneven literature on the Second Republic and the Spanish Civil War. In general I have followed Gerald Brenan, *The Spanish Labyrinth* (Cambridge: Cambridge University Press, 1950); Gabriel Jackson, *The Spanish Republic and the Civil War* (Princeton, N.J.: Princeton University Press, 1965); Pierre Broué and Émile Témime, *The Revolution and the Civil War in Spain* (Cambridge: MIT Press, 1970); Paul Preston, *The Coming of the Spanish Civil War* (London: Macmillan, 1978); Paul Preston ed., *Revolution and War in Spain: 1931–1939* (London: Methuen, 1984); Ronald Fraser, *Blood of Spain: An Oral History of the Spanish Civil War* (New York: Pantheon, 1979).

2. On the ritual nature of such coups d'états, see Leach, *Culture and Communication*, pp. 31–32.

3. Of the seven largest cities, only two fell to the insurgents (Seville and Saragossa), as did Oviedo, Valladolid, Burgos, Salamanca, Córdoba, Granada, Huesca, and Teruel. Although the insurgents held geographically sizable portions of Spain after the *pronunciamiento*, population, wealth, and the means of industrial production were concentrated in those areas where the rising was defeated.

4. Works on this topic are understandably often quite extreme in their rhetoric and presentation of data. Among the more reliable of the older sources are Justo Peréz de Urbel, *Los martires de la iglesia* (Barcelona: Editorial AHR, 1956); and Antonio Montero Moreno, *Historia de la persecución religiosa en España 1936–1939* (Madrid: Biblioteca de Autores Cristianos, 1961). The latter of these documents the murder of 4,184 priests, 2,365 monks, and 283 nuns, most during the first few weeks of the Civil War (pp. 762–883). More recently and dispassionately, see José M. Sánchez, *The Spanish Civil War as a Religious Tragedy* (Notre Dame, Ind.: University of Notre Dame Press, 1987).

5. The fullest account of the events at the Iglesia de la Enseñanza is found in Antonio Peréz de Olaguer, *El terror rojo en Cataluña* (Burgos: Ediciones Antisectarias, 1937), pp. 18–21, although the nature of the source does not inspire confidence. It is this incident that continues to be mentioned in most general histories of the Civil War.

6. Fraser, *Blood of Spain*, p. 152.

7. See in particular the important July 1937 *Joint Letter of the Spanish Episcopate to the Bishops of the Entire World,* the text of which is found in (Archbishop) Isidro Goma y Tomas, *Por Dios y por España* (Barcelona: Rafael Casulleras, 1940), p. 575.

8. We see here another instance of the political use of myth, discussed earlier, especially in chaps. 1 and 2. For example, see such works as Constantino Bayle, S.J., *Qué pasa en España? A los católicos del mundo* (Salamanca, Sp.: Delegación del Estado para Prensa y Propaganda, 1937); A. de Castro Albarran, *Guerra santa: El sentido católico del movimiento nacional español* (Burgos, Sp.: Editorial Española, 1938); idem, *La gran victima: La iglesia española martir de la revolución roja*

(Salamanca, Sp.: n.p., 1940); and Joaquin Arrarás Iribarren, *Historia de la cruzada española* (Madrid: Ediciones Españolas, 1940–44). For attempts to deprive this myth of its authority and even its credibility, see Juan de Iturralde, *El catolicismo y la cruzada de Franco* (Bayonne, Fr.: Editorial Egi-Indarra, 1956–65); and Herbert R. Southworth, *El mito de la cruzada de Franco* (Paris: Ruedo Ibérico, 1963).

9. For example, Hugh Thomas, *The Spanish Civil War* (New York: Harper & Row, 1977), p. 174; G. Jackson, *Spanish Republic,* p. 290; Broué and Témime, *Spanish Revolution,* p. 126.

10. In general on Church-State relations and anticlerical violence, see Brenan, *Spanish Labyrinth,* pp. 37–56; José M. Sánchez, *Reform and Reaction: The Politico-Religious Background of the Spanish Civil War* (Chapel Hill: University of North Carolina Press, 1964); idem, *Spanish Civil War as a Religious Tragedy;* Joan Connelly Ullman, *The Tragic Week: A Study of Anti-Clericalism in Spain, 1875–1912* (Cambridge: Harvard University Press, 1968); Julio Caro Baroja, *Introdución a una historia contemporánea del anti-clericalismo español* (Madrid: Ediciones ISTMO, 1977); F. García de Cortazar, "La iglesia en la crisis del estado español (1898–1923)," in M. Tuñon de Lara et al., *VIII Coloquio de Pau: La crisis del estado Español 1898–1936* (Madrid: Editorial Cuadernos para el Dialogo, 1978), pp. 343–377; Frances Lannon, "The Sociopolitical Role of the Spanish Church—A Case Study," *Journal of Contemporary History* 14 (1979): 193–210; idem "The Church's Crusade Against the Republic," in Preston, *Revolution and War in Spain,* pp. 35–58; and David Gilmore, "Andalusian Anti-clericalism: An Eroticized Rural Protest," *Anthropology* 8 (1984): 31–44.

11. Lincoln, "Theory of Religion and Revolution," pp. 268–72.

12. The first, Cardinal Segura, was banished from Spain as the result of violently antirepublican sentiments expressed in a pastoral letter of 7 May 1931. He was discovered trying to return incognito one month later and expelled again. Although holding quite similar views, his replacement, Cardinal Goma, was somewhat more discreet—at least until the outbreak of the Civil War.

13. One of the few serious—if idiosyncratic—attempts to consider the significance of the exhumations was made by Salvador Dali, whose 1940 canvas *Visage of War* seems to have been strongly influenced by the spectre of the exhumed corpses. He wrote, apropos of the Civil War in general:

> At one fell swoop, from the middle of the Spanish cadaver springs up, half-devoured by vermin and ideological worms, the Iberian penis in erection, huge like a cathedral filled with the white dynamite of hatred. Bury and Unbury! Disinter and Inter! In order to unbury again! Such was the charnel desire of the Civil War in the impatient Spain. One would see how she was capable of suffering; of making others suffer, of burying and unburying, of killing and resurrecting. It was necessary to scratch the earth to exhume tradition and to profane everything in order to be dazzled anew by all the treasures that the land was hiding in its entrails" (cited in Robert Descharnes, *Salvador Dali* [New York: Abrams, 1976], p. 136).

14. Mircea Eliade, *Yoga: Immortality and Freedom* (Princeton, N.J.: Princeton University Press, 1969), pp. 296–301; Jonathan Parry, "Sacrificial Death and the Necrophagous Ascetic," in M. Bloch and J. Parry, eds., *Death and the Regeneration of Life* (Cambridge: Cambridge University Press, 1982), pp. 74–110.

15. Franz Boas, *Kwakiutl Ethnography,* edited by Helen Codere (Chicago: University of Chicago Press, 1966), pp. 171–279; Stanley Walens, *Feasting with Cannibals: An Essay on Kwakiutl Cosmology* (Princeton, N.J.: Princeton University Press, 1981).

16. Worsley, *The Trumpet Shall Sound,* p. 250.

17. Kenelm Burridge, *New Heaven, New Earth* (New York: Schocken, 1969), pp. 166–68.

18. The most celebrated testimonial is, of course, George Orwell, *Homage to Catalonia* (New York: Harcourt, Brace & World, 1952). See also, however, such works as H.-E. Kaminski, *Ceux de Barcelone* (Paris: Éditions DeNoel, 1937); John Langdon-Davies, *Behind Spanish Barricades* (New York: Robert M. Mcbride, 1937); Franz Borkenau, *The Spanish Cockpit* (Ann Arbor: University of Michigan Press, 1974); Mary Low and Juan Brea, *Red Spanish Notebook* (San Francisco: City Lights, 1979); and Augustin Souchy Bauer, *With the Peasants of Aragon* (Minneapolis, Minn.: Soil of Liberty, 1982). Some caution is necessary in considering such sources, as has been shown by Gerd-Rainer Horn, "The Language of Symbols and the Barriers of Language: Foreigners' Perceptions of Social Revolution (Barcelona: 1936–1937)," seminar paper, University of Michigan at Ann Arbor, Department of History, Spring 1988.

19. Kenelm Burridge, remarks in "Final Discussion," *Religion, Rebellion, Revolution,* p. 296. Emphasis added.

20. Cited in Robert Buijtenhuijs, *Le mouvement "Mau-Mau"* (The Hague, Neth.: Moulton, 1971), p. 260; more broadly, see pp. 255–98.

21. Gluckman, *Order and Rebellion,* pp. 137–45.

22. Hodgson, *The Order of Assassins,* pp. 148–58; Bernard Lewis, *The Assassins: A Radical Sect in Islam* (London: Weidenfeld & Nicolson, 1967), p. 73.

23. Cited in Christopher Dawson, *The Gods of Revolution* (New York: Minerva, 1975), p. 80. Emphasis added.

24. There are a few exceptions to this, as in the exhumation of prominent persons subject to particular scorn for one reason or another: Queen Maria of Castile, Bishop Torras y Bages, and Vilfredo el Velloso, the conqueror of Catalonia.

25. I am indebted here to the astute remarks of Comaroff, *Body of Power, Spirit of Resistance,* p. 198. See also the observations of M. Warnke, ed., *Bildersturm: Die Zerstörung des Kunstwerks* (Munich: Hanser, 1973); David Freedberg, "The Structure of Byzantine and European Iconoclasm," in A. Bryer and J. Herrin, eds., *Iconoclasm* (Birmingham, Eng.: University of Birmingham Centre for Byzantine Studies, 1977), pp. 165–77; James C. Scott, "Protest and Profanation," *Theory and Society* 4 (1977): 1–38, 211–46; Carlos M.N. Eire, *War Against the Idols: The Reformation of Worship from Erasmus to Calvin* (Cambridge: Cambridge University Press, 1986); and Yves-Marie Bercé, *Revolt and Revolution in Early Modern Europe* (New York: St. Martin's, Press, 1987), pp. 19–20 in addition to the literature cited in note 26.

26. See S. Idzerda, "Iconoclasm During the French Revolution," *American Historical Review* 60 (1954): 13–26; Michel Vovelle, *Religion et révolution. La déchristianisation de l'an II* (Paris: Hachette, 1976); Ozouf, *La fête révolutionnaire,* pp. 99–124; John Ransome Phillips, *The Reformation of Images: Destruction of Art in England, 1535–1660* (Berkeley: University of California Press, 1973); and Vincent Y.C. Shih, *The Taiping Ideology* (Seattle: University of Washington Press, 1967), pp. 23–29.

27. The story is taken from a source sympathetic to the Right, and is provided with an appropriately satisfying conclusion, given its intended audience. Thus, we are told that as they sought to burn the statue, two of the *milicianos* strayed into the line of fire from the "heroes of the Alcázar," whereupon they were shot and themselves pitched into the pyre (Luis Carreras, *The Glory of Martyred Spain*

(London: Burns, Oates & Washbourne, 1945), p. 99. The same structure and moral are evident in other countericonoclasm stories favored by the Right, as in that of a leftist who urinated against a church door, and was fatally stricken with cancer of the anus directly thereafter (Fraser, *Blood of Spain,* p. 88).

28. Bayle, *Qué pasa en España?* p. 53.
29. Montero Moreno, *Historia de la persecución religiosa,* pp. 64, 432.
30. Ullman, *Tragic Week.*

Chapter 8

1. In practice, of course, things are rather more complex than this summary description indicates because age, unlike gender, is neither fully amenable to straightforward binary categorization (however much societies may attempt to define it as such) nor something that remains invariant. In practice the relative and changing ages of children has considerable importance for familial hierarchies, interacting with gender in complex ways. To cite one example, if in a patriarchal system the firstborn child is a girl and the second a boy, the girl may outrank her brother for a time (considerations of age initially prevailing over those of gender), but as he grows older and the relative difference between their ages narrows, both will be classified simply as children, without major distinction being made between them on the basis of age. At such a moment the boy will come to outrank his sister as considerations of gender are called into play and a period of stress or crisis may ensue. Again, as a son and daughter approach the age of majority, pressures mount for their reclassification as adults, in which form they become hierarchically equal to their parent of the same sex. The usual resolution of this situation (which commonly involves stress or even crisis) is for the children-become-adults to leave home and form new family units in which they will occupy the foremost positions. Daughters, however, are more free to remain at home than are sons, for their elevation to adult status threatens to demote no one, whereas an adult son (who has moved from the status of − Age/ + Gender to that of + Age/ + Gender) threatens to displace his mother in the family hierarchy. On the classificatory complexities of gender, the discussion of Sherry Ortner, "Is Female to Male as Nature Is to Culture?" in M.Z. Rosaldo and L. Lamphere, eds., *Woman, Culture, Society* (Stanford, Calif.: Stanford University Press, 1974), pp. 67–88, remains fundamental.

2. One of the boldest statements in an extremely daring book is Durkheim and Mauss's affirmation that "every mythology is fundamentally a classification" (*Primitive Classification,* p. 77). Although this overstates the case somewhat, the researches of Claude Lévi-Strauss on Amerindian mythology (*Introduction to a Science of Mythology,* 4 vols. [New York: Harper & Row, 1969–81]) have shown how intertwined myth and taxonomy can be. For his part, however, Lévi-Strauss undervalued the interrelations of taxonomy and social hierarchy rightly emphasized by Durkheim and Mauss.

3. Malinowski, *Magic, Science and Religion,* p. 112.

4. Bronislaw Malinowski, *Soil-Tilling and Agricultural Rites in the Trobriand Islands* (Bloomington: Indiana University Press, 1965), pp. 160–64, passim.

5. Elsewhere, in "The Tyranny of Taxonomies," *Occasional Papers of the University of Minnesota Center for Humanistic Studies,* No. 1 (Minneapolis: University of Minnesota, 1985), I have shown this for the myth of ethnogenesis via

Noah's sons in *Genesis* 9.20–10.32 and the account of the Scythian peoples found in the fourth book of Herodotus's *Histories* (esp. 4.2, 4.17, and 4.20).

6. For all that it is obvious, it should still be noted that nature expresses no hierarchy in simple verticality. Yet the representation of hierarchic relations through images in which relative vertical position is at issue (*X* being above, superior to, or higher than *Y*) is so common—and nearly universal in its distribution—that the association of the two comes to seem almost "natural." On this pattern, see most extensively Barry Schwartz, *Vertical Classification* (Chicago: University of Chicago Press, 1981).

7. Durkheim and Mauss, *Primitive Classification*. Notwithstanding the brilliance of this pioneer work, it is now clear that Durkheim and Mauss erred in the evolutionistic and essentially unilinear way that they conceptualized the relations between social and other forms of categorization. Had they spoken of the social focus, import, or utility of taxonomic systems rather than their social origins, they would have served their intentions better and would have offered less ground for criticism.

8. Bourdieu, *A Theory of Practice*, esp. pp. 97, 163–66.

9. This tendency is particularly characteristic of the structuralist movement in anthropology, for example, Claude Lévi-Strauss, *Totemism* (London: Merlin Press, 1964); idem, *The Savage Mind* (Chicago: University of Chicago Press, 1966); Leach, *Culture and Communication;* Needham, *Right and Left;* idem, *Symbolic Classification* (Santa Monica, Calif.: Goodyear Publishing Co., 1979). In a very different vein, see the attempt of Don Handelman—"The Idea of Bureaucratic Organization," *Social Analysis* 9 (1981): 5–23, esp. pp. 6–12—to connect taxonomic structures both logically and historically to the emergence of bureaucratic systems of organization in seventeenth- and eighteenth-century Europe.

10. One must, of course, grant that the diverse data of the phenomenal world being too numerous, varied, and complex for any individual mind or cultural aggregate to process, it is a move born of necessity to organize disparate bits of information into categories and to organize those categories into taxonomic systems. Such systems always remain, however, impoverished, oversimplified, and tendentious models of a fuller reality. Nor should their necessity or utility be taken uncritically: although taxonomies may render thought and action possible, it must be stressed that any given system renders only *certain kinds* of thought and action possible, simultaneously precluding infinite others. Along these lines, Schwartz's comparison of classification to dreams, both involving the "work" of distortion whereby "vague ideas and sentiments [are converted] into tangible representations" is extremely attractive (*Vertical Classification*, p. 76).

11. In a celebrated article, Victor Turner, *Forest of Symbols*, pp. 59–92, compared the system of Three Forms to other systems of classification (particularly those of Central Africa) in which the colors red, white, and black appear as master categories. On the basis of this comparison, he went on to argue: First, that this taxonomic pattern was extremely widespread, if not universal; second (*pace* Durkheim and Mauss), that it had the natural world as its basis, not the social, for he took the fundamental significance of these three colors to be their association to certain bodily products: red for blood (and thus conflict); white for milk and semen (and thus creation and nurturance); black for feces (and thus processes of decay). Beyond his having missed the social content and significance of the Indic system, Turner erred in numerous details, distorting the Indic materials so as to make them resemble the African data more closely than they actually do.

12. This module provides a convenient example of the way in which a complex taxonomy both reinforces and creates problems for itself through the interrelation of its many modules. Thus, when one correlates bodily fluids to vertical mapping, things work nicely, breath being located most palpably in the nose (= highest), blood in the heart (= intermediate), and urine in the bladder (= lowest). But when one seeks correlation to the colors, it is a different story, for according to the givens of the system, breath ought be red, blood white, and urine dark.

13. The systems we have considered all deploy two taxonomizers to create either three or four master categories (depending on whether the second-order taxonomizer is applied to both subclasses produced by the first-order taxonomizer or not). Systems having up to eight master categories could be produced by the deployment of a third-order taxonomizer, and up to sixteen with a fourth (in all cases the maximum number of master categories equals 2^t, where t equals the number of taxonomizers deployed). Theoretically, there is no limit to the number of master categories that might be included in such a system, but the capacities of the human memory set certain practical limits.

14. Two specifications are necessary. First, there are two different systems of social classification in India that are sometimes called caste. It is the older and simpler of these with which we are concerned here, that of color (Sanskrit, *varṇa*), not that of birth (Sanskrit *jāti*). Second, this system organizes four classes, drawing a radical distinction between the upper three (the twice-born, or Aryan, castes) and the lowest (the Shudras), members of which are denied initiation; refused access to rituals, sacred texts, and religious instruction; and are defined as racially alien. The system of the Three Forms ignores them altogether. For more detail, see Georges Dumézil, "La préhistoire indo-iranienne des castes," *Journal asiatique* 216 (1930): 109–30; Louis Dumont, *Homo Hierarchicus* (Chicago: University of Chicago Press, 1970), and the forthcoming work of Brian Smith, *Classifying the World: The Ancient Indian Varṇa System* (New York: Oxford University Press).

15. See, for instance, the *Laws of Manu* 12.24–50, the *Bhagavad Gītā* 18.7–48, or the *Vishnu Purana* 16.

Chapter 9

1. See, for example: Davis, *Society and Culture,* pp. 97–151; Gluckman, *Order and Rebellion,* pp. 110–36; Barbara Babcock, ed., *The Reversible World: Symbolic Inversion in Art and Society* (Ithaca, N. Y.: Cornell University Press, 1978); Marc Augé, "Quando i segni si invertono: A proposito di alcuni riti africani," in Francesco Maiello, ed., *Antropologia e potere* (Rome: Lerici, 1979), pp. 73–94; Stuart Clark, "Inversion, Misrule, and the Meaning of Witchcraft," *Past and Present* 87 (1980): 98–127; Giuseppe Cocchiara, *Il mondo alla rovescia* (Turin, It.: Boringheri, 1981), plus the literature on carnival cited in Chap. 6 n. 5.

2. Marcel Granet, "Right and Left in China," in Needham, *Right and Left,* p. 48.

3. As always with Duchamp, the choice of a pseudonym involved complex word play. Of most interest in the present context is his statement that the initial R. stood for *Richard*, which in French slang denotes a rich man, observing "That's not bad for a *pissotière*" (Arturo Schwarz, *The Complete Works of Marcel Duchamp* [New York: Abrams, 1970], p. 466). But one must also note the pun that

exists between R. Mutt and the German *Armut* (poverty). We see here again inversions upon inversions and a general confusion of categories.

4. On this group and its relations to other component groups within the New York avant-garde of the period, see Louise Hassett Lincoln, "New York Dada and the Arensberg Circle," in William Innes Homer, *Alfred Stieglitz and the American Avant-garde* (Boston: New York Graphic Society, 1977), pp. 179–85.

5. Turner, *Schism and Continuity;* idem, *Dramas, Fields, and Metaphors: Symbolic Action in Human Society* (Ithaca, N.Y.: Cornell University Press, 1974), pp. 23–59.

6. Most recently and extensively on the conflicts between patricians and plebes, see Jean-Claude Richard, *Les origines de la plèbe romaine: Essai sur la formation du dualisme patricio-plébéien* (Rome: École française de Rome, 1978); and Kurt A. Raaflaub, ed., *Social Struggles in Archaic Rome: New Perspectives on the Conflict of the Orders* (Berkeley: University of California Press, 1986).

7. Livy appears to contradict himself on this point, stating in consecutive sentences of 2.32.8 first that Menenius was "an eloquent man" (Latin, *facundum virum*), and then that he spoke in a "crude manner" (*horrido modo*). Although some commentators have sought to reconcile these statements, arguing that Livy was casting judgment on the favored oratorical styles of the distant past, I prefer to see this as yet another means whereby the interstitial class identity of the mediator was noted, his eloquence being part of his more recently established patrician nature, and the roughness of his speech deriving from his plebeian origins. Being possessed of the potential for both sorts of verbal style, he emerges once again as the ideal figure to bear a message from the patricians to the plebes.

8. Bercé, *Revolt and Revolution,* p. 54. Also of interest is a 1536 pamphlet written against the English Catholic uprising of the Pilgrimage of Grace, which Bercé cites on the same page. The author of this text asked: "Would it not be foolish and unheard of for a foot to say it wanted to wear a hat just as the head does or for a knee to say it wanted to have eyes, or some such caprice?" The Apologue of Menenius Agrippa remains a required part of the curriculum in Italian public schools, purportedly for its stylistic excellence.

9. This program was initially chosen to provide material for discussion in a course offered at the University of Minnesota in the Fall of 1984 on "Analysis of Ritual." I am most grateful to the students in this class, who contributed significantly to the analysis that follows. I do not claim that the pattern adduced here governs all of professional wrestling, which employs numerous other formulaic structures as well. The specific pattern evident within this broadcast is a popular and influential one, which is evidenced in roughly 25 percent of the televised cards I have considered since the initial study. It is also clear that this dialectic figure often unfolds over time in a sequence of matches between two opponents rather than being condensed within the matches of a single card. A thorough study of professional wrestling would thus have to consider successive cards—televised and those for which admission is charged—staged within a given viewing area over a period of months or even years.

10. An instructive distribution is evident in the costumes of the four villains who won, two of whom wore particularly flamboyant costumes and two of whom were distinctively disheveled. The former—who tended toward the foppish in their grooming and demeanor as well—might be classified as displaying a superabundance of culture, overly cooked as it were, whereas the others were villains of a

brutish type, exhibiting an excess of nature. Those who fell in the latter category bore the names of beasts ("The Animal," "The Moondogs") and in one instance used raw meat as a prop for their team performance.

11.   Barthes, *Mythologies*, pp. 15–25.

12.   The ethnic and racial coding implicit within the matches was raised to explicitude during an interview aired between the fourth and fifth matches. Here, a wrestler not featured on this card, one Ivan Putski, discussed his upcoming bout with "Dr. D." David Schultz, whom he accused of employing ethnic slurs and "treating his opponents like trash." Putski vowed, on behalf of his fans (whom he identified as living primarily in northern Minneapolis, an area of heavy Eastern European population, in contrast to Germanic and Scandinavian predominance in the rest of the city), to treat Schultz, whom he characterized as a "big mouth redneck," to a demonstration of "Polish power."

13.   Students in my seminar, when called on to remember Hayes's appearance two days after the match, almost uniformly referred to him as a "California type," by which they—who live and for the most part have their roots in the upper Midwest—meant to identify him as one culturally as well as geographically on the margins of American society.

14.   Jim Freedman, "Will the Sheik Use His Amazing Fireball: The Ideology of Professional Wrestling," in Frank Manning, ed., *The Celebration of Society* (Bowling Green, Ohio: Bowling Green University Press, 1982), pp. 67–79.

15.   The sponsors of "All-Star Wrestling" provide a convenient index to the socioeconomic status of the audience, at least as it is understood by the TV network and its advertisers. These included a bargain tire outlet, two fast-food chains, a used-car dealer, a diet formula, economy razors, and a mail-order firm that offered "genuine diamelle rings" for "an incredible $10.00."

16.   I am grateful to Don Handelman, who suggested aspects of the preceding analysis to me in the course of discussions during the fall of 1982. In particular it was he who first recognized the dialectic processes described here, which he terms a "dialectic of encapsulation."

Chapter 10

1.   Although, following convention, I refer to Namuci as a demon, this is somewhat misleading. The texts call him an Asura, a term better rendered as anti-god, the Asuras being an older, more sinister, and slightly less powerful group of deities who struggle constantly with another set of divine beings, called Devas (conventionally translated as gods). The *Brāhmanas* teem with stories of their struggles, always on the pattern of Indra and Namuci: (1) supremacy of the Devas (usually marked by their possession of the implements and knowledge necessary for performance of the sacrifice), (2) threat of the Asuras, (3) supremacy of the Devas reestablished. This, of course, is the same dialectic structure that was explored in chapter 9, which is also evident in the myth of Nuer and Dinka discussed in chapters 1 and 2. Thus (1) preferred brother (= Nuer) is given younger cow, (2) other brother (= Dinka) takes younger cow, (3) preferred brother is given right to retake younger cow and all others.

2.   Quotations are from *Shatapatha Brāhmana* 12.7.3.1–4. Variants are found in numerous other texts; for a full listing see Maurice Bloomfield, "The Story of

Indra and Namuci," *Journal of the American Oriental Society* 15 (1893): 143–63.

3. *Math* is one "branch" of *The Four Branches of the Mabinogi*. Its similarity to the myth of Indra and Namuci was first noted by Alwyn Rees and Brinley Rees (*Celtic Heritage* [London: Thames & Hudson, 1961], p. 333) and developed more fully by José Carlos Gomes da Silva, "Mythe et idéologie," *L'Homme* 16 (1976): 49–75.

4. See Bruce Lincoln, "Places Outside Space, Moments Outside Time," in Polomé, *Homage to Georges Dumézil*, pp. 69–84, with citation of relevant primary and secondary sources, to which should be added Jan de Vries, *Die Märchen von klugen Rätsellöserin* (Helsinki, Fin.: *Folklore Fellows Communication* No. 73, 1928). An apparent difference in the two stories treated here should be noted, for one evokes sympathy for the killer (Indra) and the other for the victim (Lleu). Further scrutiny reveals this difference to be more superficial than real. Thus, both stories present a three-part drama: (1) hero (Indra, Lleu) possesses a prized good (soma, Blodeuedd), (2) villain (Namuci, Gronw) overcomes hero and seizes this prize, (3) hero overcomes villain in definitive fashion. The sole major difference is that the Indic narrative emphasizes Act Three of the drama by placing the incident of the anomalous assault there, whereas the Welsh does the same for Act Two. One should also note that the heroes in both tales are (or originally were) gods, for the name *Lleu* is but the Welsh equivalent of a name born by one of the foremost deities of the pre-Christian Celts: Old Irish *Lug*, Gallo-Roman *Lugus*.

5. Things are, of course, somewhat more complicated than this simple formulation indicates, for Blodeuedd is not only a resource desired by the others, but also an active agent in her own right.

6. That is to say, they do not cease to exist. In a certain sense, however, they do disappear to the extent that the system renders them unacknowledged, unacknowledgeable, and thus quasi-invisible. Such lovers themselves frequent places where they will "not be seen," and an acquaintance who encounters them confronts the dilemma of whether or not to acknowledge—or even perceive—their presence. A favored metaphor for extramarital relations is that they are shadowy, an expression that, like the literary convention of lovers' meetings at dawn (on which, see Arthur Hatto, ed., *Eos: An Enquiry into the Theme of Lovers' Meetings and Partings at Dawn in Poetry* [The Hague, Neth.: Mouton, 1965]), marks their anomalous or interstitial quality: neither light nor dark, open nor closed, and so on.

7. Marriages in which there are no sexual relations logically pose an equal threat, and such ascetic challenges have at times been quite prominent, for instance, in India and in the religious orders of medieval Europe. (Note that nuns still wear wedding bands as the non-sexual brides of Christ). The anomaly most corrosive of all to social-sexual order is, as Lévi-Strauss argued in *Elementary Structures of Kinship*, incest, which annihilates the distinction between wife-givers and wife-takers, yet one should note that there have been situations in which even this anomaly has been embraced (e.g., royal marriages, as in Ptolemaic Egypt, and within classic Zoroastrianism more broadly).

8. That such formulations as these were actually employed by official power centers to their own benefit is seen in a royal inscription of Darius the Great, in which, he boasts, "These are the lands which came to me. They were bound to me by the will of Ahura Mazda. They bore me tribute. What I said to them—*by day or by night*—that was done," that is, disobedience was tolerated "neither by day nor by night." (Behistun Inscription, par. 7).

9. See further Marcel Detienne and Jean-Pierre Vernant, *Cunning Intelligence in Greek Culture and Society* (New York: Humanities Press, 1978).

10. Arnold van Gennep, *The Rites of Passage* (Chicago: University of Chicago Press, 1960); Edmund Leach, "Anthropological Aspects of Language: Animal Categories and Verbal Abuse," in Eric H. Lenneberg, ed., *New Directions in the Study of Language* (Cambridge: MIT Press, 1964); Mary Douglas, *Purity and Danger: An Analysis of Concepts of Pollution and Taboo* (London: Routledge & Kegan Paul, 1966); Turner, *Forest of Symbols*, pp. 93–111; idem, *Ritual Process;* Michael Thompson, *Rubbish Theory* (Oxford: Oxford University Press, 1979).

11. Needham, *Symbolic Classification*, p. 46; cf. S.O. Murray, "Fuzzy Sets and Abominations," *Man* 18 (1983): 396–99.

12. See Hans-Peter Hasenfratz, *Die Toten Lebenden: Eine religionsphäno-menologische Studie zum sozialen Tod in archaischen Gesellschaften* (Leiden, Neth.: E.J. Brill, 1982); and Bruce Lincoln, "The Living Dead: Outlaws and Others," *History of Religions* 23 (1984): 387–389.

13. Thomas Kuhn, *The Structure of Scientific Revolutions* (Chicago: University of Chicago Press, 1962).

14. On whom see Vittorio Lanternari, *Crisi e ricerca d'identità* (Naples: Liguori Editore, 1977), pp. 125–32.

15. For recent uses of the androgyne image, see, inter alia, Pamela Butler, *Self-assertion for Women: A Guide to Becoming Androgynous* (San Francisco: Canfield Press, 1976); June K. Singer, *Androgyny: Toward a New Theory of Sexuality* (Garden City, N.Y.: Doubleday, Anchor, 1976); James Richard Broughton, *The Androgyne Journal* (Oakland: Scrimshaw Press, 1977); Sukie Colgrave, *The Spirit of the Valley: The Masculine and Feminine in the Human Psyche* (Los Angeles: J.P. Tarcher, 1979); Mary Vetterling-Braggin, ed., *"Femininity," "Masculinity," and "Androgyny": A Modern Philosophical Discussion* (Totowa, N.J.: Rowman & Littlefield, 1982); and Michel Foucault, ed., *Herculine Barbin: Being the Recently Discovered Memoirs of a Nineteenth-Century French Hermaphrodite* (New York: Pantheon, 1980). Within antiquity, note, for instance, the use of androgyny in the rhetoric and ideology of dissident religious groups in the first few centuries of our era, as discussed, for instance, in Wayne Meeks, "The Image of the Androgyne: Some Uses of a Symbol in Earliest Christianity," *History of Religions* 13 (1974): 165–209. Among other anomalies that figured in the symbolic arsenal of the early Church, one ought also note virgin births, carpenter kings, crucified gods, and words made flesh.

16. Within the *Symposium,* these views are explicitly rejected (205D), and Plato returns to attack them again in *Laws* 731D–732B, where, however, they are associated neither with Aristophanes nor any other individual but are treated as a fairly widespread and popular view. On Greek sexual politics, with particular reference to the position of homosexuals, male and female, see K.J. Dover, *Greek Homosexuality* (Cambridge: Harvard University Press, 1978), noting also Félix Buffière, *Eros adolescent: La pédérastie dans la Grèce antique* (Paris: Collection "Les belles lettres," 1980); and Bernard Sergent, *L'homosexualité dans la mythologie grecque* (Paris: Payot, 1984).

17. Geertz, *Interpretation of Cultures*, p. 100.

18. Ibid., p. 101. Emphasis in the original.

19. Michael Walzer, *Regicide and Revolution* (Cambridge: Cambridge University Press, 1974).

Postscripts

1. The precise ethymological sense of familiarity is of some interest here, as those things with which one is familiar are those with which one enjoys a familial relation of sorts, whether by birth or adoption. Alternatively, one might say that parochialism is a stance of uncritical engagement with those data for which one feels or has come to feel affinity, and a corrseponding disengagement from those from which one remains estranged.

2. The move of parochialism involves the construction of a socio-epistemological border and a hierarchico-taxonomic distinction between the knower, known, and worth-knowing, on the one hand, and the unknown and unworthy of knowledge, on the other hand. Generalizations based on the known thus either leave the unknown unacknowledged and unknowable or misconstrue it as nothing more than a set of variants on the known.

3. Although important beginnings have been made, as in Michel Foucault, *The Archaeology of Knowledge* (New York: Pantheon, 1972), there remains much to be said regarding the discourse of discipline and the sociology of the modern university. As a starting point one might consider the semantic range of the English common noun *discipline,* for which *The Compact Edition of the Oxford English Dictionary* (Oxford: Oxford University Press, 1971), Vol. 1, p. 741, lists these definitions:

1. Instruction imparted to disciples or scholars . . .
2. A branch of instruction or education . . .
3. Instruction having for its aim to form the pupil to proper conduct and action . . .
4. The orderly conduct and action which result from training . . .
5. The order maintained and observed among pupils, or other persons under control or command, such as soldiers, sailors, the inmates of a religious house, a prison etc. . . .
6. The system or method by which order is maintained in a church and control exercised over the conduct of its members . . .
7. Correction; chastisement; punishment inflicted by way of correction and training . . .

The further you go, the worse it gets, moving from processes of instruction (1) to institutionalization (2), indoctrination (3–4), and finally repression (5–7). All this stands in contrast to the Latin origins of the term, for *disciplina* marks nothing other than the practice of the student (Latin, *discipulus*), as opposed to *doctrina* or doctrine, the discourse of the teacher (Latin, *doctor*).

4. This observation could equally well be inverted: It is also true that those persons who regard one another as members of different societies feel more estrangement than affinity toward one another, for this is a process the products of which are also its preconditions. How such processes are set in motion *ab origine* remains ever mysterious (cf. the banal example of chickens and eggs), but what is clear is the extreme efficiency with which they secure their own replication.

Bibliography

Akhavi, Shahrough (1983). "The Ideology and Praxis of Shi'ism in the Iranian Revolution," *Comparative Studies in Society and History* 25: 195–221.

Aneer, Gudmar (1985). *Imam Ruhullah Khumaini, Shah Muhammad Riza Pahlavi and the Religious Traditions of Iran*. Uppsala, Swed.: Almquist & Wiksell.

Appadurai, Arjun (1981). "The Past as a Scarce Resource," *Man* 16: 201–19.

Apter, Andrew (1983). "In Dispraise of the King: Rituals 'Against' Rebellion in South-east Africa." *Man* 18: 521–34.

Arnold, Walter (1871). *The Life and Death of the Sublime Society of Steaks*. London: Bradbury, Evans & Co.

Arrarás Iribarren, Joaquin (1940–44). *Historia de la cruzada española*. Madrid: Ediciones Españolas.

Augé, Marc (1979). "Quando i segni si invertono: A proposito di alcuni riti africani." In Francesco Maiello, ed., *Antropologia e potere* (Rome: Lerici), pp. 73–94.

Babcock, Barbara, ed. (1978). *The Reversible World: Symbolic Inversion in Art and Society*. Ithaca, N.Y.: Cornell University Press.

Bakhtin, Mikhail (1984). *Rabelais and His World*. Bloomington: Indiana University Press.

Barletta, Laura (1981). *Il carnevale del 1764 a Napoli: Protesta e integrazione in uno spazio urbano*. Naples: Società Editrice Napoletana.

Barthes, Roland (1972). *Mythologies*. London: Jonathan Cape.

Bastide, Roger (1960). "Mythes et utopies," *Cahiers internationaux de sociologie* 28: 3–12.

Bateson, Gregory (1958). *Naven*. Stanford, Calif.: Stanford University Press.

Baudy, Gerhard J. (1983). "Hierarchie oder: Die Verteilung des Fleisches." In B. Gladigow and H.G. Kippenberg, eds., *Neue Ansätze in der Religionswissenschaft* (Munich: Kösel Verlag), pp. 131–74.

Bauer, Augustin Souchy (1982). *With the Peasants of Aragon*. Minneapolis, Minn.: Soil of Liberty.

Bayle, Constantino, S.J. (1937). *Qué pasa en España? A los Católicos del mundo*. Salamanca, Sp.: Delegación del Estado para Prensa y Propaganda.

Beidelman, T.O. (1966). "Swazi Royal Ritual." *Africa* 36: 373–405.

Benveniste, Émile (1929). *The Persian Religion According to the Chief Greek Texts*. Paris: Paul Geuthner.

Bercé, Yves-Marie (1976). *Fête et revolte: Des mentalités populaires du XVIe au XVIIe siècle*. Paris: Hachette.

────── (1987). *Revolt and Revolution in Early Modern Europe*. New York: St. Martin's Press.

Berghe, Pierre L. van den (1963). "Institutionalized Licence and Normative Stability." *Cahiers d'études africaines* 3: 413–23.

Berglund, Axel-Iver (1976). *Zulu Thought Patterns and Symbolism*. Uppsala: Swedish Institute of Missionary Research.

Bertelli, Sergio, and Giuliano Crifo, eds. (1985). *Rituale, Cerimoniale, Etichetta*. Milan: Bompiano.

Bidez, Joseph, and Franz Cumont (1938). *Les mages hellénisés*, Vol. 2. Paris: Société "Les belles lettres."

Biersack, Aletta (forthcoming). "Prisoners of Time: Millenarian Praxis in a Melanesian Valley." In Aletta Biersack, ed., *Clio in Oceania* (Washington, D.C.: Smithsonian Institution Press).

Bloch, Maurice (1974). "Symbols, Song, Dance and Features of Articulation: Or Is Religion an Extreme Form of Traditional Authority?" *Archives européennes de sociologie* 15: 55–81.

────── (1977). "The Past and the Present in the Present," *Man* 18: 278–92.

──────, ed. (1984). *Marxist Analyses and Social Anthropology*. London: Tavistock.

────── (1986). *From Blessing to Violence: History and Ideology in the Circumcision Ritual of the Merina of Madagascar*. Cambridge: Cambridge University Press.

Bloomfield, Maurice (1893). "The Story of Indra and Namuci." *Journal of the American Oriental Society* 15: 143–63.

Boas, Franz (1966). *Kwakiutl Ethnography*. Edited by Helen Codere. Chicago: University of Chicago Press.

Bohannon, Laura (1952). "A Genealogical Charter," *Africa* 22: 301–15.

Bonner, Philip (1980). "Classes, the Mode of Production and the State in Precolonial Swaziland." In Shula Marks and Anthony Atmore, eds., *Economy and Society in Pre-industrial South Africa* (London: Longman), pp. 80–101.

────── (1983). *Kings, Commoners and Concessionaires: The Evolution and Dissolution of the Nineteenth-Century Swazi State*. Cambridge: Cambridge University Press.

Booth, Alan R. (1983). *Swaziland: Tradition and Change in a Southern African Kingdom*. Boulder, Colorado: Westview Press.

Borkenau, Franz (1974). *The Spanish Cockpit*. Ann Arbor: University of Michigan Press.

Bourdieu, Pierre (1977). *Outline of a Theory of Practice*. Cambridge: Cambridge University Press.

Bourdillon, M.F.C. (1978). "Knowing the World or Hiding It? A Response to Maurice Bloch," *Man* 13:591–99.

Brenan, Gerald (1950). *The Spanish Labyrinth*. Cambridge: Cambridge University Press.

Bromberger, Christian (1986). "La seduzione del potere: Procedure simboliche di legittimazione nel Islam rivoluzionario." In Carla Pasquinelli, ed., *Potere senza stato* (Rome: Riuniti), pp. 115–34.

Broué, Pierre, and Émile Témime (1970). *The Revolution and the Civil War in Spain.* Cambridge: MIT Press.

Broughton, James Richard (1977). *The Androgyne Journal.* Oakland: Scrimshaw Press.

Buffière, Félix (1980). *Eros adolescent: La pédérastie dans la Grèce antique.* Paris: Collection "Les belles lettres."

Buijtenhuijs, Robert (1971). *Le mouvement "Mau-Mau."* The Hague, Neth.: Mouton.

Burguière, André (1982). "The Marriage Ritual in France: Ecclesiastical Practices and Popular Practices (Sixteenth to Eighteenth Centuries)." In Robert Forster and Orest Ranum, eds., *Ritual, Religion, and the Sacred: Selections from the Annales,* Vol. 7 (Baltimore, Md.: The Johns Hopkins University Press), pp. 8–23.

Burridge, Kenelm (1969). *New Heaven, New Earth.* New York: Schocken.

——— (1985). Remarks in "Final Discussion." In B. Lincoln, ed., *Religion, Rebellion, Revolution: An Interdisciplinary and Cross-cultural Collection of Essays.* (London: Macmillan), pp. 293–299.

Burton, John W. (1981). "Ethnicity on the Hoof: On the Economics of Nuer Identity," *Ethnology* 20: 157–62.

Butler, Pamela (1976). *Self-assertion for Women: A Guide to Becoming Androgynous.* San Francisco: Canfield Press.

Buttitta, Antonio (1979). *Semiotica e antropologia.* Palermo, It.: Sellerio.

Byrne, Francis J. (1973). *Irish Kings and High-Kings.* New York: St. Martin's Press.

Caro Baroja, Julio (1977). *Introdución a una historia contemporánea del anticlericalismo español.* Madrid: Ediciones ISTMO.

——— (1979). *Le carnaval.* Paris: Gallimard.

Carreras, Luis (1945). *The Glory of Martyred Spain.* London: Burns, Oates & Washbourne.

Castro Albarran, A. de (1938). *Guerra santa: El sentido católico del movimiento nacional español.* Burgos, Sp.: Editorial Española.

——— (1940). *La gran victima: La iglesia española martir de la revolución roja.* Salamanca, Sp.: n.p.

Chan, Hok-lam (1969). "The White Lotus-Maitreya Doctrine and Popular Uprisings in Ming and Ch'ing China," *Sinologica* 10: 211–33.

Clark, Stuart (1980). "Inversion, Misrule, and the Meaning of Witchcraft," *Past and Present* 87: 98–127.

Clemente, Pietro et al. (1983). *Il linguaggio, il corpo, la festa: Per un ripensamento della tematica di Michail Bachtin.* Milan: Franco Angeli (= *Metamorfosi,* Vol. 7).

Cocchiara, Giuseppe (1981). *Il mondo alla rovescia.* Turin: Boringheri.

Cohen, Alvin P. (1978). "Coercing the Rain Deities in Ancient China," *History of Religions* 17: 224–65.

Cohn, Norman (1970). *The Pursuit of the Millennium.* New York: Oxford University Press.

Colgrave, Sukie (1979). *The Spirit of the Valley: The Masculine and Feminine in the Human Psyche.* Los Angeles: J.P. Tarcher.

Comaroff, Jean (1985). *Body of Power, Spirit of Resistance: The Culture and History of a South African People.* Chicago: University of Chicago Press.

Cooper, Charles (n.d.) *The English Table in History and Literature.* London: Sampson, Low, Marston.

Crazzolara, J.P. (1953). *Zur Gesellschaft und Religion der Nueer.* Vienna: Missionsdruckerei St. Gabriel.

Davis, J.C. (1986). *Fear, Myth, and History: The Ranters and the Historians.* Cambridge: Cambridge University Press.

Davis, Natalie Zemon (1975). "A Rejoinder," *Past and Present* 67: 131–35.

———— (1975). *Society and Culture in Early Modern France.* Stanford, Calif.: Stanford University Press.

Dawson, Christopher (1975). *The Gods of Revolution.* New York: Minerva.

Descharnes, Robert (1976). *Salvador Dali.* New York: Abrams.

Detienne, Marcel, and Jean-Pierre Vernant (1978). *Cunning Intelligence in Greek Culture and Society.* New York: Humanities Press.

————, eds. (1979). *La cuisine du sacrifice en pays grec.* Paris: Gallimard.

Diefendorf, Barbara (1985). "Prolouge to a Massacre: Popular Unrest in Paris, 1557–1572," *American Historical Review* 90: 1067–91.

Dirks, Robert (1987). *The Black Saturnalia: Conflict and Its Ritual Expression on British West Indian Slave Plantations.* Gainesville: University of Florida Press.

Douglas, Mary (1954). "The Lele of Kasai." In Daryll Forde, ed., *African Worlds: Studies in the Cosmological Ideas and Social Values of African Peoples* (London: Oxford University Press), pp. 1–26.

———— (1966). *Purity and Danger: An Analysis of Concepts of Pollution and Taboo.* London: Routledge & Kegan Paul.

Dover, K.J. (1978). *Greek Homosexuality.* Cambridge: Harvard University Press.

Dumézil, Georges (1930). "La préhistoire indo-iranienne des castes," *Journal asiatique* 216: 109–30.

Dumont, Louis (1970). *Homo Hierarchicus.* Chicago: University of Chicago Press.

Durkheim, Émile (1915). *The Elementary Forms of the Religious Life,* J.M. Swain, trans. London: Allen & Unwin.

Durkheim, Émile and Marcel Mauss (1963). *Primitive Classification.* Chicago: University of Chicago Press.

Eire, Carlos M.N. (1986). *War Against the Idols: The Reformation of Worship from Erasmus to Calvin.* Cambridge: Cambridge University Press.

Eliade, Mircea (1969). *Yoga: Immortality and Freedom.* Princeton, N.J.: Princeton University Press.

Elias, Norbert (1982). *The History of Manners,* 2 vols., New York: Pantheon.

———— (1983). *The Court Society.* New York: Pantheon.

Estèbe, Janine (1968). *Tocsin pour un massacre: La saison des Saint-Barthélemy.* Paris: Éditions du Centurion.

———— (1975). "The Rites of Violence: Religious Riot in 16th Century France: A Comment," *Past and Present* 67: 127–30.

[Estelrich, Juan] (1937). *La persécution religieuse en Espagñe.* Paris: Plon. (Work initially published without indication of authorship).

Evans-Pritchard, E.E. (1934). "The Nuer, Tribe and Clan," *Sudan Notes and Records* 17: 1–58.

———— (1940). *The Nuer.* Oxford: Oxford University Press.

———— (1956). *Nuer Religion.* Oxford: Clarendon Press.

Fergusson, V.H. (1921). "The Nuong Nuer," *Sudan Notes and Records* 4: 146–55.

Fischer, Michael M.J. (1980). *Iran: From Religious Dispute to Revolution.* Cambridge: Harvard University Press.

Fortes, Meyer, and E.E. Evans-Pritchard, eds. (1940). *African Political Systems*. Oxford: Oxford University Press.

Foucault, Michel (1972). *The Archaeology of Knowledge*. New York: Pantheon.

—— (1979). *Discipline and Punish: The Birth of the Prison*. New York: Random House.

—— ed. (1980). *Herculine Barbin: Being the Recently Discovered Memoirs of a Nineteenth-Century French Hermaphrodite*. New York: Pantheon.

Fraser, Ronald (1979). *Blood of Spain: An Oral History of the Spanish Civil War*. New York: Pantheon.

Freedberg, David (1977). "The Structure of Byzantine and European Iconoclasm." In A. Bryer and J. Herrin, eds., *Iconoclasm* (Birmingham, Eng.: University of Birmingham Centre for Byzantine Studies), pp. 165–77.

Freedman, Jim (1982). "Will the Sheik Use His Amazing Fireball: The Ideology of Professional Wrestling." In Frank Manning, ed., *The Celebration of Society* (Bowling Green, Ohio: Bowling Green University Press, pp. 67–79.

Friedman, Jerome (1987). *Blasphemy, Immorality and Anarchy: The Ranters and the English Revolution*. Athens, Ohio: Ohio University Press.

Galaty, John (1981). "Models and Metaphors: On the Semiotic Explanation of Segmentary Systems." In L. Holy and M. Stuchlik, eds., *The Structure of Folk Models* (New York: Academic Press), pp. 63–92.

García de Cortazar, F. (1978). "La iglesia en la crisis del estado español (1898–1923)." In M. Tuñon de Lara et al., *VIII Coloquio de Pau: La crisis del estado español 1898–1936* (Madrid: Editorial Cuadernos para el Dialogo), pp. 343–77.

Geertz, Clifford (1973). *The Interpretation of Cultures*. New York: Basic Books.

—— (1980). *Negara: The Theatre State in Bali*. Princeton, N.J.: Princeton University Press.

Gennep, Arnold van (1960). *The Rites of Passage*. Chicago: University of Chicago Press.

Georgoudi, Stella (1979). "L'égorgement sanctifié en Grèce moderne: Les Kourbánia des saints." In Marcel Detienne and Jean-Pierre Vernant, eds., *La cuisine du sacrifice en pays grec* (Paris: Gallimard), pp. 271–307.

—— (1985). "Viande sacrificielle et structures sociales dans la pratique du kourbani néo-grec," *L'Uomo* 9: 201–14.

Gilmore, David (1984). "Andalusian Anti-clericalism: An Eroticized Rural Protest," *Anthropology* 8: 31–44.

Glickman, Maurice (1972). "The Nuer and the Dinka: A Further Note," *Man* 7: 586–94.

Gluckman, Max (1940). "Analysis of a Social Situation in Modern Zululand." *Bantu Studies* 14: 1–30, 147–74.

—— ed. (1962). *Essays on the Ritual of Social Relations*. Manchester, Eng.: Manchester University Press.

—— (1963). *Order and Rebellion in Tribal Africa*. New York: Free Press of Glencoe.

Goma y Tomas, (Archbishop) Isidro (1940). *Por Dios y por España*. Barcelona: Rafael Casulleras.

Gomes da Silva, José Carlos (1976). "Mythe et idéologie." *L'Homme* 16: 49–75.

Goody, Jack (1982). *Cooking, Cuisine and Class: A Study in Comparative Sociology*. Cambridge: Cambridge University Press.

Graham, A.C., trans. (1960). *The Book of Lieh-tzü.* London: John Murray.

Gramsci, Antonio (1973). *Letters from Prison.* New York: Harper and Row.

Granet, Marcel (1973). "Right and Left in China." In Rodney Needham, ed., *Right and Left* (Chicago: University of Chicago Press), pp. 43–58.

Green, Jerrold D. (1982). *Revolution in Iran: The Politics of Countermobilization.* New York: Praeger.

Griffiths, J. Gwyn, ed. (1970). *Apuleius of Madauros, The Isis-Book (Metamorphoses, Book XI).* Leiden, Neth.: E.J. Brill.

Grotpeter, John J. (1975). *Historical Dictionary of Swaziland.* Metuchen, N.J.: Scarecrow Press.

Grottanelli, Cristiano (1985). "Archaic Forms of Rebellion and Their Religious Background," in Bruce Lincoln, ed., *Religion, Rebellion, Revolution* (London: Macmillan), pp. 15–45.

——— (1981). "L'ideologia del banchetto e l'ospite ambiguo," *Dialoghi d'Archeologia* 3: 122–54.

——— (1985). "Cibo, istini, divieti." In Sergio Bertelli and Giuliano Crifo, eds., *Rituale, Cerimoniale, Etichetta* (Milan: Bompiano), pp. 31–52.

Grottanelli, Cristiano, and Nicola Parise, eds. (1988). *Sacrificio e società nel mondo antico.* Rome: Laterza.

Grottanelli, Cristiano, Nicola Parise, and Pier Giorgio Solinas, eds. (1984). "Sacrificio, organizzazione del cosmo, dinamica sociale," *Studi storici* 25: 829–956.

———, eds. (1985). "Divisione delle carni: Dinamica sociale e organizzazione del cosmo," *L'Uomo* 9: 3–298.

Hall, Stuart, and Tony Jefferson (1976). *Resistance Through Rituals: Youth Subcultures in Post-war Britain.* New York: Holmes & Meier.

Handelman, Don (1976). "Rethinking Banana Time: Symbolic Integration in a Work Setting," *Urban Life* 4: 433–448.

——— (1981). "The Idea of Bureaucratic Organization," *Social Analysis* 9: 5–23.

Hasenfratz, Hans-Peter (1982). *Die Toten Lebenden: Eine religionsphänomenologische Studie zum sozialen Tod in archaischen Gesellschaften.* Leiden, Neth.: E.J. Brill.

Hatto, Arthur, ed. (1965). *Eos: An Enquiry into the Theme of Lovers' Meetings and Partings at Dawn in Poetry.* The Hague, Neth.: Mouton.

Hegland, Mary (1983). "Two Images of Husain: Accommodation and Revolution in an Iranian Village." In Nikki R. Keddie, ed., *Religion and Politics in Iran* (New Haven, Conn.: Yale University Press), pp. 218–35.

Hill, Christopher (1954). "The Norman Yoke." In John Saville, ed., *Democracy and the Labour Movement: Essays in Honour of Dona Torr* (London: Lawrence & Wishart), pp. 11–66.

——— (1961). *The Century of Revolution: 1603–1714.* Edinburgh: Thomas Nelson.

——— (1972). *The World Turned Upside Down.* New York: Viking Press.

Hill, Christopher, and Edmund Dell, eds. (1969). *The Good Old Cause: The English Revolution of 1640–1660.* London: Frank Cass.

Hinnells, John R. (1973). "The Zoroastrian Doctrine of Salvation in the Roman World: A Study of the Oracle of Hystaspes." In J.R. Hinnells and E.J. Sharpe, eds., *Man and His Salvation: Studies in Memory of S.G.F. Brandon* (Manchester, Eng.: Manchester University Press), pp. 125–48.

Hobsbawm, E.J. (1972). "The Social Function of the Past: Some Questions," *Past and Present* 55: 3–17.

Hobsbawm, Eric, and Terence Ranger, eds. (1983). *The Invention of Tradition.* Cambridge: Cambridge University Press.

Hodgson, Marshall G.S. (1955). *The Order of Assassins.* The Hague, Neth.: Mouton.

—— (1974). *The Venture of Islam,* Vol. 1. *The Classical Age of Islam.* Chicago: University of Chicago Press.

Horn, Gerd-Rainer (Spring 1988). "The Language of Symbols and the Barriers of Language: Foreigners' Perceptions of Social Revolution (Barcelona 1936–1937)." Seminar paper, University of Michigan, Department of History.

Howe, Leopold E.A. (1981). "The Social Determination of Knowledge: Maurice Bloch and Balinese Time," *Man* 16: 220–34.

Howell, P.P. (1954). *A Manual of Nuer Law.* London: Oxford University Press.

Hussain, Asaf (1985). *Islamic Iran: Revolution and Counter-revolution.* New York: St. Martin's Press.

Idzerda, S. (1954). "Iconoclasm During the French Revolution," *American Historical Review* 60: 13–26.

Iturralde, Juan de (1956–65). *El catolicismo y la cruzada de Franco.* Bayonne, Fr.: Editorial Egi-Indarra.

Jackson, Gabriel (1965). *The Spanish Republic and the Civil War.* Princeton, N.J.: Princeton University Press.

Jackson, H.C. (1923). "The Nuer of the Upper Nile Province," *Sudan Notes and Records* 6: 59–107, 123–89.

Johnson, Douglas H. (1981). "The Fighting Nuer: Primary Sources and the Origins of a Stereotype," *Africa* 51: 508–27.

—— (1982). "Tribal Boundaries and Border Wars: Nuer–Dinka Relations in the Sobat and Zaraf Valleys, c. 1860–1976," *Journal of African History* 23: 183–203.

Jones, Louis C. (1942). *The Clubs of the Georgian Rakes.* New York: Columbia University Press.

Kaminski, H.-E. (1937). *Ceux de Barcelone.* Paris: Éditions DeNoel.

Kapferer, Bruce (1988). *Legends of People, Myths of State: Violence, Intolerance, and Political Culture in Sri Lanka and Australia.* Washington, D.C.: Smithsonian Institution Press.

Karp, Ivan, and Kent Maynard (1983). "Reading The Nuer," *Current Anthropology* 24: 481–503.

Keddie, Nikki (1981). *Roots of Revolution.* New Haven, Conn.: Yale University Press.

Kelley, Donald R. (1974). "Martyrs, Myths, and the Massacre: The Background of St. Bartholomew." In Alfred Soman, ed., *The Massacre of St. Bartholomew: Reappraisals and Documents* (The Hague, Neth.: Martinus Nijhoff), pp. 171–202.

Kelly, Raymond C. (1985). *The Nuer Conquest: The Structure and Development of an Expansionist System.* Ann Arbor: University of Michigan Press.

Kingdon, Robert M. (1988). *Myths About the St. Bartholomew's Day Massacres: 1572–1576.* Cambridge, Mass.: Harvard University Press.

Kippenburg, Hans (1981). "Jeder Tag 'Ashura, Jedes Grab Kerbala." In Kurt Greussing, ed., *Religion und Politik im Iran: Mardom Nameh-Jahrbuch zur Geschichte und Gesellschaft des mittleren Orients* (Frankfurt am Main: Syndikat), pp. 217–56.

Kuhn, Thomas (1962). *The Structure of Scientific Revolutions.* Chicago: University of Chicago Press.

Kuper, Hilda (1947/1961). *An African Aristocracy: Rank Among the Swazi.* London: Oxford University Press.

——— (1947). *The Uniform of Colour: A Study of White–Black Relationships in Swaziland.* Johannesburg, S. Afr.: Witwatersrand University Press.

——— (1972). "A Royal Ritual in a Changing Political Context," *Cahiers d'études africaines* 12: 593–615.

——— (1973). "Costume and Cosmology: The Animal Symbolism of the Ncwala," *Man* 8: 613–30.

——— (1973). "Costume and Identity," *Comparative Studies in Society and History* 15: 348–67.

——— (1978). "The Monarchy and the Military in Swaziland." In J. Argyle and E.P. White, eds., *Social System and Tradition in Southern Africa: Essays in Honour of Eileen Krige* (Cape Town, S. Afr.: Oxford University Press), pp. 222–39.

——— (1978). *Sobhuza II: Ngwenyama and King of Swaziland.* New York: Africana Publishing Co.

Kuper, Leo, and M.G. Smith, eds. (1969). *Pluralism in Africa.* Berkeley: University of California Press.

Ladurie, Emmanuel Le Roy (1979). *Carnival in Romans.* New York: George Braziller.

Lane, Christel (1981). *The Rites of Rulers: Ritual in Industrial Society—the Soviet Case.* Cambridge: Cambridge University Press.

Langdon-Davies, John (1937). *Behind Spanish Barricades.* New York: Robert M. Mcbride.

Lannon, Frances (1979). "The Sociopolitical Role of the Spanish Church—A Case Study," *Journal of Contemporary History* 14: 193–210.

——— (1984). "The Church's Crusade Against the Republic." In Paul Preston, ed., *Revolution and War in Spain 1931–1939* (London: Methuen), pp. 35–58.

Lanternari, Vittorio (1977). *Crisi e ricerca d'identità.* Naples: Liguori Editore.

Larsen, S. Saugestad (1982). "The Glorious Twelfth: The Politics of Legitimation in Kilbroney." In A.P. Cohen, ed., *Belonging: Identity and Social Organisation in British Rural Cultures* (Manchester, Eng.: Manchester University Press), pp. 278–91.

Leach, Edmund (1954). *Political Systems of Highland Burma.* London: Athlone Press.

——— (1964). "Anthropological Aspects of Language: Animal Categories and Verbal Abuse." In Eric H. Lenneberg, ed., *New Directions in the Study of Language* (Cambridge: MIT Press).

——— (1968). "Ritual." In *International Encyclopedia of the Social Sciences* (New York: Macmillan), 13: 523–27.

——— (1976). *Culture and Communication.* Cambridge: Cambridge University Press.

Lévi-Strauss, Claude (1964). *Totemism.* London: Merlin Press.

——— (1966). *The Savage Mind.* Chicago: University of Chicago Press.

——— (1969). *The Elementary Structures of Kinship.* Boston: Beacon Press.

——— (1969–81). *Introduction to a Science of Mythology,* 4 vols. New York: Harper & Row.

Lewis, Bernard (1967). *The Assassins: A Radical Sect in Islam.* London: Weidenfeld & Nicolson.

Lienhardt, R. Godfrey (1975). "Getting Your Own Back: Themes in Nilotic Myth."

In J.H.M. Beattie and R.G. Lienhardt, eds., *Studies in Social Anthropology: Essays in Memory of E. E. Evans-Pritchard* (Oxford: Clarendon Press), pp. 213–37.

Lincoln, Bruce (1981). *Priests, Warriors, and Cattle: A Study in the Ecology of Religions.* Berkeley: University of California Press.

—— (1982). "Places Outside Space, Moments Outside Time." In Edgar Polomé, ed., *Homage to Georges Dumézil* (Washington, D.C.: Journal of Indo-European Studies Monograph Series), 69–84.

—— (1983). "Der politische Gehalt des Mythos," in Hans-Peter Duerr, ed., *Alcheringa, oder die beginnende Zeit: Studien zu Mythologie, Schamanismus, und Religion* (Frankfurt am Main: Qumran Verlag), pp. 9–25.

—— (1984). "The Living Dead: Outlaws and Others," *History of Religions* 23: 387–89.

—— (1985). "Notes Toward a Theory of Religion and Revolution." In B. Lincoln, ed., *Religion, Rebellion, Revolution: An Interdisciplinary and Cross-cultural Collection of Essays* (London: Macmillan), pp. 266–92.

—— (1985). "The Tyranny of Taxonomies," *Occasional Papers of the University of Minnesota Center for Humanistic Studies,* No. 1 (Minneapolis: University of Minnesota).

—— (1986). *Myth, Cosmos, and History: Indo-European Themes of Creation and Destruction.* Cambridge: Harvard University Press.

Lincoln, Louise Hassett (1977). "New York Dada and the Arensberg Circle." In William Innes Homer, *Alfred Stieglitz and the American Avant-garde* (Boston: New York Graphic Society), pp. 179–85.

Low, Mary, and Juan Brea (1979). *Red Spanish Notebook.* San Francisco: City Lights.

MacNeill, Eoin (1923). "Ancient Irish Law. The Law of Status or Franchise," *Proceedings of the Royal Irish Academy,* sec. C, (N.S.) 16: 265–316.

Makarius, Laura (1973). "Une interprétation de l'Incwala Swazi: Étude du symbolisme dans la pensée et les rites d'un peuple africain." *Annales économies société civilisation* 28: 1403–22.

Malinowski, Bronislaw (1954). *Magic, Science and Religion and Other Essays.* Garden City, N.Y.: Doubleday, Anchor Books.

—— (1965). *Soil-Tilling and Agricultural Rites in the Trobriand Islands.* Bloomington: Indiana University Press.

Matsebula, J.S.M. (1976). *A History of Swaziland,* 2d ed. Cape Town, S. Afr.: Longman/Penguin Southern Africa.

Marx, Karl (1970). *Critique of Hegel's 'Philosophy of Right.'* Cambridge: Cambrige University Press.

Marx, Karl, and Friedrich Engels (1938). *The German Ideology.* London: Lawrence and Wishart.

Mauss, Marcel (1967). *The Gift.* New York: Norton.

—— (1969). *Oeuvres.* Vol. 3. *Cohésion sociale et divisions de la sociologie.* Paris: Éditions de Minuit.

McGregor, J.F., and B. Reay, eds. (1984). *Radical Religion in the English Revolution.* London: Oxford University Press.

McLeod, Neil (1986–87). "Interpreting Early Irish Law: Status and Currency," *Zeitschrift für celtische Philologie* 41: 46–65 and 42: 41–115.

Meeks, Wayne (1974). "The Image of the Androgyne: Some Uses of a Symbol in Earliest Christianity." *History of Religions* 13: 165–209.

Meid, Wolfgang (1971). *Dichter und Dichtkunst im alten Irland*. Innsbruck, Aus. Innsbrucker Beiträge zur Sprachwissenschaft.

———— (1974). "Dichtkunst, Rechtspflege und Medizin im alten Irland: Zur Struktur der altirischen Gesellschaft." In W. Meid, et al., eds., *Antiquitates Indogermanicae: Gedenkschrift für Hermann Güntert* (Innsbruck, Aus.: Innsbrucker Beiträge zur Sprachwissenschaft), pp. 21–34.

Mélis, Antonio (1983). "Figure del rovesciamento e figure dell' alterità," *Metamorfosi* 7: 153–68.

Montero Moreno, Antonio (1961). *Historia de la persecución religiosa en España 1936–1939*. Madrid: Biblioteca de Autores Cristianos.

Moore, Sally F., and Barbara Myerhoff, eds. (1977). *Secular Ritual*. Amsterdam, Neth.: Van Gorcum.

Morton, A.L. (1970). *The World of the Ranters*. London: Lawrence and Wishart.

Motto, Anna Lydia, and John R. Clark (1969). "Isē Dais: The Honor of Achilles," *Arethusa* 2: 109–125.

Moulton, James Hope (1913). *Early Zoroastrianism*. London: Williams & Norgate.

Murray, S.O. (1983). "Fuzzy Sets and Abominations," *Man* 18: 396–99.

Nagy, Gregory (1979). *Best of the Achaeans*. Baltimore, Md.: The Johns Hopkins University Press.

Needham, Rodney, ed., (1973). *Right and Left: Essays on Dual Symbolic Classification*. Chicago: University of Chicago Press.

———— (1979). *Symbolic Classification*. Santa Monica, Calif.: Goodyear Publishing Co.

Newcomer, Peter J. (1972). "The Nuer Are Dinka," *Man* 7: 5–11.

Ngubane, Harriet (1977). *Body and Mind in Zulu Medicine*. London: Academic Press.

Norbeck, Edward (1963). "African Rituals of Conflict," *American Anthropologist* 65: 1254–79.

O'Leary, Philip (1984). "Contention at Feasts in Early Irish Literature," *Eigse* 20: 115–27.

Ortner, Sherry (1974). "Is Female to Male as Nature Is to Culture?" In M.Z. Rosaldo and L. Lamphere, eds., *Woman, Culture, Society* (Stanford, Calif.: Stanford University Press), pp. 67–88.

———— (1978). *Sherpas Through Their Rituals*. Cambridge: Cambridge University Press.

———— (1984). "Theory in Anthropology Since the Sixties," *Comparative Studies in Society and History* 26: 126–66.

Orwell, George (1952). *Homage to Catalonia*. New York: Harcourt, Brace & World.

Ozouf, Mona (1976). *La fête révolutionnaire 1789–1799*. Paris: Gallimard.

Parry, Jonathan (1982). "Sacrificial Death and the Necrophagous Ascetic." In M. Bloch and J. Parry, eds., *Death and the Regeneration of Life* (Cambridge: Cambridge University Press), pp. 74–110.

Peel, J.D.Y. (1984). "Making History: The Past in the Ijesha Present," *Man* 19: 111–32.

Pemán, José Maria (1967). *Comentarios a mil imagenes de la guerra civil española*. Barcelona: Editorial AHR.

Peréz de Olaguer, Antonio (1937). *El terror rojo en Cataluña*. Burgos, Sp.: Ediciones Antisectarias.

Peréz de Urbel, Justo (Fray) (1956). *Los martires de la iglesia*. Barcelona: Editorial AHR.

Petrie, George (1839). "On the History and Antiquities of Tara Hill," *Proceedings of the Royal Irish Academy*, sect. C, 18: 25–232.

Pettazzoni, Raffaele (1967). *Essays on the History of Religions*. Leiden, Neth.: E.J. Brill.

Phillips, John Ransome (1973). *The Reformation of Images: Destruction of Art in England, 1535–1660*. Berkeley: University of California Press.

Poli, Diego (1985). "La distribuzione nel banchetto celtico," *L'Uomo* 9: 75–97.

Potholm, Christian P. (1977). "The Ngwenyama of Swaziland: The Dynamics of Political Adaptation." In R. Lemarchand, ed., *African Kingships in Perspective: Political Change and Modernization in Monarchical Settings* (London: Frank Cass), pp. 129–59.

Preston, Paul (1978). *The Coming of the Spanish Civil War*. London: Macmillan.

———, ed. (1984). *Revolution and War in Spain: 1931–1939*. London: Methuen.

Raaflaub, Kurt A., ed. (1986). *Social Struggles in Archaic Rome: New Perspectives on the Conflict of the Orders*. Berkeley: University of California Press.

Raum, O.F. (1967). "The Interpretation of the Nguni First Fruit Ceremony," *Paideuma* 13: 148–63.

Rees, Alwyn, and Brinley Rees, (1961). *Celtic Heritage*. London: Thames & Hudson.

Richard, Jean-Claude (1978). *Les origines de la plèbe romaine: Essai sur la formation du dualisme patricio-plébéien*. Rome: École française de Rome.

Richet, Denis (1982). "Sociocultural Aspects of Religious Conflicts in Paris During the Second Half of the Sixteenth Century." In Robert Forster and Orest Ranum, eds., *Ritual, Religion, and the Sacred: Selections from the Annales*, Vol. 7 (Baltimore, Md.: The Johns Hopkins University Press), pp. 182–212.

Roelker, Nancy Lyman (1968). *Queen of Navarre: Jeanne d'Albret, 1528–1572*. Cambridge: Harvard University Press.

Sahlins, Marshall (1961). "The Segmentary Lineage: An Organization of Predatory Expansion," *American Anthropoloigst* 63: 322–45.

——— (1981). *Historical Metaphors and Mythical Realities: Structure in the Early History of the Sandwich Islands Kingdoms*. Ann Arbor: University of Michigan Press.

——— (1985). *Islands of History*. Chicago: University of Chicago Press.

Salzman, P.C. (1978). "Does Complementary Opposition Exist?" *American Anthropologist* 80: 53–70.

Sánchez, José M. (1964). *Reform and Reaction: The Politico-Religious Background of the Spanish Civil War*. Chapel Hill: University of North Carolina Press.

——— (1987). *The Spanish Civil War as a Religious Tragedy*. Notre Dame, Ind.: University of Notre Dame Press.

Schapera, Isaac (1938). "Contact Between European and Native in South Africa: Bechuanaland." In Lucy Mair, ed., *Methods of Study of Culture Contact in Africa* (London: Oxford University Press), pp. 25–37.

Scheiner, Irwin (1973). "The Mindful Peasant: Sketches for a Study of Rebellion," *Journal of Asian Studies* 32: 579–91.

Schwartz, Barry (1981). *Vertical Classification*. Chicago: University of Chicago Press.

Schwarz, Arturo (1970). *The Complete Works of Marcel Duchamp*. New York: Abrams.

Scott, James C. (1977). "Protest and Profanation," *Theory and Society* 4: 1–38, 211–46.

——— (1985). *Weapons of the Weak: Everyday Forms of Peasant Resistance*. New Haven, Conn.: Yale University Press.

Scribner, Bob (1978). "Reformation, Carnival, and the World Turned Upside Down," *Social History* 3: 303–29.

Sergent, Bernard (1984). *L'homosexualité dans la mythologie grecque*. Paris: Payot.

Sheikholeslami, Ali Reza (1986). "From Religious Accommodation to Religious Revolution: The Transformation of Shi'ism in Iran." In A. Banuazizi and M. Weiner, eds., *The State, Religion, and Ethnic Politics* (Syracuse, N.Y.: Syracuse University Press), pp. 227–55.

Shih, Vincent Y.C. (1967). *The Taiping Ideology*. Seattle: University of Washington Press.

Singer, June K. (1976). *Androgyny: Toward a New Theory of Sexuality*. Garden City, N.Y.: Doubleday, Anchor.

Skocpol, Theda (1982). "Rentier State and Shi'a Islam in the Iranian Revolution," *Theory and Society* 11: 265–84.

Smith, Brian (forthcoming). *Classifying the World: The Ancient Indian Varna System*. New York: Oxford University Press.

Smith, M.G. (1956). "Segmentary Lineage Systems," *Journal of the Royal Anthropological Institute* 86: 39–80.

Smith, Pierre (1982). "Aspects of the Organization of Rites." In M. Izard and P. Smith, eds., *Between Belief and Transgression: Structuralist Essays in Religion, History, and Myth* (Chicago: University of Chicago Press), pp. 103–26.

Solinas, Pier Giorgio (1986). "Guerra e matrimonio." In Carla Pasquinelli, ed., *Potere senza stato* (Rome: Riuniti), pp. 21–47.

Southall, Aidan (1976). "Nuer and Dinka Are People: Ecology, Ethnicity and Logical Possibility," *Man* 11: 463–91.

———— (1986). "The Illusion of Nath Agnation," *Ethnology* 25: 1–20.

Southworth, Herbert R. (1963). *El mito de la cruzada de Franco*. Paris: Ruedo Ibérico.

Strong, Roy (1984). *Art and Power: Renaissance Festivals 1450–1650*. Berkeley: University of California Press.

Sutherland, N.M. (1973). *The Massacre of St. Bartholomew and the European Conflict 1559–1572*. London: Macmillan.

———— (1974). "The Massacre of St. Bartholomew and the Problem of Spain." In Alfred Soman, ed., *The Massacre of St. Bartholomew: Reappraisals and Documents* (The Hague: Martinus Nijhoff), pp. 15–24.

Sypher, G. Wylie (1980). "Faisant ce qu'il leur vient à plaisir: The Image of Protestantism in French Catholic Polemic on the Eve of the Religious Wars," *Sixteenth Century Journal* 11: 59–84.

Taussig, Michael (1983). *The Devil and Commodity Fetishism in South America*. Chapel Hill: University of North Carolina Press.

Tcherkézoff, Serge (1983). *Le roi Nyamwezi, la droite, et la gauche: Révision comparative des classifications dualistes*. Cambridge: Cambridge University Press.

Thomas, Hugh (1977). *The Spanish Civil War*. New York: Harper & Row.

Thompson, E.P. (1971). "The Moral Economy of the English Crowd in the 18th Century," *Past and Present* 50: 76–136.

———— (1980). *The Making of the English Working Class*, rev. ed. New York: Penguin.

Thompson, Michael (1979). *Rubbish Theory*. Oxford: Oxford University Press.

Tierney, J.J. (1960). "The Celtic Ethnography of Posidonius," *Proceedings of the Royal Irish Academy*, sect. C, 60: 189–275.

Trotsky, Leon (1973). *The Spanish Revolution (1931–1939)*. New York: Pathfinder Press.

Turner, Victor W. (1957). *Schism and Continuity in an African Society*. Manchester, Eng.: Manchester University Press.

—————— (1967). *The Forest of Symbols: Aspects of Ndembu Ritual*. Ithaca, N.Y.: Cornell University Press.

—————— (1969). *The Ritual Process: Structure and Anti-structure*. Chicago: Aldine.

—————— (1974). *Dramas, Fields, and Metaphors: Symbolic Action in Human Society*. Ithaca, N.Y.: Cornell University Press.

Ullman, Joan Connelly (1968). *The Tragic Week: A Study of Anti-clericalism in Spain, 1875–1912*. Cambridge: Harvard University Press.

Vernant, Jean-Pierre (1980). *Myth and Society in Ancient Greece*. Atlantic Highlands, N.J.: Humanities Press.

—————— (1982). *The Origins of Greek Thought*. Ithaca, N.Y.: Cornell University Press.

Vetterling-Braggin, Mary, ed. (1982). *"Feminity," "Masculinity," and "Androgyny": A Modern Philosophical Discussion*. Totowa, N.J.: Rowman & Littlefield.

Vovelle, Michel (1976). *Religion et révolution. La déchristianisation de l'an II*. Paris: Hachette.

Vries, Jan de (1928). *Die Märchen von klugen Rätsellöserin, Folklore Fellows Communication* No. 73.

Walens, Stanley (1981). *Feasting with Cannibals: An Essay on Kwakiutl Cosmology*. Princeton, N.J.: Princeton University Press.

Walzer, Michael (1965). *The Revolution of the Saints: A Study in the Origins of Radical Politics*. Cambridge: Harvard University Press.

—————— (1974). *Regicide and Revolution*. Cambridge: Cambridge University Press.

Warnke, M., ed. (1973). *Bildersturm: Die Zerstörung des Kunstwerks*. Munich: Hanser.

Windisch, H. (1929). *Die Orakel des Hystaspes. Verhandelingen der koninklijke Akademie van Wetenschappen te Amsterdam*, Afdeeling Letterkunde, Nieuwe Reeks 28/3.

Woodhouse, A.S.P., ed. (1974). *Puritanism and Liberty: Being the Army Debates, 1647–1649, from the Clarke Manuscripts*, 2d ed. London: J.M. Kemp.

Woolrych, Austin (1987). *Soldiers and Statesmen: The General Council of the Army and Its Debates, 1647–1648*. London: Oxford University Press.

Worsley, Peter (1968). *The Trumpet Shall Sound: A Study of Cargo Cults in Melanesia*. New York: Schocken.

Acknowledgments

The chapters of this book have evolved gradually toward their present form, and I have benefited from the astute comments and criticisms of colleagues at numerous institutions. The prehistory of each piece prior to its thoroughgoing revision in 1986–88 follows.

Chapters 1 and 2 were written in Italian in December 1984 and delivered as a public lecture for the Faculty of Letters and Philosophy of the University of Siena. They were published together as "Mito, storia, sentimento, e società: Osservazioni preliminari su un grande tema" in *Thélema* 9 (1986): 43–54. Revised English versions were presented as the lead paper in a Mellon colloquium on "Religion and Political Culture" held at Princeton University in October 1986, and at meetings on the theme "Comparative History of European Revolutions," organized by the International Society for the Study of European Ideas (Amsterdam, September 1988).

Chapter 3 was written in winter 1981–82 and was presented as a lecture for the University of Chicago's Department of History of Religions (November 1982). It was published in *Comparative Studies in Society and History* 25 (1983): 136–53.

Chapter 4 was written in Italian in November 1984 and delivered as a seminar held by the University of Siena's Institute of Anthropology and Folklore. A revised version in English was published in *Man* 22 (1987): 132–56; earlier versions were presented in seminars sponsored by the University of Copenhagen's Institute of History of Religions (May 1985) and the University of Minnesota's Department of Anthropology (April 1986).

Chapter 5 was written in two parts. *Beef and Liberty* was prepared in the summer of 1983 and formed part of the lead paper presented at a conference on "The Division of Meat, the Organization of the Cosmos, and Social

Dynamics" held at the University of Siena (September 1984). This paper was subsequently published in *L'Uomo* 9 (1985): 9–29 and in Italian translation in *Studi storici* 25 (1984): 859–74. The discussions on *The Royal Feast at Tara* and *Battles over the "Champion's Portion"* were written in Spring 1988 and were presented at the annual meetings of the American Society for the Study of Religion (April 1988).

Chapter 6 was written in the spring of 1984 and delivered at a conference on "Religion and Social Integration/Disintegration" organized by the University of Minnesota's Religious Studies Program (May 1984). Subsequent versions were delivered at a seminar of the University of Siena's Institute of Anthropology and Folklore (December 1984), in public lectures organized by the University of Rome's Faculty of Anthropology (March 1985), the University of Stockholm's Institute of Comparative Religion (March 1985), and as the inaugural lecture of Carnegie-Mellon University's College of Humanities and Social Sciences Distinguished Lecture Series (September 1985). The Italian text presented in Rome and Siena was published under the title "Feste e massacri: Riflessioni antropologiche sulla notte di San Bartolomeo," in *Studi e materiali di storia delle religioni* 52 (1986): 275–90.

Chapter 7 was written in winter 1982–83. It was presented in a lecture series held at St. Cloud State University on the topic "Ritual, Metaphor, and Power" (April 1983) and was published in *Comparative Studies in Society and History* 27 (1985): 241–60. An Italian version was presented as a seminar of the University of Siena's Institute of Anthropology and Folklore in November 1984; a German translation is scheduled for publication in the journal *Unter den Pflaster liegt der Strand*.

Chapter 8 was written in December 1983 and was presented as the inaugural lecture of the University of Minnesota's Center for Humanistic Studies. Subsequent versions were presented in seminars sponsored by the University of Siena's Institute of Anthropology and Folklore (November 1984), the University of Lund's Institute of Comparative Religion (May 1985), and Carnegie-Mellon University's Department of Philosophy (September 1985). The original text was published as a University of Minnesota Center for Humanistic Studies Occasional Paper (no. 1: 1985).

Chapter 9 was written in Italian in November 1984 and presented in a seminar held by the University of Siena's Institute of Anthropology and Folklore. A revised Italian text was published under the title "Ancora il mondo alla rovescia: Aspetti dell'inversione simbolica," in *Annali della facoltà di lettere e filosofia, università di Siena* 6 (1985): 185–200.

Chapter 10 was originally written in late 1980 and was published under the title "Places Outside Space, Moments Outside Time," in Edgar Polomé, ed., *Homage to Georges Dumézil* (Washington, D.C.: 1982: 69–84). This was thoroughly revised in March 1985 and presented in Italian at a seminar of the University of Siena's Institute of Anthropology and Folklore.

Index